THE DEATH AND LIFE OF THE URBAN COMMONWEALTH

THE DEATH AND LIFE OF THE URBAN COMMONWEALTH

Margaret Kohn

OXFORD
UNIVERSITY PRESS

OXFORD
UNIVERSITY PRESS

Oxford University Press is a department of the University of Oxford. It furthers
the University's objective of excellence in research, scholarship, and education
by publishing worldwide. Oxford is a registered trade mark of Oxford University
Press in the UK and certain other countries.

Published in the United States of America by Oxford University Press
198 Madison Avenue, New York, NY 10016, United States of America.

Library of Congress Cataloging-in-Publication Data
Names: Kohn, Margaret, 1970– author.
Title: The death and life of the urban commonwealth / Margaret Kohn.
Description: New York, NY : Oxford University Press, [2016] |
Includes bibliographical references and index. | Description based on print version
record and CIP data provided by publisher; resource not viewed.
Identifiers: LCCN 2016019135 (print) | LCCN 2016006205 (ebook) |
ISBN 9780190606619 (Updf) | ISBN 9780190606626 (Epub) |
ISBN 9780190606596 (hardcover : alk. paper) | ISBN 9780190606602 (pbk. : alk. paper)
Subjects: LCSH: Urbanization—Political aspects. | Municipal government. |
Sociology, Urban. | Political geography. | Common good. |
Commons—Political aspects. | Public spaces—Political aspects.
Classification: LCC HT361 (print) | LCC HT361 .K64 2016 (ebook) |
DDC 307.76—dc23
LC record available at https://lccn.loc.gov/2016019135

1 3 5 7 9 8 6 4 2

Paperback printed by Webcom Inc., Canada
Hardback printed by Bridgeport National Bindery, Inc., United States of America

CONTENTS

ACKNOWLEDGMENTS

I began this book at the Centre for Ethics at the University of Toronto, where I was inspired to think about how to bring normative and critical theory together. I am grateful for the institutional and collegial support that I received there. The first chapters of the book used political theory to think about the physical space around me. I had recently moved to a neighborhood filled with check-cashing places, dollar stores, and men-only sports bars. In theory I was a critic of gentrification and in practice I was a gentrifier. In order to clarify these issues, I decided to try to examine the harm of gentrification, and suddenly the concept of the right to the city, which I had always found confusing, began to make sense. It was like a lens that brought the struggles over sharing social value and against dispossession into focus. It helped me see and explain the link between local conflicts over parks, transit, and public housing and connect them to more extreme forms of dispossession happening around the world. The book project was born.

The theoretical ideas were developed and refined through conversations with colleagues and in response to their work. I especially benefitted from the following workshops, conferences, and colloquia: Centre de Recherche en Étique de l'Université de Montreal (Spatiality and Justice); European Urban Research Association (City Futures); University of Minnesota; Université Paris Diderot (Radical Democracy and Utopia); Annenberg School, University of Pennsylvania (Context Collapse,

Reassembling the Spatial); Brock University (Public Space/Urban Crisis); University of British Columbia (Strong Democracies, Smart Cities?); Canadian Political Science Association; several American Political Science Association meetings; Urban Affairs Association meeting; University of Toronto (Law, Justice, and Urbanity Working Group); and Washington University (Justice and the American Metropolis).

I wish to express particular gratitude to the following people who have commented on parts of the book or helped me improve it through their support, inspiration, and encouragement: Clarissa Hayward, Daniel Weinstock, Loren King, Patrick Turmel, Joan Tronto, Michael Kessler, Jane Bennett, Ryan Hurl, Keally McBride, Theresa Enright, Avigail Ferdman, Frank Cunningham, Ronit Levine-Schnur, Mariana Valverde, Nancy Love, Thad Williamson, David Imbroscio, Ali Aslam, Oliver Dlabac, Mark Warren, Barbara Arneil, Jeffrey Isaac, Roger Keil, and Paul Apostolidis. Several graduate research assistants—Chris Enman, Emma Planinc, and Eric Rossett—were enormously helpful in providing feedback and editing.

This book is deeply influenced by the collegial and pluralistic political theory community at the University of Toronto. I would like to thank the faculty members and former grad students in the Political Science Department and friends in the theory community: Joe Carens, Melissa Williams, Simone Chambers, Jennifer Nedelsky, Ronnie Beiner, Rebecca Kingston, Nancy Bertoldi, Ruth Marshall, Ryan Balot, Dan Lee, Clifford Orwin, Stephanie Silverman, Monique Deveaux, Stefan Dolgert, Clifton Mark, Alex Livingston, Margarete Haderer, Mara Marin, and Inder Marwah. And, while this project began over a decade after I finished my doctoral dissertation, it still reflects the influence of my mentors from graduate school, who are creative thinkers and inspiring scholars: Susan Buck-Morss, Anna Marie Smith, Jonas Pontusson, and Sidney Tarrow.

My biggest debt, however, is to my editor, Angela Chnapko, who was extremely supportive and encouraging through the process of turning an assortment of essays into a coherent book.

The final stages of writing and revising this book were completed in the library of the beautiful Camargo Foundation in Cassis, France. I would like to thank the foundation, the director, Julie Chenot, and the residential fellows who created such a warm environment. I am also

grateful for financial support from the Social Science and Humanities
Research Council of Canada and a sabbatical from the University of
Toronto.

All of the chapters have been significantly revised, but earlier versions
of some of them have appeared in print. I am grateful for the permission to
republish them in this revised form: chapter 2, "The Critique of Possessive
Individualism: Solidarism and the City," *Political Theory*, July 24, 2015.
http://ptx.sagepub.com/content/early/2015/07/23/009059171559
6559.full.pdf+html; chapter 5, "What Is Wrong with Gentrification?,"
Urban Research and Practice 6, no. 3 (2013); chapter 7, "Privatization and
Protest: Occupy Wall Street, Occupy Toronto, and the Occupation of Public
Space in a Democracy," *Perspectives on Politics* 11, no. 1 (2013): 99–110.
A short section from Chapter 8 will appear as part of my contribution to a
forthcoming Critical Exchange in *Contemporary Political Theory*.

ix

THE DEATH AND LIFE OF THE URBAN COMMONWEALTH

[1]

INTRODUCTION

Toronto is not one of the most expensive cities in the world. Nevertheless, in 2016, the median price for a detached home was over $1.2 million.[1] Two hundred miles away, a nice home in a good part of town costs $114,000. The difference in price is entirely due to its location in Windsor, Ontario, a Canadian town of 216,000 people across the bridge from Detroit.

This tale of two cities is so familiar that it hardly seems like a puzzle to be explained or a moral problem to be explored.[2] As any real estate agent will remind you, there are three things that matter in real estate: "location, location, location." The difference between real estate prices in cities like Windsor and Toronto seems like the variation in the natural landscape, which includes verdant hills and flat, desert terrain. Only a complete collapse of property values becomes a matter of political concern. The most notorious case of real estate devaluation in the United States is Detroit, Michigan. In 2013, when city officials tried to auction off tax-foreclosed properties with an opening bid of $500, over 7,000 properties remained unsold. These severely depressed prices reflect the low value of the neighborhoods and cities where they are located. When we purchase a house or rent an apartment we are also securing access to the city itself, to a common world made up of streets that connect us with jobs, entertainment, necessities, visual delights, encounters, barriers, threats, beneficial relationships, educational opportunities, sports facilities, and places that are more or less protected from surveillance. Our lives are fundamentally affected by these outside spaces and the opportunities and restrictions that they place upon on us. Economists find this unremarkable. The price of a home reflects the value buyers place on the location. A home located on a busy road costs less than a similar one on a quiet street because buyers know that they are purchasing both the home and the surrounding area. They intuitively subtract the cost of noise and traffic from the value of the home. It doesn't take a degree in economics to know that houses in good school districts command higher prices. This is because these homeowners purchase more than a building; they also acquire exclusive access to a scarce and much-desired good: high-quality education.

Yet why should access to public goods be tied to the ability to acquire private property? To most people this link seems natural and therefore not a matter of justice or injustice. A good neighborhood is a luxury like a BMW or the newest iPhone. In this book, I challenge this view and argue that the public goods of the city are not the same as consumer goods.[3] The city should be understood as a form of common-wealth, a concentration of value created by past generations and current residents.[4] When people lose access to the urban commons, they are effectively dispossessed of something to which they have a rightful claim. Dispossession can take a variety of forms: slum clearance, gentrification, foreclosure, demolition of public housing, and the privatization of public space. This book criticizes exclusion and dispossession in cities and argues that these are matters of justice.[5]

Political economists such as John Logan and Harvey Molotch have convincingly argued that the built environment and institutional structure of the city are organized around the pursuit of exchange value and rents.[6] The political economy approach explains why homeowners mobilize when their neighborhood is reassigned to the catchment of a less elite school and politicians collaborate with big developers on stadiums and waterfront parks to attract tourists, the creative class, and economic growth. This literature provides an astute analysis of the way that economic and political power shape urban space.[7] It is critical of the way that local political institutions exacerbate inequality and promote exchange value over use value, but the reasons for this critique are implicit rather than explicit. This book builds on this analysis but, by carefully examining, reconstructing, and defending the underlying normative assumptions, it makes a distinctive contribution to our thinking about urban inequality and social justice. The enormous popularity of the concept of the right to the city, I believe, reflects the growing sense that there is a need for a richer account of these normative issues.

The concept of the right to the city was introduced by the French philosopher Henri Lefebvre in 1968 to criticize the spatial segregation in capitalist cities and to inspire people to experiment with new forms of popular control. The right to the city has been an extremely influential concept, particularly in geography, urban sociology, and city planning. It is a statute in Brazil, the name of an anti-gentrification and anti-foreclosure movement in the United States, and the theme of an art exhibition in Sydney. The right to the city has also informed legal doctrines that protect, expand, and democratize access to public space.[8] Judges have used the right to free speech or movement to strike down laws criminalizing homelessness, thereby providing homeless people with greater access to the city. This book tries to gain a new perspective on the right to the city by drawing on thinkers and concepts from political theory that have not been prominent in the existing literature.

My definition of the right to the city is simple, but it has radical implications for urban politics. Rights protect fundamental interests that are recognized by, and entail obligations for, others. The right to the city protects access, enjoyment, and co-determination of the common-wealth of the city.[9] I use the term "city" to describe material places that bring together diverse strangers engaged in a wide range of activities, including production, culture, domesticity, and politics rather than in the narrower sense of jurisdiction. The city is often figured as a commodity and this book treats it as a commons and a public good.[10] It is the materialization of value that was created collectively by past generations who built the city and diverse contemporaries who repair and animate it. This book tries to show that displacement and exclusion from cities entails the dispossession of social property. In settler-colonial contexts, however, cities were built on indigenous land and therefore the urban commonwealth is itself the site of a prior dispossession. Confronting this fact profoundly challenges the picture of the common-wealth as a product of voluntary collaboration. This book tries to sustain a productive tension between an account of the common-wealth as an object of struggle and a source of solidarity. Both are necessary in order to explain why the city has flourished as a refuge for the dispossessed and shouldn't become the exclusive property of the wealthy.

The right to the city is a complex and paradoxical notion. The right to the city protects the fundamental interest in shaping, accessing, and enjoying this commons, but this means that it asserts a claim to something that cannot be possessed. It confounds the categories of public and private, individual and state, use and ownership. The goal of this book is to explain and justify the concept by examining normative claims that underpin specific aspects of the right to the city. I consider different types of rights claims: equality, social property, life, and occupancy. These rights-based theories help us explain the harm of displacement, but they are unable to fully resolve conflicting claims to place. This book approaches these issues from the perspective of rights, but it also argues that rights are claims that must be weighed against other, sometimes conflicting claims. In other words, rights are internal to rather than external to politics. The final chapters of the book take a popular solution[11]—democracy—and turn it back into a problem. Democracy is a way of imagining that these conflicts about place and power can be reconciled. Even some of the most forceful critics of the abstract character of rights fail to recognize that democracy too is an abstract concept. Democratic procedures and egalitarian principles are treated as intrinsically linked when in fact this connection is contingent and unstable. The rhetoric of democracy can legitimize state power, but it can also dismantle and reconfigure it. Democracy is Janus-faced; one side foments critique and popular mobilization while the other mystifies and legitimizes state power.

Struggles over the use and control of physical space are visible manifestations of two conflicting logics, those of use value and exchange value. In each case, poorer residents are forced to move to areas where property values are lower in order to make land available for profitable reinvestment. The rooming house in a transitional neighborhood can be renovated and sold to bourgeois bohemians who are willing and able to pay high prices for proximity to downtown. At least since Neil Smith and David Harvey's pioneering work, however, we have known that the process of urban transformation is not simply a matter of individual consumer choice.[12] It is part of a cycle of disinvestment and reinvestment in which large developers and investors play a key role. The American housing bubble was created not only by the demand of homeowners but also by the supply of capital that was funneled into low-cost mortgages. This had an inflationary effect on prices, which pulled new investors into the market. By pursuing exchange value, investors drove up prices to the point where families seeking to use their homes for shelter were excluded from the market.[13]

It is particularly problematic when investors purchase real estate not in order to rent it out or renovate it and flip it for a profit but simply as a low-risk place to preserve capital. While the extent of this phenomenon is difficult to document, the Census Bureau's American Community Survey showed that almost one-third of residential units on the Upper East Side of Manhattan are vacant at least ten months of the year. In a city where demand dramatically exceeds supply and need exceeds ability to pay,[14] prices are driven higher and scarce housing is left empty, creating even more competition for the remaining housing stock.

Not all cities, however, follow this model. In Toronto, the booming market in single-family homes is not driven by speculation but by the value that people place on urban amenities. Most homes are owner occupied and prices reflect the strong demand for a limited supply of housing stock that is close to the central city.[15] The exclusion of low- and even middle-income people is produced not only by the actions of capitalists who approach the housing market as an investment but also by fellow city dwellers who love the city for its own sake. Economists suggest that the allocation of housing reflects preferences and the willingness to trade one good (say size of dwelling, quality, or commute time) for another (money),[16] but this way of characterizing the distribution of housing as a choice makes sense only within income brackets, not across them. Friedrich Hayek was right to remind us that there must be some way of allocating scarce goods that are desired by lots of people, but he was wrong to treat the market as a non-coercive alternative to authoritative allocation. This book challenges the assumption that the market is a natural and fair way to distribute access to the urban commonwealth and explores alternative principles of distribution.[17]

What would it mean to imagine the city as something other than a collection of individual-private, corporate, and state-controlled places? Charles Taylor defines social imaginaries as "the ways in which people imagine their social existence, how they fit together with others, how things go on between them and their fellows, the expectations that are normally met, and the deeper normative notions and images that underlie these expectations."[18] Urban policy is informed by urban imaginaries, idealized images of the city that underpin the perception of facts and legitimize norms. The key concept in this book, "the urban commonwealth" is an alternative to the other ways of imagining the city, as a growth machine, a community, or a phantasmagoria for the creative class. The urban commonwealth is more like a pair of glasses than a set of parameters. It helps us see the value in the interstices of the city, the "in-between" sites that nourish the lifeworld: streets that facilitate encounters and imagination, visual delights that can astound or comfort, institutional safety nets that can provide for the needy, and the libraries and parks that educate and entertain.

The term "urban commonwealth" can also be understood literally. The city is value that is shared by residents. It is meant to remind us that the city is a form of property that cannot be broken up into individual parcels. A sidewalk loses its usefulness for transportation if each person has exclusive control over a small section. By its intrinsic character, the city belongs to a collective. It is res publica: the public thing. What then, is the difference between the commons and the public? "Public" is a complex concept that can signal a connection to the state, the community, or the quality of being open, accessible, shared, or universal.[19] The "commons" usually describes land or resources that are shared by a group. Throughout this book, I use "common-wealth," "social property," and "commons" interchangeably and the terms are meant to convey that social property is prior to and logically independent of state ownership or control. When the commons is regulated, owned, or administered by an institution that is accountable to the people, I describe it as public. These definitions, however, are only provisional, since the concepts will be discussed in more detail in subsequent chapters. Moreover, consistency is impossible, since the meaning of the term "public" changes when it is used as part of the phrase "public goods" (a technical term in economics), "public good" (a normative theory), or "public space" (a normative and descriptive term).

Economists have two specialized terms that they use to define public goods: non-severable and non-excludable. Clean air, for example, cannot be divided into individual parcels and the benefit of clean air cannot be reserved for those who pay for it. The urban commonwealth is different: it is non-severable but excludable.[20] How can you exclude people from sharing something that is, by nature, collective? In China, the Hukou system secures exclusion through law. Without a permit, rural people are not allowed to settle in cities or to use urban public services. In other places, exclusion is achieved through a shifting array of norms, rules, tactics, and practices such as exclusionary zoning, by-laws, transit deserts, and slum clearance. The primary mechanism of exclusion is the market, which allocates housing based on the ability to pay. The market produces a certain kind of built environment and regulates access to it; yet it depends upon government and the public; it is regulated by law, refereed by judges, sustained by norms, and subsidized by taxpayers. This is why examination of the urban imaginary and normative judgments that derive from this imaginary is so important.

The urban commonwealth also has a more precise, even technical meaning. This builds on the concept of "unearned increment" or rent, which describes the way that the return on urban land privatizes the value generated by public goods (policing, roads, sewers, transit, education) and social goods (urban scenes, street culture, neighborhood effects). In this book, I argue that this unearned increment should be shared. Planners and activists have already experimented with ways of putting this idea into practice; inclusionary zoning, value capture, and community benefit agreements are all applications of the idea that some of the profit from real estate development should be reinvested in public goods.[21] These policies are best justified by the theory of social property that I explain in this book. The theory of the urban commonwealth provides a more comprehensive justification of these policies and also the strategies of contentious politics that stake a claim to a right to the city.

PLAN AND METHOD OF THE BOOK

Many of the chapters of the book present examples or illustrations of dispossession in cities. These include the demolition of public housing in Chicago, the removal of informal settlements in Delhi and Mumbai, gentrification in San Francisco, and the eviction of Occupy encampments in Toronto and New York. These examples are not intended as empirical case studies that advance expert knowledge of these particular conflicts. Most of the information is drawn from a variety of textual sources: newspaper and magazine articles, court briefs, judicial opinions, online forums, scholarly articles, and documentary films. These vignettes are true stories of struggles over the right to the city, but they are meant to function as narratives that help us see more vividly.[22] My goal is to describe key features of a conflict in order to help the reader see the political stakes or normative dilemmas more clearly, to recognize structural patterns by focusing on their concrete manifestations, and thereby to make connections with similar conflicts in other times and places.

This book is primarily a work of critical and normative theory. The arguments about social property, debt, dispossession, and commonwealth are meant for two different audiences. I hope to convince the skeptics and to provide sympathetic citizens, students, and scholars with better arguments against dispossession. Without a good understanding of the theoretical issues it is easy to miss cases of injustice and difficult to explain what is wrong with them to someone who does not already agree. This requires a language that both builds on common ideas and derives new conclusions from these ideas. Normative arguments about the rights to occupancy, housing, equality, mobility, and life illuminate the wrong of dispossession, but they also raise new questions. If dispossession is wrong because it is coercive, then how do we evaluate the coercion of market forces? If the right to shelter is a basic component of the right to life, then shouldn't it trump private as well as public property rights? If the public is not synonymous with the state, how do we resolve conflicts between the public and the state? This book is not simply a celebration of the urban commonwealth but rather an attempt to use the concept to deepen our understanding of the challenges entailed in the struggle for local justice.

This book focuses on three dimensions of the right to the city: housing, public transit, and public space. The right to housing in particular falls into the category of "social rights," but the meaning of social rights is not well understood.[23] Chapter 2 introduces the theory of solidarism and explains the distinctive theory of social rights associated with this movement. Solidarism is a strand of French republicanism that emerged in the late 19th century. The leading theorists explained and defended the concepts that are foundational for the theory of the urban common-wealth: social property, unearned increment, and debt. Chapter 2 provides an intellectual history of solidarism and deals only indirectly with urban issues; some readers may prefer to focus on the following chapters, which explain how solidarism can inform legal and political debates about social justice in cities.

Chapter 3 examines *Olga Tellis v. Bombay Municipal Corporation* (1985), an Indian court case that recognized that shelter is part of the right to life that is protected in the Indian constitution.[24] This decision was heralded as a victory for proponents of social rights, but I argue that this reading is incorrect. The court decision drew on the liberal, Lockean concept of the right to life, and rejected the slum dwellers' claim to property rights. The unconventional property rights argument was not persuasive to the Indian Supreme Court, because it was rested on an approach that was unfamiliar: the theory of solidarism. The slum dwellers asserted a collective right to share the common-wealth based on the fact that they built their dwellings, their neighborhood, and the infrastructure of the city itself. The common law concept of adverse possession provides some additional arguments in favor of this position.

Scholars of global justice and territorial rights have developed a concept known as "the right to occupancy." The right to occupancy helps explain why individuals who are living in an area, and have come to live there justly, have a moral entitlement to continue to live there. The concept is used to evaluate the legitimacy of claims to territorial jurisdiction and to explain the harm of forced relocation of indigenous people. Chapter 4 asks whether there is a right to occupancy for city dwellers. It focuses on the destruction of public housing in the United States that was financed by a government program called Hope VI, particularly the demolition of the Cabrini-Green housing project in Chicago.

Chapter 5 poses the question, "What is wrong with gentrification?" It explores five harms that are associated with gentrification: residential displacement; exclusion; transformation of public and commercial space; polarization; and homogenization. The strongest normative argument against gentrification, I will argue, is based upon the wrong of displacement. Drawing on a philosophical theory called luck egalitarianism, I explain why we should adopt policies that limit displacement, even though such policies are inconsistent with market allocations. The desire to remain in a gentrifying neighborhood is one example of what philosophers call "the problem of expensive tastes" and luck egalitarian theory provides reasons to accommodate this preference. The transformation of public/social space, exclusion, polarization, and homogenization may be harmful or beneficial depending on the composition of the city as a whole and the power dynamics involved in the transformations.

Chapter 6 argues that mobility is part of the right to the city. Following Thad Williamson, I define mobility as "the capacity to access and participate in the economic, civic, and social life of one's community, without respect to social class or personal economic circumstances."[25] There are two ways to share the urban commonwealth. One is through direct proximity. Living in an amenity-rich area makes it easy to enjoy its benefits and contribute to its ongoing construction. The other possibility is to access such areas through efficient transportation. Transit, however, seems like a particularly unlikely topic to approach through the lens of rights. In fact, traffic control is used as a paradigmatic example of a governmental responsibility that does not implicate fundamental rights. The chapter draws on the Kantian distinction between public and private right in order to explain why access to transit is a public responsibility and why it should be distributed equally. I discuss the strengths and limitations of theories of rights in connection with three contemporary debates about fair access to mobility: the Google shuttle, the expansion of the subway in Toronto, and intra-regional transit in metro Richmond.

The first part of the book draws on normative theory in order to critique practices of dispossession, but the final chapters explore the role of democracy in resolving conflicting claims. Democracy involves both deliberation and mobilization.[26] As a society we have to decide how to structure the terms of living together: who to coerce and what freedoms to protect.[27] We have to ask both "what is the public good" and "what procedures do we use to decide"? Chapter 7 reads Occupy Wall Street as an event that posed these questions. In both New York City and Toronto, the courts relied on a theory that Habermas called "German Hobbesianism." This sovereigntist theory of the public was used to justify removing the protesters and disbanding the encampments. The alternative is what I call the "populist model of the public," a term which describes the political mobilization of the people outside the institutional structures of the state. While my focus is on public *space*, I suggest that the appropriation of space was the most visible aspect of a broader call for collective control of the common-wealth of society. In other words, we should understand the occupations synecdochally as struggles over the meaning and power of public and private.

Chapter 8 also examines the use of civil disobedience to protect access to public space. A conflict over a soccer pitch in the Mission District of San Francisco highlights the connection between gentrification and the commodification of public space. The two sides of this conflict defended very different theories of public space. One side drew on the sovereign-tist theory of the public and the other emphasized community traditions. Community, however, is problematic because it can be used to legitimize exclusive, hierarchical, and exploitive traditions. This chapter looks at two forms of citizen mobilization about land use (NIMBYism [Not-in-my-back-yard] and environmental justice) and explains how the concept of the common-wealth helps us distinguish between them.

In *Rebel Cities*, David Harvey explains his reservations about the concept of "the right to the city." The term seems to rely on a theory of politics that is antithetical to two key ideas of the left. It emphasizes the rights-bearing individual rather than the political group, and focuses on the distribution of goods ("the city") rather than the production of inequalities. Chapter 9 responds to these concerns by examining the Marxian critique of rights and introducing the concept of hetero-rights. A hetero-right uses rights claims to advance fundamental interests, but it does so in a way that forces us to confront the limits that are embedded in the tradition of liberal rights. It is a dialectical-political rather than an abstract-philosophical approach to right. From the perspective of private property, a right to the city is incomprehensible in so far as no one can assert a conventional property right to the city. This paradox forces us to think about the city through the lens of social rather than private property. In this last chapter I offer a reading of Lefebvre's *Le Droit à la Ville* and explain how it fits together with the rest of this book.

Some forms of enclosure are easy to recognize. Gated communities, for example, advertise their exclusivity.[28] Contemporary cities do not seem exclusive in the same way, but the real estate market becomes a de facto form of enclosure when access to the urban commons is not afford-able to the middle class and poor.[29]

The critique of enclosure began in the 16th century with Thomas More's book *Utopia* and was developed more forcefully by 17th-century writers like Gerrard Winstanley, the founder of a group that called them-selves the *true* Levellers, because they claimed more than the right to vote: they wanted to preserve access to the commons. In the belle epoque, an era of economic inequality similar to our own,[30] the French solidarists developed a new, distinctively modern critique of enclosure and a the-ory of social rights. The key idea was that the division of labor produces a social product and the division of the product into public and private shares is not a law of nature but rather the outcome of political struggle. Political struggle, however, is not just about the strength of groups. It requires normative theory because it involves making claims about how things *should* be arranged and it also requires critical theory, which shifts our understanding of what is natural or subject to change.

This book draws on the theory of social property to provide a new perspective on struggles over the right to the city. From the solidarist perspective, the city is the site of conflicts over ownership, use, control, and access, but it is not only that. It is also something more than the sum of its parts. The city is vibrant and vital precisely because it is shared with other people. This variety can itself be a source of visual delight and social opportunity. People choose to live in cities because proxim-ity makes it possible to build networks with others who share idiosyn-cratic tastes, to encounter strangers, and to have new experiences. From the solidarist perspective, the city does not have to be the tragic com-mons where acquisitive individuals exploit limited resources. It can be lived as the comedy of the commons where we build something and enjoy it together.

[2]

SOLIDARISM AND SOCIAL
PROPERTY

On July 13, 2012, Barack Obama gave a campaign speech that was widely derided by right-wing commentators. The speech featured the notorious line, "If you've got a business, you didn't build that." Obama's point was that productivity and innovation stem from the confluence of individual initiative and social and physical infrastructure: roads, technology, knowledge, and communication.[1] Some of this infrastructure is created by government and much of it is inherited from past generations. Obama introduced an unfamiliar political claim that was difficult for Americans to understand because it did not fit neatly into the two dominant political rationalities of our time. The first, neo-liberalism or market conservatism, governs through market rationality. It privileges economic exchange, de-emphasizes responsibility for redistribution, and legitimizes the resulting economic inequality.[2] The rival framework is welfare-state capitalism. This approach recognizes that the prosperity produced through market competition fails to satisfy the basic needs of all residents and concludes that the state must redistribute some resources to alleviate suffering.[3]

In recent years, there has been increased awareness of economic inequality, and this has fostered interest in theories that illuminate or critique inequality.[4] For example, political theorists have written about John Rawls's brief but suggestive remarks on "property owning democracy."[5] Others have turned to T. H. Marshall's concept of social rights, which provides a compelling descriptive account of the historical emergence of the welfare state and a useful typology for categorizing rights claims, but it does not advance a normative theory.[6] The alternative theory that I examine in this book is called solidarism, a strand of left-republicanism that emerged in France in the late 19th and early 20th centuries.[7] Solidarism rests on the claim that the division of labor creates a social product that does not naturally belong to the individuals who control it as their private property.[8] This claim provides the foundation for the principle that the wealthy have a quasi-contractual debt to society that they are obliged to repay. Solidarism provides a justification of social rights, and does so in a way that is distinct from the welfare-as-charity model. Solidarism also helps makes sense of "the right to the city." It does so in three ways. It shows how something shared like the city could *be* the subject of a rights claim; it helps us see how the city generates resources that could help dismantle urban inequality; and it is a normative theory that explains why resources should be allocated to benefit the disadvantaged. By reconstructing the distinctive intellectual history of "solidarism," I hope to provide a more convincing account of social property and show how this approach is relevant to conflicts over inclusion and exclusion in cities.

SOCIAL PROPERTY BEFORE AND AFTER SOLIDARISM

The French solidarists were not the only theorists to promote the idea that all members of society have a rightful claim to a share of the social wealth. This argument dates back at least as far as Thomas Paine. In 1795 Paine wrote a pamphlet addressed to the Legislature and Executive of the French Republic entitled *Agrarian Justice*.[9] The bulk of the pamphlet is devoted to defending the view that people without property are owed a share of private property. He argues that in the state of nature, land was the common property of mankind. While Paine concedes that the *products* of the land legitimately belong to the person who invests his labor by cultivating or gathering them, he insists that such labor does not generate ownership of the land itself. He concludes that private property is an illegitimate usurpation and owners owe land-rent to non-owners. According to Paine, this rent should be collected in the form of a tax on inherited property and paid out in grants to all citizens: he proposes one grant to help young adults get started in life and another to support the elderly in old age.

If Paine stopped here, "Agrarian Justice" would simply be an updated and radicalized version of classic republican ideas about the need to limit the size of landed estates and to help citizens maintain economic independence, but he goes a step farther. Paine also argues that society is entitled to a share of non-landed property. Why? Paine explains,

> Personal property is the effect of society and it is impossible for an individual to acquire personal property without the aid of society, as it is for him to make land originally. Separate an individual from society, and give him an island or a continent to possess, and he cannot acquire personal property. He cannot be rich. So inseparably are the means connected with the end, in all cases, that where the former do not exist the latter cannot be obtained. All accumulation, therefore, of personal property, beyond what a man's own hands produce, is derived to him by living in society; and he owes on every principle of justice, of gratitude, and of civilization, a part of that accumulation back again to society from whence the whole came.

This passage succinctly presents some of the core ideas that the solidarists would elaborate, defend, and put into practice one hundred years later.

Similar arguments have appeared in other times and places. In a number of publications written in the 1920s and 1930s, the Guild socialist G. D. H. Cole promoted the idea of a "social dividend" that would distribute social wealth and ensure that basic social needs were met, regardless of one's success in the labor market. The Nobel Prize–winning economist James Meade used a social dividend to justify a universal and unconditional income funded through "the revenue from a stock of public assets jointly owned by citizens but managed through market criteria through a multiplicity of investment funds."[10] Intellectual archeology reveals a family of related concepts—social debt, rent, dividend, and inheritance—that all get at a similar idea: a portion of privately owned value legitimately belongs to society and should be shared.[11]

As long as state socialism and market liberalism were the two dominant frameworks, this third alternative remained obscure, but it experienced a brief resurgence after the fall of Soviet communism. In the early 1990s, leftist theorists looking for a third way began to promote a universal minimum income as a way of reconciling the liberal emphasis on individual freedom with the socialist commitment to prioritizing basic needs. In a series of books and articles, the philosopher Philippe Van Parijs advocated an unconditional basic income to be paid to all citizens.[12] He argued that this would be the best way to promote social justice because it would enable everyone to pursue their vision of the good, including the enjoyment of leisure. The main objection to such a proposal is based on another strong moral intuition: that people deserve the fruits of their own labor and no capable person should live parasitically on the labor of others. The proponent of the welfare state accepts the obligation to provide for the disabled but questions whether the able-bodied person who foregoes work for pleasure should be supported at public expense. Van Parijs framed this question provocatively by asking "why should surfers be fed?"[13]

His answer to this question draws on the theory of social property. According to Van Parijs, basic income should not be understood as a form of redistribution, whereby resources that belong to one person are transferred to another. Nor is it a largesse provided to people who deserve help because they have tried to support themselves and have been unsuccessful through no fault of their own. Instead, it is an entitlement. The basic income rests on the notion that each member has a legitimate claim on an equal share of society's external resources. External resources include not only land but also useable objects such as infrastructure, factories, and technologies.[14] According to Van Parijs, a fair distribution of the income produced by a share of these resources could enable each member of society to enjoy the greatest possible freedom. Some people would choose to maximize leisure (a category which includes not just surfing but all non-income-generating pursuits such as volunteerism, homemaking, creativity, study) and others would augment their basic income with paid labor in order to maximize income and consumption. Since this arrangement privileges neither leisure nor income, it genuinely allows each individual to pursue his or her own vision of the good life, which is a key principle of liberalism.

SOLIDARISM AND SOCIAL PROPERTY

Van Parijs uses the theory of social property—or what he calls external resources—to provide a largely convincing argument in favor of a universal basic income. Such an income—if set at the high level he endorses—would greatly decrease economic inequality, which would in turn help dismantle spatial injustice. Nevertheless, I have some concerns about this approach. First, it is a moral theory that remains too disconnected from political analysis. It is not able to answer the following question: what are the social forces that might be able to bring about this change? Another related issue is the "problem of the second best."[15] According to the economists Richard Lipsey and Kelvin Lancaster, the attempt to achieve the best—but impossible—outcome can sometimes have the unintended consequence of making it more difficult to achieve the second best—but more feasible—outcome. Promoting a universal basic income in the way that Van Parijs does—by using the language of choice and individualism—may reinforce neo-liberal ideology and undermine a politics of solidarity that could bring about the basic income that he endorses.

A final objection is that the link between the argument that all members of society have an "equal claim on external resources" and the argument that "freedom is secured through equal distribution of these resources to individuals" is not a necessary one. It is also possible to conclude that these resources are social products—created through a process of collaboration that builds on a rich inheritance—and therefore society has the right to decide how to allocate them. Following Michael Walzer, I argue that the allocation of scarce and desirable things will reflect socially determined ideas about justice.[16] If justice is determined socially and not deduced from abstract reason, then what role does political theorizing play in thinking and writing about urban justice? Couldn't we just carry out a deliberative opinion poll or anthropological study to determine what is just?

I will return to this issue at more length in the conclusion, but my view is that the answer to this question rests on a prior question: how are socially determined ideas about justice actually determined? They are at least partially determined through the process of giving reasons, making arguments, examining the consistency of different positions, and considering examples that bring out the tension between different normative commitments and judgments. Political theorizing is a critical practice that

17

works on existing assumptions, ideas, and traditions. The theory of social property that I defend in this chapter serves to refute the conventional understanding of private property rights as natural rights. The theory of social property does not tell us whether justice requires equal distribution of resources, or opportunity for welfare, or whether priority should be given to the worst off, or to meeting the needs that make it possible to live a minimally good life. It primarily serves a negative function, which is to refute the entitlement theory of property. This theory is defended most forcefully by libertarians like Nozick but it is also an important feature of conventional wisdom in capitalist democracies, especially in the United States. The entitlement theory holds that ownership is legitimate and absolute as long as property was acquired justly and transferred consensually.

As we will see later, the solidarists challenged the assumption that the original privatization of common property was just acquisition. Once we come to see property as naturally social—as composed of an individual and a collective portion—then we can begin to imagine the provision of public goods as something other than a zero-sum game. Instead of resenting the fact that the fruits of one's labor must be redistributed to collective projects or needy individuals, we can think about how our social resources should be allocated for the common good. We may even begin to feel grateful that the enriching soil of the common-wealth has made our labor so fruitful. The theory of the common-wealth is less an abstract theory of justice that provides definitive solutions to conflicts about distribution and more a rhetoric and ethos that enables us to think about these issues in new ways.

This chapter is devoted primarily to presenting and defending solidarism and the following chapters use it to think about urban issues. Solidarism, of course, could also be used to think about other issues at different scales, but it is beyond the scope of this project to examine these broader implications. I start with the city because it is the place where we experience the visceral and material dimension of social property, where the fact of physical proximity forces us to figure out how to live together.

The theory of the urban commonwealth is an application of solidarist perspective to urban issues. A distinctively spatial approach is necessary because space differs from other commodities. It is indispensable to human existence, yet it is limited. This creates an asymmetrical relationship between owners and non-owners. Furthermore, some spaces are sites of great emotional investment or even sanctity that exceed their economic value. Finally, owners and users of adjacent properties have shared interests and conflicts in a way that owners of other products do not.[17] This makes property ownership a social and political relationship. Solidarism provides a cogent justification for the right to the city, and this book tries to show what this means for specific conflicts over use, access, and control of space.

THE PHILOSOPHY OF SOLIDARISM

In this book I use the term "solidarism" to describe an ideal type that draws largely on the eponymous French political movement, but I also broaden it to incorporate more contemporary appropriations of these ideas. I focus on the French solidarists not because their theory is unique, but rather because it is a particularly detailed and systematic account of an important alternative framework. In what follows I present the version of solidarism promoted by the Radical Party in France in the late 19th and early 20th centuries. This is an ideal type that draws on works by the statesman Léon Bourgeois, the political economist Charles Gide, the philosopher Alfred Fouillée, and the jurist Léon Duguit. Their theory of solidarism was a critique of possessive individualism and the economic inequalities that it legitimized. According to the solidarists, the modern division of labor produces a social product. Once this fact is acknowledged, it becomes necessary to reconsider the unquestioned status of the right to private property in liberal-republican thought.[18]

For the proponents of solidarism, solidarity was more than just a feeling of benevolence or fraternity.[19] According to the 1765 *Encyclopédie Commercial*, the term "solidarity" had a distinctive and precise legal meaning. *Solidarité* referred to the obligation of a group of borrowers to discharge the debt of others. It was the opposite of a limited liability corporation. The members were each liable for the entire contracted obligation.[20] The solidarists expanded this notion and used it to describe society's joint obligation for the well-being of its citizens.

The legal and moral theory of solidarism also built on a growing recognition in the natural sciences of the importance of cooperation. A new generation of biologists, economists, and sociologists were also beginning to challenge the ideas of Herbert Spencer, insisting that the key to survival and success was association and collaboration rather than competition. They argued that social organization among men could modify the forces of nature through intentional action and conscious solidarity.

Alfred Fouillée was a philosopher and prolific writer who first brought together a number of ideas that became the key elements of solidarism: a naturalist account of solidarity; the theory of collective property/social debt; and a normative principle of obligation.[21] Fouillée begins his book *La Propriété Sociale et la Démocratie* with the claim that all products are the collective work (*oeuvre commune*) of the individual and society, and they therefore contain a dimension of both private and social property. Both socialism and laissez-faire are incomplete because they deny this hybrid character. Denial is a way of avoiding the difficult task of determining the respective shares. Fouillée makes it clear that his focus is not the common property of the state of nature. He notes that modern societies do not have large amounts of unclaimed and unused property. The kind of *terra nullis* that John Locke thought existed in the Americas no longer exists: "The entire earth is already occupied and enclosed by fences."[22] The type of property that Fouillée describes as "social and collective" includes the physical, technological, intellectual, and social infrastructure of modern society. He also includes collective power, or democracy, as a component of the common-wealth. Social property is created by diverse contributions by a vast array of people over generations and is the patrimony of all members of society. He argues that this *"richesse collective"* (common-wealth) could be effectively employed by governments and used to subsidize a universal insurance system that would provide for those in need. At the same time, however, he recognizes that the market system of free enterprise has generated growing material prosperity.[23]

Fouillée's goal was to develop an alternative to the laissez-faire ideology that he thought predominated in the United States, and the statism of both right (Bismarck) and left (the socialist party in France). He approached this task from his position as a philosopher and asked about the scientific basis of the right to property. Answering this fundamental question, he thought, could provide some guidance about the practical issues of redistribution and state intervention. He criticized the individualist (laissez-faire) school on the grounds that it fundamentally misconstrued the nature of property. Only the God of Genesis created something out of nothing. Humans, by contrast, create products and value by shaping or giving form to existing objects such as soil, stone, or wood. According to Fouillée, the exclusive right to private property rests on a mistaken conflation of shape (*forme*) and substance (*fond*).[24]

Fouillée asks what rights humans have in relation to substance (the unformed material conditions of life) and notes that there are two important dimensions of this question: the right of the first occupant and the right of the last occupant. While the former has received considerable attention, the latter has been ignored. The right of the first occupant stems from labor. Modifying the classic Lockean account, Fouillée points out that improvement through labor justifies a partial claim upon the product, in proportion to the labor invested. In a state of natural abundance, the materials may have little value since anyone can take what they want, but under conditions of scarcity—and this is the situation faced by the "last occupant"—these materials become the source of considerable value.[25] At this point, the acquisition of individual, private property *does* harm those who come afterward and no longer have access to the same opportunity to transform labor into property. Writing in the 17th century, John Locke anticipated this objection and conceded that unlimited acquisition did, in a certain sense, violate fairness since it meant that similarly situated people had vastly different opportunities to acquire property and material things.[26] He insisted, however, that this disadvantage was outweighed by a greater advantage. The landless laborer could not simply acquire private property by cultivating unclaimed common land, but he could still gain a share of the benefits of the system of private property as a whole. Locke argued that enclosure and cultivation of common land yielded enormous gains in productivity, which benefitted the laborer. To support this claim, Locke notoriously insisted that a landless laborer in England had a better standard of living than a native king in the wilds of America.[27]

21

Fouillée astutely identified both the strength and weakness of this argument. He agreed that "civilized" (e.g., economically developed) societies had indeed developed the knowledge, technology, infrastructure, transportation networks, and markets that dramatically increased material well-being, and he also conceded that the market system (private property, commodification of labor, and individual freedom) played a role in unleashing the creativity and initiative that generated growth. The problem with Locke and his 19th-century followers like Bastiat was that they wouldn't acknowledge that landless laborers seldom got a fair share of the social product. The market system had no way to ensure that landless laborers actually received any share, let alone one that was proportional to their contribution or one that was larger than the share they would have received if the system of common property had not been dismantled. Fouillée agreed that the market system created an enormous stock of common-wealth but also recognized that this meant very little if there was no way of ensuring that it be used to meet everyone's basic needs.

The paradox of "private property" is that the institutions and ideologies that generated an enormous stock of social wealth also prevented it from being used for its original purpose. Even Locke admitted that the fundamental purpose of the right to property was securing "life" by meeting the material needs of all people.[28] But the right to *private* property, when interpreted in an abstract and absolutist way, prevented some people from accessing the share of the common-wealth that they needed to survive and flourish. Many writers recognized this and emphasized the duty of charity as the preferred solution. Hospitals and poorhouses were often supported by religious orders or the voluntary contributions of wealthy individuals.[29] In an increasingly secular age, however, the religious arguments in favor of charity became less prominent, and the doctrines of Social Darwinism and individualism posed strong challenges to secular theories of moral obligation.[30]

Fouillée thought that the concept of charity had to be reconfigured in order to address the problems of private property and the challenges of Social Darwinism. Fouillée's position differed from Lockean charity in an important way. For Locke, the right to private property is in principle unlimited, but it is trumped by a higher obligation to preserve life.[31] For Fouillée, existing private property is composed of a legitimate portion and an illegitimate portion, which was acquired when people mixed their labor with raw materials and then claimed the entire product, rather than just the value of their contribution, as their own.[32] To put this in contemporary language, we could call it "accumulation through dispossession."[33] It is important to note that this argument does not apply only to agrarian, pre-industrial societies. Unlike earlier forms of republicanism, which took the yeoman farmer or independent craftsman as the model of independence, Fouillée was writing about an urban society with an advanced division of labor. The simplified account of labor and raw materials was intended to illustrate a logic that applied to complex industrial societies. The key idea was that labor productivity, including the entrepreneurial labor of the business person, is created by leveraging the value of an enormous amount of "material" that one does not and cannot own. This "material" includes social, technological, economic, and physical infrastructure. The upshot is that the social right to common property is just as strong as the individual right to private property.

As many critics of Locke's labor theory of property rights have pointed out, it is unclear why mixing my labor with material should make it mine.[34] The reverse is just as plausible. Mixing my labor with materials could turn my labor into something that belongs to all, which is exactly Fouillée's point. This argument introduces a great deal of uncertainty about how to allocate property, but it also provides a framework for justifying an assertion of social rights against those who have usurped the common-wealth. In an increasingly secular age in which religious arguments in favor of charity were becoming less influential and the doctrines of Social Darwinism and individualism were flourishing, a new way of thinking about social obligation was necessary.[35]

Fouillée argued that individual freedom and social obligation could be reconciled, but he acknowledged that maintaining a balance between them was difficult, and he identified excessive individualism as a particularly powerful threat in his own day. In opposition to the dominant social contract tradition, which depicted people as atomistic individuals and derived political obligation from consent, Fouillée emphasized the sociality of the self.[36] He noted that babies are born utterly dependent on their mothers, and they could not survive without the shelter, nourishment, and education provided by their families. From this starting point, obligation is not the result of intentional contract and choice; obligation precedes the ability to choose and it is not something that can simply be denied or avoided. The conscious and intentional component is the process of deliberating about the extent, distribution, and limits of obligation, as well as the best of way of meeting it. A theory and practice of social responsibility comes about through critical reflection that brings general principles and logic to bear on specific problems. Other solidarists, notably the politician Léon Bourgeois and the political economist Charles Gide, used these principles to justify new and controversial policies such as a national income tax, universal public education, and social rights.

THE POLITICAL ECONOMY OF SOLIDARISM

The theory of solidarism drew not only on philosophy but also on the new empirical social sciences. The emerging disciplines of anthropology and sociology and the growing importance of the division of labor reinforced the conviction that the social must be a primary object of inquiry.[37] Durkheim's distinction between mechanical and organic solidarity had enormous influence in late-19th-century France. In contrast to mechanical solidarity, which emerged from shared beliefs and similar lifestyles, organic solidarity described the kind of interdependence that stemmed from specialization and differentiation.[38] This concept made it possible to see the division of labor not only as a source of class conflict but also as the basis of a new kind of solidarity. At the same time, increasing urbanization made it obvious that individuals were connected with one another through urban infrastructure and through what we today call the externalities of private action: sewage in the street, industrial pollution, noise, and so on. Research on infectious diseases made it clear that even something as apparently private as one's own body could have enormous impact on others. According to the solidarists, increased vulnerability to the effects of others' actions changes the nature of our responsibilities.[39]

The solidarists acknowledged that the mere fact of interconnectedness did not automatically generate a corresponding sense of obligation toward others.[40] In fact, a goal of the theory was to encourage critical thinking about the sentiment of natural solidarity that people often feel toward family or social class, and to promote a more comprehensive understanding of solidarity. In *Solidarité*, Bourgeois advanced the notion of quasi-contractual obligations.[41] This was an alternative to the dominant view of rights, which was understood first and foremost as the individual's ability to control his property for his own benefit. Bourgeois built on Fouillée's argument that private property (in the sense of productive property or capital) was mistakenly treated as individual private property, when in fact it was a social product that had been illegitimately appropriated by capitalists. Bourgeois expanded the original argument about moral obligation into a claim about legal obligation.

According to Bourgeois, the existing French legal code recognized a wide range of "non-conventional contracts." This concept of "quasi-contract" was used to describe obligations that were legally binding, even though they did not rest on the explicit consent of the parties. For example, the obligation of an heir to repay debts of the deceased would fall into this category. Bourgeois drew on the general idea of quasi-contractual obligation, and the notion of debt in particular, to justify the progressive taxes necessary to pay for redistributive measures such as a minimum income, public insurance, and universal education. According to Gide, "as a result of the division of labor, of the influence of heredity, and of a thousand other causes which have just been described, every man owes either his forebears or his contemporaries the best part of what he has, and even of what he is."[42] For the solidarists, the way to pay off this debt is to make those with a disproportionate share of the social product redistribute it to "the disinherited," those who have "suffered loss" through the operation of natural solidarity.[43] The solidarists acknowledged that this debt could be repaid in different ways, and conceded there could be no perfect way of calculating the exact amount owed to specific individuals; the quasi-legal concept of debt provided a normative principle that justified redistribution.

The final component of solidarism is an explicit defense of the economic theory that is implicit in the critique of dispossession: the theory of rent. It builds on Ricardo's famous definition of rent as "unearned increment." Ricardo pointed out that the same amount of labor and capital, when applied to the same amount of land, can yield vastly different amounts of revenue for the owner. The difference between the two yields is "unearned increment," and this makes it possible to distinguish between the value that is created through the labor of the entrepreneur and the capitalist. Gide points out that rapid urbanization and the resulting increase in land prices is a striking illustration of this phenomenon. He notes that a quarter-acre of land in Chicago that cost $20 in 1830 was valued at $1,250,000 in 1894.[44] "Rent," however, is not simply a term that applies to land and real estate. It applies to all analogous differences in revenue from identical inputs. Several factors help explain the different rates of return: some factors may be natural like soil fertility; others, like demand for the product or position relative to the market, are social. In the case of the quarter-acre in Chicago, the increased value did not reflect entrepreneurial activity or improvement, but simply the fact that other people decided to build a bustling city around it, a city that for many complicated reasons became the dominant metropolis of the region.

This concept of rent underpins the solidarist idea of the social product and the normative theory derived from it. The unearned increment that is created socially does not naturally belong to the property owner and should be reallocated to benefit society. In principle this could apply to agricultural land, but the most striking examples of rent occur in places where the division of labor, infrastructure, and social networks inflate the value of land and labor. The solidarists were the first to propose an embryonic version of the theory of the urban commonwealth and to use it to justify social rights: free public education, including adult education and enough leisure to learn; comprehensive insurance against disability, illness, and poverty; and a basic standard of living. Solidarism inspired a passionate debate and elicited criticism from both the left and the right. For the purposes of my theory of the urban commonwealth, the most important objection is the one leveled by the economists, who challenged the accuracy of the solidarist notion of debt. The classical economists insisted that wages reflect each individual's contribution to the social product. The distributions that result from voluntary exchange are fair because both parties consent to the labor contract, and therefore there is no "debt." The solidarists made two responses. First, they pointed out that this is a distorted picture of exchange because it hides the fact that contracting parties do not start out on a footing of equality. According to Gide, the classical economists would have to view Esau's exchange of his birthright for a bowl of pottage as fair. Gide reminds his readers that Esau agreed to this exchange when he was on the point of death. He did consent and, in the short term, benefitted from the exchange, but that doesn't mean that it wasn't an exploitative arrangement. For Gide, the piece-worker and the rubber tapper in the Congo are modern-day Esaus.[45] The example of the Congo, a notoriously brutal colony which was privately owned by King Leopold, reminds the reader of the role of violence in the current allocation of wealth. The first response to the economists' critique is that pay reflects the bargaining power of the parties rather than their contribution, but there is a second response. Gide also notes that a business- or crafts-man often introduces some new process or innovation only to be bankrupted when a competitor adopts the innovation, sells at a lower price, and dominates the market. In a "winner-takes-all" marketplace, the profit from a new product is captured by one dominant player, even though it is developed through the contributions of many competitors. They key idea is that the allocation of benefit does not reflect desert.[46]

The strong version of the economic critique, the claim that everyone gets what they deserve on the market, is unpersuasive, but the weaker version, that there is no objective way to decide who gets what, has some validity. This is the basis of the third critique, which emphasizes the indeterminacy of the theory. The concepts of social product and social property are most useful when used to criticize and denaturalize the absolutist theories of private property that were hegemonic in the late 19th century, theories used to discredit the idea of economic regulation and progressive taxation. Yet while solidarism legitimizes the concept of a social share, solidarism does not explain how to divide the social product between private and public shares or among individuals.[47]

Once having justified the concept of social debt, Bourgeois draws on related but distinct arguments for guidance in addressing the issue of redistribution, and interestingly, some of these arguments are ones that are today associated with liberal-egalitarian theory. First, Bourgeois argues that individuals are responsible only for the consequences of their choices, not for conditions caused by bad luck. He uses this version of luck egalitarianism to justify comprehensive social insurance.[48] Second, in *Philosophie de la Solidarité* he suggests that the level of contribution to solidaristic initiatives should be decided through democratic deliberation under the guidance of a thought experiment that looks a great deal like John Rawls's veil of ignorance.[49]

The veil of ignorance is a thought experiment introduced in Rawls's pathbreaking book *A Theory of Justice*.[50] Rawls asks his readers to think about what principle of justice they would select if they did not know their own social position. He argues that they would want "equality in the assignment of basic rights and duties" and would accept economic inequality only in so far as it benefits the least advantaged. This latter idea is called "the difference principle." Bourgeois does not use the same term, but he asks people to think about the types of social and tax policy that they would endorse if they did not know whether they were rich or poor. Contemporary critics have faulted Rawls and liberal-egalitarian theory more generally for excessive individualism, but the solidarist use of similar arguments shows that they are not *intrinsically* linked to a deeply individualist worldview. They may be even more persuasive when reconnected with the idea of common-wealth.

In his own day, Bourgeois's critics faulted him for presenting a theory that could justify a whole range of solutions, from a minimalist safety net to a socialist revolution. Of course, this indeterminacy may have been strategic. He was the leader of the dominant group in the National Assembly and the principle of solidarism helped him to appeal to socialists and liberal-republicans alike. From a contemporary perspective, a certain degree of flexibility can also be viewed as a positive feature in so far as it recognizes the need for deliberation, experimentation, and contestation about what is a fair way to share common-wealth.[51] The theory of solidarism forces us to pose this question and provides some tools for answering it, while also recognizing that the answer will vary in different historical periods and cultures. For example, a deeply religious society might devote a large portion of the common-wealth to endowing religious institutions and a more individualist society might adopt a minimum income.

SOLIDARISM AND THE CITY

The solidarist theory of the common-wealth can also help us think about urban policy in new and creative ways and to imagine alternatives to the neo-liberal city.[52] The city itself is a striking illustration of Obama's claim "you didn't build that," because it is obvious that no individual built the city by him- or herself. Once we begin to think in solidarist terms, a new set of policies becomes possible to imagine. For example, the concepts of social property and rent explain why it is legitimate to capture part of the value created through urban real estate markets and use this value to pay for public goods. "Rent" highlights the fact that investments in different locations yield different returns and this difference is directly linked to location, which is value created by others. The government provides public transit, schools, urban infrastructure, and policing; neighbors foster community, aesthetics, and eyes-on-the-street; and businesses create opportunities for work, leisure activities, and consumption. Some of this social value can be captured and reallocated to solve the social problems of urban life such as lack of affordable housing and transit infrastructure. Many countries including Canada and the United States do not tax all or part of the capital gains on the sale of a primary residence. Simply taxing this unearned increment and eliminating the mortgage interest deduction could almost triple the budget for public housing in the United States.[53] Inclusionary zoning, value capture, and community benefit agreements are all applications of the idea that some of the profit from real estate development should be reinvested in public goods.[54]

As we will see in chapter 6, transit activists in San Francisco used an updated version of solidarism to promote a novel way of funding public transit through a property tax levy on commercial real estate in the downtown core. They argued that both public and private actors contribute to the value of the commercial rents in downtown high-rises, but the profit is appropriated almost entirely by the private sector. A portion of these rents should go to the public and could be allocated to fund public transit. While San Francisco's "Transit Assessment District" was not adopted, a similar logic has convinced lawmakers in cities across the United States to pass inclusionary zoning legislation. The final chapter of the book introduces a recent decision by the California State Supreme Court, which upheld the city of San Jose's solidarist defense of a law requiring large developments to include affordable units. In court cases about inclusionary zoning, the removal of informal settlements, the privatization of public space, and the destruction of public housing, we see the relevance of the archeological work of unearthing the theory of solidarism. Judges are asked to decide between claims based on the right to private property and arguments that draw on social rights and the public good, concepts that need to be more fully and persuasively defended. Neo-liberalism—itself an archeological project—has been very successful at persuading people to perceive themselves and their relationship to others in a certain way, as possessive individuals rather than citizens linked together through common projects. Solidarism works on subjectivities in a similar way but with an opposite objective. It recasts public life as composed of ties of obligation. In the writings of solidarists like Gide, these ties are not described as webs that immobilize but as similar to the ropes linking mountain climbers; they are supports that help us climb higher and protect us when we fall.[55]

The text of solidarism is a palimpsest. Solidarism was a very influential theory, but its history has been almost entirely effaced.[56] The contemporary traces take the form of social policies and claims about the public interest and social rights, but these claims, like Obama's "you didn't build that" speech, remain inchoate. This chapter has tried to provide a comprehensive account of solidarism that renders these claims intelligible and politically salient.

Given the theoretical sophistication of solidarism, it is puzzling that the concept has largely been forgotten. The main reason seems to be political and historical. In the early 20th century, the ideological terrain was increasingly polarized between socialist parties that opposed collaboration with the capitalist state and bourgeois parties opposed to state intervention. Today the ideological terrain has shifted dramatically. Both the left and right basically agree on the legitimacy of a minimal welfare state and the capitalist economy but differ over the degree and form of redistribution. The right, however, has been more effective in the past 20 years at shifting the terrain by convincing people that privatization and low taxes increase freedom and unleash initiative that creates prosperity for all, or at least for those who deserve it. The left needs an alternative to the welfare-as-state-charity model, which has several defects. By describing recipients as those who have failed to achieve self-sufficiency, it depicts them as bare life.[57] This erodes equality and establishes a relationship of paternalism/dependency. The welfare-as-state-charity model also undermines political support by framing taxation as coercive (as a way of forcing the individual to give his resources to someone else). This frame can reinforce the view that the poor and working class are "takers."[58] This frame also reinforces the belief that the rich deserve the increasingly large share that they have claimed for themselves.

Libertarian legal theorists have been extremely successful at promoting a distinct but related legal concept: regulatory takings.[59] The basic premise is that government regulation that decreases the market value of property is equivalent to expropriation and therefore the loss must be compensated by the government. This book asks readers to consider the inverse: when government action increases the value of property, then the collectivity has a legitimate claim on this value. This helps us see that there are untapped resources that could be reallocated to address injustice in cities. Looking at justice and injustice in the cities, however, makes things more complicated rather than less complicated. Through the lens of the urban, justice is not only a question of how to distribute something abstract like money but how to live together, side by side. Justice in cities has a concrete, material, and visceral dimension that more abstract theories of equality do not have to address. The following chapters look at such conflicts, which take place in courtrooms and parks and plazas, sites where processes of dislocation are resisted and challenged. The first conflict that I examine is a struggle over the constitutional right to shelter in India, a case that shows how the right to the city was built on the unstable foundation of the liberal approach to the right to life.

[3]

THE RIGHT TO LIFE AND SHELTER
IN HOMEGROWN NEIGHBORHOODS

On July 13, 1981, the chief minister of Maharashtra, India, announced that all pavement dwellers would be evicted from public property. Their makeshift shelters would be destroyed and the inhabitants would be sent back to their villages. One of the pavement dwellers was P. Angamuthu, a landless laborer who migrated to Bombay in 1961 in order to find work. He left Salem, Tamil Nadu, because of a drought which exacerbated unemployment and hunger in his village. He found a low-paying job in a chemical company. Unable to afford even the most basic dwelling, he paid a "landlord" for plastic sheeting and access to a bit of pavement adjacent to the Western Express Highway. Some of his neighbors were construction workers who built the highway and then remained after it was finished. Angamuthu lived there with his wife and three daughters until July 23, 1981, when his shack was destroyed and his entire family was forced onto a bus to Salem. Unable to find work, he soon returned to Bombay.

Angamuthu's story is not unique. In India alone, 64 million people live in urban slums. According to the 2011 census, 41 percent of the residents of Mumbai live in informal settlements.[1] Angamuthu's name is known because he was one of the petitioners who challenged the dispossession and deportation in a case that made it to the Indian Supreme Court (ISC). The resulting decision, *Olga Tellis v. Bombay Municipal Corporation* (1985), is considered a pathbreaking case of public interest litigation.[2]

In *Olga Tellis* the ISC cautiously recognized the legitimacy of some of the claims made by people living in informal settlements, but subsequent decisions have scaled back even this limited recognition of social rights.[3]

For example, in 2002 the Delhi High Court ordered the eviction of tens of thousands of people living in informal settlements along the Yamuna River. The informal settlements did not encroach on privately owned property, but they were an anathema to people living in adjacent neighborhoods. A neighborhood association brought a suit demanding that the police remove the slum. The Court agreed. In the judicial opinion, Justice Sikri emphasized that it would be wrong to prioritize "social justice" for slum dwellers over the rights of the people in the adjacent neighborhoods.[4] According to the judge, the existence of slums threatened the lives not of those who had to live *in* them but of those who lived *near* them.

Article 21 of the Indian Constitution states, "No person shall be deprived of his life or personal liberty except according to procedure established by law." Invoking article 21 in this way was a significant reversal of the logic of *Olga Tellis*, which first acknowledged that the meaningful enjoyment of the right to life rests on the ability to find work, and the need to work is what forces people to live in urban slums. In *Olga Tellis*, the ISC did not require that the government provide alternative land to people left homeless through slum clearance projects, but it did recognize, in principle, that the right to life could imply a right to reside in the city, even if this meant occupying the least desirable marginal spaces.[5]

Illegally occupying state or privately owned land is a way of claiming a right to the city. This chapter asks whether it is acceptable to clear informal squatter settlements, and if so, under what circumstances. The court cases make it clear that these decisions involve conflicting rights. In some cases, the legal rights of private property owners come into direct conflict with the needs of homeless people. How do we balance the right to subsistence against the right to private property? Does it matter how the property is used and whether it is owned by an individual or the state?

In *Olga Tellis*, the ISC acknowledged that the right to shelter can be derived from the right to life, and this seemed like a huge victory. By drawing out the implicitly Lockean logic of the decision, however, I show that the Court placed the doctrine of social rights on a very unstable foundation. The right to housing should be understood as composed of two parts: the right to shelter and the right to a share of the common-wealth. Both are necessary to explain why it is wrong to displace people with insecure tenure.

According to UN-Habitat there are three levels of the right to housing: basic shelter, secure tenure, and adequacy.[6] Basic shelter means that an individual or family has protection from the elements, a place to store belongings, and the ability to fulfill basic physical needs such as sleeping, washing, and consuming food. Secure tenure refers to legal recognition of control over living space, which can come through ownership or usufruct (tenancy in private, cooperative, or public housing). A squatter is someone who lacks secure tenure. Adequacy is a more difficult concept, since adequacy is related to cultural norms, technological development, and economic context. According to UN-Habitat, slums lack one or more of the following: structural quality and durability of dwellings; access to safe water; access to sanitation facilities; and sufficient living area. These concepts, however, seem to fit imperfectly with the complex negotiations and social relations that underpin the diverse forms of tenure in contemporary cities like Mumbai. As Arjun Appadurai points out, many poor people pay rent to secure a spot in one of the vast *bastis* (slums) or *jopadpattis* (settlements composed of shacks with amenities), while others live with relatives or in the interstices of the city: storage rooms, sidewalks, roofs, parapets, alleys, and compound walls.[7] In this chapter, I argue that the right to housing also has a fourth, less familiar but equally important component: proximity. By proximity I mean access to non-commodified sources of value (social networks, cultural activities) and to public and social goods, including employment.

OLGA TELLIS

The *Olga Tellis* decision has been cited as a pathbreaking example of the legal recognition of social rights.[8] A closer examination, however, shows that this is not an accurate characterization. In what follows, I will provide a brief overview of the logic of the court decision and the issues that it raises. This decision implicitly relies on the Lockean theory of property, which is not surprising given that Locke provided an extremely influential defense of private property, which has been assimilated into the English legal tradition. By making the Lockean assumptions explicit, we can see both the usefulness and limitations of this framework.

In *Olga Tellis*, the ISC considered a petition brought by slum dwellers in Bombay (now Mumbai) who were facing imminent displacement. The petitioners challenged the slum clearance project on procedural and substantive grounds. They argued that there is a right to occupy public land and this right is derived from the constitutional protection of the right to life in article 21 of the Indian Constitution. They also claimed that the municipal statute that allowed for eviction without prior notice was unreasonable in so far as it failed to provide the opportunity for those affected to plead their case. Finally, the Court considered the underlying issue, which was the paradoxical assertion that an individual could have a natural right to public property.

One of the challenges faced by Angamuthu and his fellow petitioners was the language of the Indian Constitution, which did not incorporate a right to housing or shelter.[9] Although 95.9 percent of constitutions in developing countries recognize the right to private property, only 40.2 percent recognize the right to housing.[10] The rights to land, housing, food/water, and development are among the "social and economic" rights that are least likely to be constitutionalized. The ISC, however, accepted the petitioners' argument that shelter is closely linked to the right to life, which is protected in the Indian Constitution. The Court agreed that life itself depended on the ability to secure basic necessities through work and, given the extreme poverty in many rural parts of India, this meant moving to the cities to eke out a living. The ISC pointed out the enormous disparity between the cost of renting a modest apartment in Bombay and a laborer's monthly salary. It would be literally impossible to rent any kind of legal housing, let alone to pay for housing and other necessities such as food, clothing, and medical care. Living on the remote outskirts of the city had once been a viable option for new arrivals, but given the vast scale of the metropolis, and the huge distance between jobs and housing, the cost of transportation made this prohibitive. This meant that workers had to live in close proximity to job sites. Drawing on research presented by sympathetic journalists, the ISC also accepted that the extreme shortage of affordable housing in proximity to jobs was partially caused by the government's failure to implement its own urban plan, which had called for decentralization of commerce and production.

Olga Tellis is viewed as a decision endorsing social rights because of the way the ISC transforms the negative right to life into a potentially positive obligation on the state to consider how government policy could indirectly deprive citizens of the preconditions of life.[11] While the ISC recognized the connection between life, labor, and the right to the city, it also emphasized that individual rights are not absolute. Individual rights must be balanced against the broader public good, which the state is obliged to protect. The ISC noted that even the fundamental rights to life and liberty are not trumps;[12] the role of the Court is to examine whether policies that threaten or burden the lives of some are nevertheless reasonable in the context of the government's broader responsibilities.

Reasonableness here has both a substantive and a procedural component. The procedural dimension requires that a policy be within the mandate of state authority. The petitioners, however, challenged this definition of "reasonable" and insisted that state action must also meet the criteria of natural justice. They argued that a policy is reasonable when it is adopted after a process of consultation, so that those most directly affected have had the opportunity to explain their objections. The Bombay Municipal Corporation Act, however, did not require any prior notice before clearing encroachments on publically owned land. The ISC refused to recognize a general requirement that notice be given prior to eviction. The Court agreed that this would be preferable and appropriate in most cases but also insisted that the local authorities must have discretion to act quickly and decisively when necessary to fulfill their mandate.[13]

The Court also examined the issue of substantive reasonableness. It asked whether, all things considered, the government was justified in removing "encroachments" (informal settlements built on public land). The Court concluded that "no one has a right to make use of a public property for private use without authorisation," and it rejected the petitioners' argument that necessity—the article 21 right to life—should trump the public interest.[14] The ISC interpreted the case as a conflict between two legitimate interests: the economic needs of the poor and the safety and mobility of the broader population. It relied on the municipality's claim that the land was adjacent to a public highway and was necessary to ensure the safe circulation of pedestrians. The construction and maintenance of roads is a paradigmatic example of a government responsibility that benefits the public as a whole. The city of Bombay argued that makeshift dwellings on sidewalks make it difficult for city workers to collect trash and clear drains, maintenance work which is necessary for the health and safety of the population. The ISC agreed with the municipality's argument that there is a legitimate state interest in public safety. Pavement dwellers may act out of necessity, but they block the sidewalks, forcing pedestrians into the street, where their lives are threatened by vehicular traffic.

After carefully considering the arguments on both sides, the ISC rejected the petitioners' claim that their right to life should prevent the city from carrying out its stated intention to clear encroachments on public land. It also rejected the petitioners' demands for greater consultation, prior notice, and alternative land to rebuild on. Why then is this case sometimes described as a victory for social rights? I think there are two reasons.[15] The first is rhetorical; throughout the decision, the ISC expresses a great deal of sympathy for the plight of pavement dwellers. In principle it recognizes a limited "right to the city," but it assigns a low priority to this right. By "right to the city" I mean that the ISC recognizes that shelter alone is not enough. People must be able to live in the city where they can survive and flourish. The second reason is that the decision did provide protection for a subset of the people who were affected by the slum clearance policy. In 1976, the government had carried out a census of squatters and provided them with identity cards. This was part of a never-realized plan to provide alternative accommodation to people living in slums. The ISC decided that this registration process was evidence of a commitment to these particular people and directed the city of Bombay to provide alternative accommodations or land to this subgroup.

The "right to life" was the primary focus of the court decision, but it was not the only issue raised by the petitioners. They also asked the ISC to consider the meaning of article 39, section b of the Indian Constitution, which states that "the ownership and control of the material resources of the community are so distributed as best to subserve the common good."[16] This article is found in part 4 of the Constitution, which outlines "Directive Principles of State Policy." These principles were designated as aspirational rather than justiciable rights.

Namita Wahi has argued that the Indian Constitution included contradictory ideas about property rights in part because there was considerable disagreement among the drafters about how to balance economic development and social rights. They needed to find a way to limit the feudal power of the *zamindars* while still fostering economic growth through industrial development. In order to accomplish the first goal, the state needed to limit private property, but to accomplish the second, it needed to protect it. This resulted in a constitution with a justiciable right to property, directive principles that limited this right, and a series of court cases and constitutional amendments that tried to clarify the relation between them.[17]

In *Olga Tellis*, the Court chose not to address these complicated questions and instead relied on the dominant liberal approach to property which it inherited from the British legal tradition. This theory, however, contained its own internal tensions, which become apparent when we closely examine the Lockean account of property rights that informed the decision. Angamuthu's lawyers introduced an alternative theory of common property which was dismissed by the Court, presumably because it did not fit easily with the better known laissez-faire-liberal, welfarist-liberal, and state socialist approaches to property. The final section of this chapter suggests that the theory of the urban commonwealth advanced in this book points toward a better way of interpreting and resolving legal dispute about property in land.

LOCKE AND THE RIGHT TO PROPERTY

I begin with John Locke's paradigmatic account of private property because his theory implicitly informs and explicitly justifies the liberal approach to property rights that still predominates today. In *The Second Treatise of Government*[18] Locke discusses three different ways of acquiring property: labor, need, and agreement. He concedes that all property was originally held in common, but then he argues that private property is justified when it is created by mixing one's labor with external material. He illustrates this principle by giving examples of the individual appropriation of the bounty of nature: water in a stream, apples on a tree, a deer running through the forest. The apple on the tree belongs to everyone but an apple that was harvested becomes the legitimate private property of the person who picked it.[19] Locke argues that the same idea applies to land. The person who clears, cultivates, and improves land has mixed his labor with it and therefore deserves ownership of both the produce and the land itself.

Locke notes that there are some natural limitations on appropriation. The first is the spoilage limitation, a principle of natural law that dictates that no one should take more than he or she can use, since the bounty of the earth is not meant to be wasted. This limitation, however, loses its force after the introduction of trade and money, because these make it possible to accumulate value in durable goods that do not spoil such as gold and silver.

The second limitation is the famous Lockean proviso. According to Locke, this initial appropriation of *land*, by improving it, wasn't "any prejudice to any other man, since there was still enough, and as good left;" and more than the yet unprovided for could use.[20] The phrase "enough and as good" has been subject to considerable scrutiny. Locke claimed that modern societies met these criteria indirectly. Even if the "yet unprovided for" cannot acquire land, they can acquire a share of the goods produced on privately owned land and therefore they are not harmed by the original acquisition. As mentioned in the previous chapter, Locke's argument is that a landless laborer in England is better off than a king controlling a vast territory of common land in America.[21]

Even if we accept the empirical claim that the day laborer is better off than the person in the state of nature, this does not mean that their share is "as good" as the one taken by the first privatizers, because the first privatizers had freedom and opportunities to enlarge their possessions in a way that laborers do not. Furthermore, this framing rests on the "either/or" fallacy. By implying that the only choices are "common-property-with-low-productivity" or "large-estates-and-day-labor," it denies the possibility of other more equitable arrangements, for example distributing land more widely by limiting the size of estates or farming cooperatively. These alternatives were hardly unimaginable in Locke's day. The former was proposed by the 17th-century republican political theorist James Harrington and the latter was practiced by the Diggers, an egalitarian agrarian movement in 17th-century England.[22]

Locke also introduces two other principles that limit property rights: political agreement and the right to life. Although the right to property is described as a pre-political natural right, it can only be enforced after the social contract creates a state. Property becomes something more than mere possession when it is recognized by others, and this recognition is guaranteed through enforcement. In a puzzling passage, Locke points out that the natural-right-to-appropriate-land functions until land becomes scarce, and then people must switch to using "consent" to settle disputes over grazing lands and territorial boundaries. It is hard to overlook the fact that Locke uses the biblical families of Cain and Abel as examples of clans that might hypothetically reach the point where their expanding land claims came into conflict.[23] Not only politics but also the threat of violence haunts the text. In this formulation, political institutions are not limited to protecting property rights that are derived from natural law; they seem to create property rights, by balancing different interests and claims.

At first it might seem as if the labor theory of property could justify the claims made by squatters. If labor and improvement justify ownership, then the people who build informal settlements should have legitimate title to their dwellings and even the land underneath the buildings. But Locke specifically rejects this conclusion. He insists that there are two types of "common" property. The first is empty land, which is not under the sovereign authority of a state, and the second is land that is "common by compact." The unilateral right to take from the common stock only applies in the first situation. Locke notes:

It is true, in *land* that is common in *England*, or any other country, where there is plenty of people under government, who have money and commerce, no one can enclose or appropriate any part, without the consent of all his fellow-commoners; because this is left common by compact, i.e. by the law of the land, which is not to be violated. And though it be common, in respect of some men, it is not so to all mankind. . . .[24]

This passage reminds us that the discussion of property is part of a larger work on government, and one of the goals of the text is to justify state sovereignty. Paradoxically, the right to property is both naturalized as pre-political but also produced by state authority. Locke does not seem too troubled by the possible implications of this paradox. He concludes that the end of "political society" is the preservation of private property and the state's power is limited to those responsibilities necessary to achieve this end.[25] It can protect property rights but is not authorized to modify them.

There is, however, a factor that complicates the view that Locke is simply an apologist for an unlimited right to private property, and that is the principle of self-preservation. In the opening paragraphs of the *Second Treatise*, Locke emphasizes that humans are obliged to preserve themselves, and the law of nature commands the preservation of all mankind. In a time and place where premature death from overwork and malnutrition was common, this seems to imply some type of minimal obligation to provide charity, and Locke did defend a limited, draconian form of poor relief.[26] He also noted that the right to preservation included a right to the *means* for preservation, including subsistence, and that this entailed an obligation on others: a wealthy man could not rightfully deny another person "surplusage of his Goods" when "pressing Wants call for it."[27]

We now have all three components of Locke's theory—labor (improvement), subsistence, and politics—and we can see how they come together in the *Olga Tellis* decision. As noted above, the labor theory of acquisition is dismissed as inapplicable to societies governed by law, so the relevant components are politics and the right to "subsistence." According to Locke, self-preservation is the natural end of human beings and property is a means to that end. Human beings are naturally vulnerable to the environment and need protection from the elements in order to thrive. Building and shaping the landscape in order to create shelter is a basic human need, similar to the need for food and physical security. Even Hobbes, who had a limited view of natural law, included the right to a place to live among the most basic rights. According to the Lockean schema, the right to subsistence has priority over the natural right to property. This is the position that is taken by the ISC in *Olga Tellis*.

If the analysis stopped here, then a Lockean approach would clearly favor the pavement dwellers; the right to property is a means to the end of self-preservation, and the end takes precedence over the means. But there are two other important points to consider. The first is politics. Locke treats these principles as the source of legitimate positive law but also emphasizes that political institutions are authorized to resolve conflicts. Second, Locke insists that private property is justified because it can increase economic productivity and thereby provide subsistence for more people. The private property rights of an individual or group are subordinate to the right of self-preservation, but the implication of this principle changes if private property increases overall flourishing by increasing productivity. This is where agreement or political institutions come in. The state is authorized to decide how to allocate common resources and to adjudicate conflicts that emerge between individuals asserting subsistence rights and others seeking to protect their property.

In *Olga Tellis*, the Court endorses this Lockean view that the homeless and the poor have basic subsistence rights, but nevertheless, it concludes these rights do not limit the state; instead, they are treated as moral obligations that private individuals, institutions, and government agencies should try to fulfill. The ISC explained its position in the following terms: "The demand is not so much for less governmental interference as for positive governmental action to provide equal treatment to neglected segments of society." This is a laudable goal, but it was used to explain why the government could destroy the dwellings of the poor and displace the inhabitants without providing alternative accommodation. This is an ironic reversal of positive and negative rights. The government has a non-enforceable obligation to develop policies to improve the conditions in slums; therefore, slum dwellers do not have an enforceable right not to be deprived of shelter. Furthermore, the emphasis on the right to *life* positions the rights-bearer as bare life and severs subsistence needs from broader claims about access to public goods and social resources.[28]

LAW AND ORDER

The *Olga Tellis* decision drew on three principles: the right to bare life, deference to state authority, and developmentalism. By developmentalism

I mean the assumption that the protection of private property rights would foster the economic growth necessary to secure subsistence rights in the future. Since 2000, there have been a series of decisions which emphasize that India's economic vitality is threatened by slums because they harm India's image as a modern nation with world-class cities. This concern leads the judges to permit the clearance of slums, but it also is expressed in calls for better urban planning and a more comprehensive housing policy. The problem is that there is no way of enforcing these policy directives.[29]

In the 2002 decision *Pitam Pura Sudhar Samiti v. Union of India* (hereafter *Samiti*), we can see the themes of bare life, deference to state authority, and developmentalism in a crystalized form. One of the claims consolidated in this case was brought by Shri K. K. Manchanda, the president of the vividly named Ashok Vihar Residents Sufferers Associations. Blocks C and D of this residential development are adjacent to a piece of underdeveloped land that is designated as part of a green belt. Beyond the green belt is a railroad line and on the other side of the railway was an informal settlement with 8,000 to 10,000 residents, many of whom earn their living working in nearby factories. According to the judgment, there are no toilets and "this has caused untold miseries." In contrast to *Olga Tellis*, a decision which expressed considerable sympathy for the plight of the pavement dwellers, in *Samiti* Justice Sikri is concerned almost exclusively with the suffering of the *neighbors*. He writes,

> to the residents living in Blocks C and D . . . [the slum] has proved not only a health hazard to the locality but has also transgressed their right to decent living. People desirous of having morning walk cannot do so as these dwellers easing themselves [e.g. defecating] pose such uncultured scene. Besides young girls do not come to their own balconies throughout the day as obnoxious smell pollute [*sic*] the atmosphere and the entire environment is unconducive to public health and morality.[30]

Whereas *Olga Tellis* expressed concerns about traffic safety, this decision emphasizes public health and hygiene. In both cases, general arguments about hypothetical, indirect threats to the public are invoked to justify displacement of specific people who have no other place to go.

In *Samiti* there is a clear sense that the judge is viewing the issue from the perspective of the more affluent people living in the residential developments adjacent to the slums. He describes the landscape and the geography as if viewed from the balcony of Block C or D of Ashok Vihar. From this point of view, the green belt is closest and the settlement is farther away. He also describes the people living in the slums from that distant perspective. They are the source of obnoxious smells, pollution, and moral decay. He doesn't consider the scene from the other side of the tracks. He fails to ask what it might be like to be forced to defecate on the edge of the train tracks, visible to the resentful residents of Ashok Vihar, who are glaring with disgust from their balconies, while enjoying the privilege of being able to retreat to their own bathrooms when necessary.

This perspective, while quite distinct from the one in *Olga Tellis*, is nevertheless an extension of it. The earlier decision was more sympathetic, but from a legal perspective, it still treated the petitioners as bare life, as people who needed help to survive, rather than as agents who built the city, cared for residents, made products, moved goods, and provided services, all the while receiving very little in return. This emphasis on "need/subsistence/ life" made the petitioners seem more like animals than human beings. The *Olga Tellis* decision was a component of this broader discourse of dehumanization, which took a much more vivid, explicit, and extreme form in *Samiti*. *Samiti* is not exceptional. In *Almitra Patel* (2000), the ISC issued a judicial opinion about environmental issues which blamed slum dwellers for a range of urban problems such as pollution and garbage. According to the ISC, the solution to the garbage problem is the removal of slums. Given that slum dwellers frequently work as garbage pickers clearing trash from the city, we have to read this as a statement that treats the residents themselves as human garbage to be disposed of.[31]

The second theme that we see in a more exaggerated form in *Samiti* is developmentalism. In *Olga Tellis*, there was a faint trace of the Lockean concern that private property must be protected in order to provide the proper incentives for economic development, because such development would ultimately benefit everyone. In *Samiti*, slum dwellers are depicted as a direct threat to modernity, prosperity, and development. According to Justice Sikri,

> Delhi being the capital city of the country, is a show window to the world of our culture, heritage, traditions and way of life. A city like Delhi must act as a catalyst for building modern India. It cannot be allowed to degenerate and decay. Defecation and urination cannot be allowed to take place in open at places which are not meant for these purposes.[32]

In this passage, the harm caused by slums is not the harm experienced by the people forced to live in poor-quality dwellings, without basic amenities and without secure tenure. The harm is suffered by the city itself, and the city is imagined as a reflection of the identity of the more privileged residents. Justice Sikri concludes that "it [the city] cannot be allowed to degenerate and decay." What exactly does this mean?

This statement could be a way of justifying public investment in order to get rid of slums by regularizing tenancy, providing basic amenities, and building alternative, high-density public housing. Read in this light, it would be a step toward a justiciable approach to social rights, rather than the aspirational one presented in *Olga Tellis*. In fact, however, the intent is exactly the opposite. The judge notes that the complicated problem of creating a city without slums is the responsibility of policymakers and experts and the legal question is more circumscribed. The legal question is whether the city has an obligation to clear the slum and displace the residents in order to ensure the comfort and well-being of the people living nearby. He concludes there is an obligation to remove encroachments on public land, and he treats this obligation as an enforceable statutory duty rather than a general directive.

At first glance it might seem like this part of the decision is a departure from the Lockean logic of *Olga Tellis*, which endorsed a degree of deference to the legislative branch of the government. In *Samiti* we see that the principle of deference is not applied consistently. When are rights merely interests that the government should consider and when are they trumps or at least high cards that the government must respect? The answer to this question is more difficult than it initially seems. What makes this case so interesting is that this is not a case that pits the rights of property owners against the rights of squatters. The vast informal settlement was located on public land and the petition to evict the squatters was brought not by owners seeking to exercise their "right to exclude" but by neighbors who felt adversely impacted by the proximity of slums. The neighbors used the courts to compel city officials to enforce previous court orders banning encroachments that contravened the existing municipal plan.

According to the Court, "Public interest requires promotion of law and order, not its denigration and destruction."[33] In this statement the Court characterizes its decision as a form of legislative deference. The suit was brought in order to compel the government to follow the law by removing encroachments. The municipal plan did not allow the construction of informal settlements on undeveloped property and, according to Justice Sikri, the problem was that the executive branch (especially the corrupt police) was failing to enforce existing policy. Law is linked to order and the term "order" hints at something that is beyond or behind the law. It is not explicit and therefore not the direct focus of legal or philosophical analysis, but it underpins it. Order is the unwritten imaginary that informs the text of the law.[34] In *Samiti*, there were two sets of laws that were not being implemented: the laws directing the city to provide adequate accommodation to the poor and the laws prohibiting the erection of private dwellings on public land. Only one of these failures, however, was treated as a threat to order. Reading the court decision for what is not said as well as what is said, we see that the poor people asserting a right to the city are treated as the source of disorder, not the economic and political system that produces them.

SOLIDARISM IN THE SLUMS: WE BUILT THAT

Since there was no right to housing in the Indian Constitution, the lawyers for the pavement dwellers were compelled to frame their petition in terms of "the right to life." This was not entirely disingenuous. Given that mortality rates from both disease and suicide are higher in rural areas,[35]

securing a place to live in the city is linked to life itself, but the lawyers
and housing activists also presented another argument, which does a better job of explaining why expulsion and dispossession are wrong. Instead
of emphasizing suffering, this argument stresses the agency of the dispossessed and the fact that they have contributed to the common-wealth. It
is a rights claim, but one that emphasizes the collective right to share the
common-wealth rather than the individual right to autonomy or bare life.
Ironically, this rights claim draws on a component of Locke's theory of private property, but the one Locke himself dismissed as irrelevant to modern states: the labor theory of property. The claim is basically "we built
that" and it applies both to the informal settlements and to the city itself.
In some cases, the inhabitants literally made the land upon which they
built their dwellings. According to Gautam Bhan, the neighborhood of
Pushta on the Yamuna River in Delhi was created by families who filled in
the vacant marshy embankment with leftover debris and rubble from construction sites, gradually transforming it into a place to live.[36] Eventually
this *terra nullis* became home to 35,000 people.

   Not only did they build their own settlements, they also built much of
the infrastructure of the city. Some of the early residents of Pushta were
brought to Delhi by contractors to build the infrastructure for the Asian
Games in 1982.[37] The people who built the settlement adjacent to the
Western Express Highway in Bombay were the same workers who constructed the highway. This is true not only in India but across the developing world. In his book *The Modernist City*, James Holston documents
how migrant workers from rural areas in Brazil built the new capital city,
Brasilia, only to discover that the plan for the city had no place for the
modest dwellings of the working poor.[38] The construction workers and
their families settled on land on the urban periphery and then fought to get
municipal services and legal recognition for the second city that they built.

   In a brief submitted to the court in *Olga Tellis*, a journalist and sup-
porter of the pavement dwellers pointed out that slum dwellers "constitute about 50 per cent of the total population of Greater Bombay, [and]
that they supply the major work force for Bombay from menial jobs to the
most highly skilled jobs." The brief emphasized that some residents have
been living in their dwellings for generations. "They have been making a
significant contribution to the economic life of the city . . . and therefore,

it is unfair and unreasonable on the part of the State Government and the Municipal Corporation to destroy their homes and deport them."[39] According to this analysis, not only their needs but also their contributions entitle them to a right to the city. The ISC summarized the argument like this: "The slum dwellers are the *sine qua non* of the city. They are entitled to a *quid pro quo*."[40]

The phrase *quid pro quo* means "something for something"; the claim is that the workers have contributed their labor to build and maintain the city, but they have not received fair compensation. This is a desert-based argument and such arguments have been controversial in contemporary political philosophy because they provide reasons to reject other principles of justice such as equality and need. In his book *Principles of Social Justice*, David Miller defines desert judgments like this: "Some agent A is said to deserve some benefit B on the basis of an activity or performance P."[41] The quid pro quo argument follows this structure. Poor laborers deserve a place to live on the basis of their contribution to the economic life—and often to the physical infrastructure—of the city. Intuitively, this argument seems consistent with the solidarist position that poor workers deserve a larger share of the social product, but it differs in an important respect. The solidarist argument is not really desert based according to Miller's definition. Miller defines a performance as an intentional act and it is hard to construe "social inheritance" in this way. The right to social property could be interpreted as a kind of negative desert argument with the following structure: A's (the wealthy) do not deserve B (unlimited private property) because such property does not derive from their performance (from their own labor/contribution).

Even when reformulated in this way, however, there are still two distinct principles: (1) workers deserve a fair share of what they produce; (2) society, not private property owners, should be the steward of the social inheritance. In their book *The Myth of Ownership*, Liam Murphy and Thomas Nagel make a similar point when they argue that tax policy has two functions. It determines how the social product is distributed among individuals and also how it is divided between private and state control.[42] These issues are distinctive from both a conceptual and a normative perspective, but they are also related.

The link between them makes more sense when informed by the theory introduced by Gide, Bourgeois, and Fouillée in the late 19th century. Solidarism holds that the vast social product created by the division of labor is naturally composed of public and private shares. When a disproportionate share of the social product is appropriated by the few, then those who have the most owe a debt to society. The debt can be paid directly through taxation and appropriation of a share of productive capital or indirectly through forms of regulation that shift the distribution of surplus among different types of workers and between workers and owners. Democratic deliberation will be needed to decide among different ways of allocating the social product: collective consumption, basic income, insurance against bad luck, or claims about desert.

The "quid pro quo" claim also has a rhetorical dimension. This desert-based argument for a basic standard of living is an alternative to the welfare-as-charity model, which treats recipients as having failed to achieve personal responsibility and therefore in need of the paternalistic assistance of others. Solidarism redefines need as a structural condition rather than an individual-moral failure. In fact, it equates fault with the broader social system that allocates benefits in a fundamentally unfair way. The condition of life in slums is not interpreted as a sign of individual dysfunction that can be rectified through self-improvement or charity but as a basic structural flaw that must be corrected through political action.

In *Olga Tellis*, the ISC did not endorse this view. The case came to the Court in 1985. This was the height of a period of legal innovation, in which mobilized social movements working in conjunction with journalists and lawyers brought new issues and arguments before the courts and the public. In 1976 the preamble to the Indian Constitution had been amended to define India as a socialist state, and the right to private property was downgraded from its original status as a fundamental right. The ideological groundwork for something like solidarism was in place. In addition to the Gandhian-inspired communitarian/anti-materialist ethos, India also had a strong tradition of state regulation of private industry, public employment, and nationalized banking and insurance sectors.[43] At the same time, however, there was also a high level of stratification by caste, class, and religion. According to Lloyd and Suzanne Rudolph, India had a strong, interventionist state, but one whose policies tended to support the growing middle class of state functionaries and urban entrepreneurs. By the time the government began to turn attention to the problem of poverty, there were already growing concerns about the harmful effect of public sector inefficiency, and an emerging consensus that an over-directed economy was an obstacle to economic growth. Along with pressure from the International Monetary Fund (IMF), this set the stage for the shift away from social politics toward the pro-capitalist and market-oriented reforms promoted by Sanjay Gandhi.[44] The Court was reluctant to require that the government take on immense new responsibilities.

This background makes it clear that the theory of social property and common-wealth provides only a partial solution to conflicts over urban space. The theory explains why it is wrong to exclude and displace people from public goods including cities, but it does not tell us precisely how to balance conflicting claims in particular contexts. In some places the state can play a direct role as "debt collector" and provider of public goods, and in others the state might be more effective by implementing legislation that enables parts of civil society to flourish by building alternative economies and sites of power. The law can also shelter alternative economies. The concept of adverse possession or squatters' rights illustrates how this can be done.

ADVERSE POSSESSION

The case against dispossession and displacement rests on both a general right to the urban commonwealth and the entitlement to remain in a specific place. The latter can be understood either as a group "right to occupancy" or an individual right to property. I will introduce the right to occupancy in chapter 4. This chapter focuses on the specific features of what could be called squatters' rights. The concept of squatters' rights has Lockean roots; it rests on the contention that the continued use of land and/or the act of improving land through labor generates title to it. This idea has a long legal history. It was recognized in the Roman legal doctrine of *usucapio* and the British common law principle of adverse possession.

These terms describe a state-sanctioned transfer of land from owners to non-owners without the consent of the party who held the original title.[45] Adverse possession gives legal ownership to users after a certain number of years of continued occupancy, even though the title was never transferred. Why would the law recognize this type of acquisition? There are two main reasons. One stems from the belief that property rights exist to promote the public good. If land is meant to support human flourishing, then speculative ownership that leaves land undeveloped should be discouraged. The second reason is more pragmatic. It is linked to the view that property rights exist to secure stability and to decrease conflict. Legal title and actual possession are two different and potentially conflicting bases of ownership so legal systems try to make sure they do not become uncoupled. Possession may not be nine-tenths of the law, but there is certainly less room for dispute when the connection between use and ownership is maintained. If property owners know that they will lose their right to property if they fail to exercise ongoing control of it, then they will be more careful about maintaining such control.[46]

Adverse possession is an interesting concept because it is a way that illegality is transformed into legality. This alchemy takes place through labor and use. When a person mixes his labor with raw materials—filling in the marshy banks with sand, creating a foundation for a home with discarded concrete blocks—he creates a place to dwell and a certain kind of right to it. What about the philosophers' objection that this is incoherent, that the reverse is just as plausible: by mixing his labor with common property he loses the value of his labor rather than gaining the land? The government of New Delhi took this position. It did not recognize the terra firma of the riverbank as the property of the residents who made it. The government treated the new land on the banks of the Yamuna River as public property that could be redeveloped as a riverside promenade.

The philosophers are right that it is not logically necessary that the hybrid created by labor and common property (or in Fouillée's terms *form* and *fond*) belongs to the individual. There is a constitutive undecidability here, and this is why abstract theory alone only takes us so far. Intuitively, it seems plausible that labor generates some entitlement to the product of one's labor,[47] but this entitlement is not absolute. It does not apply when such appropriation dispossesses others, when it makes it impossible to meet the urgent needs of others, or when it is impossible to disentangle diverse contributions to the end product. How then do we know when an unauthorized occupation of land is legitimate and when it is not?

In their book *Property Outlaws: How Squatters, Pirates, and Protesters Improve the Law of Ownership*, Eduardo Peñalver and Sonia Katyal propose an answer to this question. Their approach de-emphasizes the natural right to property and instead suggests that we think about property as a social and political framework for regulating access to material things and a way of securing the public good.[48] They argue that the apparent stability and order that property law provides owes much to the destabilizing role of the lawbreaker, who occasionally forces shifts of entitlements and laws.[49] When people obey the law voluntarily, they do so for three main reasons: habit, legitimacy, and efficacy. The latter two are linked. The law appears legitimate when it works reasonably well to balance the dual goals of order and justice. What happens when the law doesn't work as it is supposed to? In democratic states, there are a range of strategies that citizens and residents can use to try to change the law. They can organize demonstrations, write op-ed pieces, vote, lobby, run for office, and petition the courts, but there is also considerable evidence that democratic deficits persist. Some people and groups have much lower capacity to influence the political system.[50] What David Harvey wrote in 1973 remains true today: democratic political institutions that rest on a philosophy of individual self-interest are unlikely to bring about social justice in cities.[51]

As we will see in chapter 8, the existence of democratic deficits is one of the main arguments in favor of civil disobedience. Peñalver and Katyal, however, go a step farther, and argue that *un-civil* disobedience may also be a necessary and legitimate form of communication and political action. They distinguish between expressive outlaws and acquisitive outlaws. Expressive outlaws, like classic practitioners of civil disobedience, violate the law, but they do so openly with the primary intent of persuading fellow citizens of the justice of their demands. Expressive outlaws accept punishment as a way of signaling that they seek to combat injustice without challenging the legitimacy of the legal order. Acquisitive outlaws, on the other hand, violate the law for their own benefit and try to avoid detection and punishment. Few theorists defend acquisitive outlaws because their conduct implies a rejection of the principle of the rule of law itself.[52]

Peñalver and Katyal point out that even if acquisitive outlaws reject the law, their actions may still be legitimate and can even have a positive impact on the evolution of the law. The violation of property law through land seizures can be justified in two ways: as a mechanism of redistribution or as a form of communication that helps overcome structural democratic deficits. One structural deficit is the lower level of political participation and influence exercised by poorer citizens.[53] Research on India confirms the trends observed in other countries: poor people have less political power than elites and the middle classes and are less effective at securing public goods.[54] When rural people migrate to cities and live on the streets, their actions more than their words persuade the government to build public housing, maintain existing affordable units, provide infrastructure to existing settlements, and defer evictions until alternative land is made available.[55]

A critic could respond that the concept of "acquisitive outlaws" rests on the claim that "might makes right": the unprincipled principle that it is acceptable to advance one's interests by taking what one wants and forcing others to accommodate them. Peñalver and Katyal, however, emphasize that law-breaking is acceptable only under strictly limited circumstances, in cases where there are barriers to market exchange or in situations of urgent necessity. Illegal downloading is an example of acquisitive outlaws responding to "barriers to market exchange." Before the introduction of services like iTunes, Netflix, and Amazon Prime, there was no platform for legally purchasing video content, including television programs that could be viewed over broadcast signals for free. Illegal actions forced media companies to develop new modes of exchange.

The second circumstance that justifies the actions of acquisitive outlaws is necessity. When a homeless person seeks shelter in the vestibule of a bank or a public park, she is violating property rights due to necessity. The underlying principle is that "it is not wrong to appropriate someone else's surplus property in order to provide for one's own need when viable legal alternatives are not available."[56] This principle could potentially justify significant levels of redistribution, especially in places where economic inequality is great and basic needs are not fulfilled.

Peñalver and Katyal concede that the application of this principle poses considerable challenges. If each person gets to decide whether his own needs are urgent and another's goods are "surplus" then we might well return to the Hobbesian war of all against all. The jurisprudence of adverse possession, however, provides some practical ways to limit this potentially overbroad reach. Adverse possession only transfers title after the squatter has invested considerable time (two to ten years) and effort in improving a place that she does not own. This is extremely risky, and the decision to do so is evidence of an urgent need that cannot be met in another way. The reverse is also true. If the property owner does not use, occupy, or assert her right to property over an extended period, this is prima facie evidence that it is "surplus." These criteria help ensure that this capillary form of redistribution does not become a source of complete disorder.

Property owners, of course, seldom see their property as surplus. The recent Indian court decisions provide a window into the way that the state responds to poor people who assert labor- and use-based claims to public property. The state raised three main objections: (1) Undeveloped government land is not surplus. It is used for necessary infrastructure that serves the public. (2) Slums are created by criminal gangs to make money, not by poor people trying to survive. (3) Building a shack on public land, like building a high-rise on public land, is a privatization of public space that harms the public good.

It is difficult to respond to these objections without invoking a theory of the urban commonwealth. Initially it might seem as if the concept of the "common-wealth" strengthens the government's claim that slum clearance is a legitimate way of protecting public property from appropriation by private actors such as criminal gangs, shady developers, and acquisitive outlaws. The idea of the common-wealth could reinforce the authority of the state to regulate public property in service of the public good. But social property is not a synonym for state property. The solidarists saw the state as an institution that could compel the rich to repay their debt to society through taxation, but they did not conflate social property and state property. The solidarists thought that non-state institutions such as labor unions and cooperatives could also advance the goal of equalizing the distribution of the social product. It is important to remember that the theory of solidarism has two components: a descriptive account of social property and a normative case for correcting unfair appropriations. It is the latter that must be brought to bear on this issue. The problem of slums is that some people's share of the social product is too small in comparison to their contributions and their needs.

Does this mean that individuals can simply take what they need or what they think they deserve? John Locke argued that in the state of nature, it is legitimate to unilaterally take water, or apples, or even land. Under conditions of abundance, the value of the material is extremely small and the value of labor is immense. Fouillée pointed out that this is not the case in the modern world, where the value of social, technological, and physical infrastructure is paramount. This is why the ISC was correct when it accused slum dwellers of privatization; they *are* taking a piece of this common-wealth and using it for their own benefit. By erecting a shack near a factory or construction site, they are leveraging the power of proximity that enables them to gain a slightly larger share of the value being produced in the city. This is legitimate when the effect is to rectify an unfair allocation, or when the act is a legitimate demand for repayment of a debt. This is why the actions of poor people in slums are morally different from the actions of property owners or developers who encroach on public lands.[57] The latter are not owed a debt. The key issue is whether a particular demand results in a more or less fair allocation of common-wealth.

A related issue is how to fairly allocate the burden of repayment or redistribution. Even if we accept that it is legitimate to distribute land from owners to non-owners, it does not seem fair to force *owner A* to repay a general social debt to the landless while *owner B* does not. We can imagine a situation in which the land owned by *A* is attractive to squatters because of its proximity to a job site while *B*'s land is not. Or, *B* violently evicts squatters from his land, but *A* has greater sympathy for the landless and allows them to temporarily squat on his land, assuming that they will soon save up the money to rent or buy property, but they do not leave and eventually acquire a right to his property through the principle of adverse possession. In both scenarios, *A* ends up paying a disproportionate share of the debt and this does not seem justified.

Legal challenges to squatters' rights often raise exactly this point. In *Samiti*, the petitioners did not object to the principle of housing the homeless but rather the practice of allowing them to build slums that created negative externalities that adversely affected those living nearby. In a South African case called *Modderklip Boerdery (Pty) Ltd v. Modder East Squatters*, a private property owner brought a suit against the local city administration for failing to evict 40,000 people living on its property.[58] Modderklip, the company that owned the land, claimed that allowing land invasions violated section 25(1) of the Bill of Rights, which states that "no one may be deprived of property except in terms of law of general application." The key provision is the second one. The petitioner did not object to the principle the property rights may be abridged to further the public good, but did object to the municipality's refusal to apply the law and carry out an eviction order. This refusal, claimed Modderklip, amounted to a de facto support of land invasion, a form of redistribution which was neither legal nor general in its application.

In this case, the right to private property came into direct conflict with the squatters' rights to shelter, to the city, and to secure tenure over the land they had made into a home. The Court recognized both sides and directed the local administration to negotiate with the parties to find a compromise solution such as the transfer of the property to the public housing authorities through sale. This is a good solution to the fairness objection because it socializes the cost of meeting the needs of the homeless rather than arbitrarily making one property owner responsible while others contribute nothing.

This case is pathbreaking because it recognizes that squatters have legitimate claims to private property and obliges the state to intervene to resolve social problems. Yet it also affirms petitioner Modderklip's view that the rectification of structural injustice must be achieved through general laws. What does this mean for a theory that legitimizes the actions of property outlaws? Somewhat counter-intuitively, I want to suggest that this decision is an illustration of the dialectical approach to the law. By using the term "dialectical," I mean to emphasize how the law is produced through the struggle between opposing forces, in this case the large landowner and the landless. The homeless people themselves were unable to compel the municipality to meet its constitutional obligation to develop public housing, but, through the tactic of land invasion, the squatters actually gained a powerful ally: the Modderklip company itself. The company conceded that it would be impossible to simply evict 40,000 squatters by forcing them onto the road because they would literally have nowhere to go and even the jails couldn't accommodate them. This gave the company no choice but to advocate for public housing and it was the company's lawsuit that was instrumental in forcing the municipality to respond to the demands of the squatters. This reminds us that the role of property outlaws is to bring about legal change by opening up new ways for disenfranchised citizens to exercise power.

The Court did accept the arguments made by the company and balanced them against the rights of the squatters, but it did not treat both claims as equally legitimate. The claims of the landless were given priority. The key move in the judicial opinion comes when the Court interprets the conflict in the context of structural inequality, noting that whites own 90 percent of arable land in South Africa, even though they are less than 10 percent of the population. The Court describes this as a violation of the principle of equity. This is a promising step, but the meaning remained open-ended. This judgment would be more compelling if it explicitly invoked the notions of power, dispossession, and debt.

CONCLUSION

It is helpful to look at conflicts over place, property, and the right to the city from the solidaristic perspective. Solidarism explains what is wrong with the suggestion that people living in informal settlements should be re-housed at a lower cost in their villages of origin or in more remote fringes of the metropolis. If the collective responsibility extends only to sustaining life, as Locke suggested, then this policy would be legitimate. If the displaced people are not simply left to fend for themselves but are given enough basic food to survive, then the "right to life" is secured. The problem is that bare life is a necessary but not sufficient condition of human flourishing. People immigrate to the city because it is a site of concentrated value. Some of this value is privatized, but the right to the city also means access to social or public goods: cultural institutions, social networks, educational opportunities, and higher wages. A garbage collector in the informal economy may earn more money than a small farmer in a remote rural area. Moreover, by virtue of physical proximity to a wide variety of economic activity, he may have more opportunities to supplement his income and develop new skills.[59] When displaced people are given housing in remote areas or villages, they are provided with shelter, but they lose proximity to, and thus a share of, the urban commons. The fact that people like Angamuthu return to the city shows that what they lose is more valuable that what they receive.

The struggle for housing and access to the city helps us imagine social rights as something distinct from individual rights. The city is not the private possession of a person or group of people. It cannot be understood as an individual accomplishment. It is created collectively by many people usually over many generations. The struggle for housing in cities is about the subsistence needs of individuals and families, but it is also a way of resisting elites' attempt to monopolize this common-wealth. The next two chapters, which focus on public housing and gentrification, explore other sides of this issue. The right to housing should be understood in relation to the right to the city. It is difficult to exercise a right to the city without a claim on a particular piece of it. Physical access to the city is a precondition of a more progressive and inclusive urban future.

[4]

PUBLIC HOUSING AND THE RIGHT TO OCCUPANCY

In a famous scene in *Democracy in America*, Alexis de Tocqueville described the forced removal of the Choctaw Indians:

> the snow had hardened on the ground, and the river swept along enormous chunks of ice. The Indians led their families with them; they dragged along behind them the wounded, the sick, the newborn babies, the elderly about to die.
>
> They had neither tents nor wagons, only a few provisions and arms.[1]

Tocqueville also astutely foretold the traumatic consequences of this displacement. He predicted that the strain of relocating to a new territory and trying to build a new way of life in inhospitable surroundings would destroy social bonds: "The social bond, long weakened, then breaks. For them, there already was no longer a native land. Soon there will no longer be a people; families will scarcely remain."[2]

Since Tocqueville's time, scholars have produced an extensive theoretical literature critiquing the normative and legal rationales for the displacement of indigenous communities from traditional lands.[3] Other forms of forced removal such as the displacement of urban dwellers from public housing projects, informal settlements, and gentrifying neighborhoods, however, have not received similar attention.[4] In the literature on indigenous rights, scholars have introduced the concept of "a right to occupancy."[5] The right to occupancy describes a right to live in a particular area and is distinct from the individual right to private property or

59

territorial jurisdiction. The right to occupancy seems like a promising way to think about displacement in an urban context. In this chapter, I draw on discussions about indigenous land rights and ask whether they provide arguments against displacement in cities. I use the right to occupancy to think critically about the Hope VI–funded destruction of public housing projects in the United States. This program provided federal funds for the demolition of more than 100,000 severely distressed public housing units, many of which were never replaced. Writing about cities focuses attention on the concrete, the material, and everyday life, and theory can be a way of transmitting concepts or arguments from one context to another. The two examples discussed in this chapter—Cabrini-Green and the Henry Horner Homes in Chicago—draw on previously published accounts in order to highlight normative questions that they raise. My goal is to describe key features of a conflict in order to help the reader see the political stakes or normative dilemmas more clearly and to recognize structural patterns by focusing on their concrete manifestations.

THE RIGHT TO OCCUPANCY

"The right to occupancy" is a concept that helps explain why individuals who are living in an area, and have come to live there justly, have a moral entitlement to continue to live there. By "right" I mean a legitimate claim that entails an obligation on the part of other people. The right to occupancy provides a normative account of the injustice of the forced expulsion of indigenous peoples from their lands. There are two different versions of the argument in favor of the right to occupy traditional lands. One rests on the individual's interest in pursuing his or her conception of the good (Stilz),[6] and the other emphasizes the importance of collective self-determination (Moore),[7] but they share a number of key features. According to Anna Stilz's Kantian approach, the right to occupancy protects the individual's ability to pursue his self-chosen project. An autonomous person is someone who has a conception of a worthwhile life and who has the capacity to carry out that conception.[8] Forced removal disrupts and sometimes destroys the individual's ability to carry out her chosen projects. This is due in part to the way that our chosen projects are often formed in a specific geographic context; they would become difficult or impossible to pursue in a different place. For example, Canada produces more professional hockey players than other countries. This is because our cold winter and many lakes create a natural environment well suited to informal hockey training. Perhaps a child exiled to Florida could still play hockey, but it is more likely that the cost or distance from an indoor rink or lack of coaching would make the goal of an NHL career much more difficult to reach. Stilz uses the term "located life-plans" to describe the way that individual choice is structured by geographical environment.[9]

Located life-plans are also deeply affected by social context. For example, certain Jewish rituals can only be carried out when there is a *minyan*, which is made up of ten adult males. Combined with the rules prohibiting driving on the Sabbath, this means that the Jewish community must be concentrated in physical space. Without such proximity, full participation in Jewish life is very difficult. Social context can also determine the viability of individual projects in more informal ways. If a mother has neighbors to watch her children after school, she can take a full-time job. Without such support, this choice is more difficult and perhaps impossible.

Margaret Moore underscores this argument about located life-plans, but also adds a distinctive emphasis on the unchosen dimension of our relationship with place.[10] While still advancing the right to occupancy as an individual right, Moore notes that our attachments to a particular place may be unchosen, yet disrupting them may still be a cause of anguish and loss. Moore also distinguishes between the right to occupancy and the right to private property.[11] She notes that a resident may have an individual right to occupy a general area even if she does not own any immoveable property. For example, a sharecropper does not own the farm, but still has a right to occupancy in the parish, village, or county. The reverse, however, is also true. The right of occupancy is not meant to protect the resident of a specific dwelling from displacement through eviction or foreclosure. This is because the right of occupancy refers to dwelling in an expansive way. It is meant to protect a way of life rather than just a particular place to live. Moving from one house to another in the same community involves transaction costs and perhaps some feelings of loss, but it does not fundamentally disrupt or destroy the individual's ability to accomplish her goals.

THE DEATH AND LIFE OF THE URBAN COMMONWEALTH

The right to occupancy is a concept developed to explain the wrong of the forced removal of indigenous communities and other cases of ethnic cleansing. It is distinct from the private property right to an individual dwelling and the collective right to self-determination.[12] Individual rights to private property do not adequately protect the need for access to social and communal spaces and do not protect sacred space and places that are tied to a people's shared history. The right to collective self-determination does not explain why a group must control a specific place. In fact, the policy of removal was originally justified using the language of self-determination. The US federal government emphasized that indigenous people could not govern themselves in areas where they lived in close proximity to European settlers, and the government concluded that removal was the only way to secure continued self-governance of Native Americans. This decision was made for indigenous peoples, not by them. Moreover, this limited ability to exercise internal self-government came at the expense of devastating disruption of economic practices, communal life, and spatial memory.

In a recent article, Margaret Moore suggested that competing theories agree on the right of non-dispossession—"a right to remain, at liberty, in one's home and community and not be removed from the place of one's projects, aims."[13] Yet the scholars who endorse this abstract principle are hesitant to apply it to urban forms of dispossession. The comparison simply doesn't occur to most scholars because urban displacement seems natural. This reminds us of one problem—but perhaps also a benefit— of abstract theory. By abstracting from the rich complexity of social and political reality, the resulting theory is not particularly able to help us see connections between cases that we perceive as dissimilar. It seems odd to us today, but this is why Americans could endorse the principle that "all men are created equal" while failing to apply it to the institution of slavery. On the other hand, an abstract theory—for example the theory of rights—can be used to think about an issue such as access to the city that has not traditionally been thought of in those terms. Linking the theory to a practice or problem that initially seems unrelated can help us see one or both in new ways. The examples presented in the following sections are intended in this vein. They are true stories that help us think about whether "the right to occupancy" could be the basis of the right to the city.

THE DECONSTRUCTION OF
PUBLIC HOUSING

In *Le Droit à la Ville* Henri Lefebvre was quite clear that the right to the city was not intended as a synonym for the right to housing.[14] The final chapter of this book closely examines Lefebvre's own use of the term, but for now I define the right to the city as a right to share and co-determine the urban commonwealth. It is particularly useful to think about the right to the city as a subset of the right to occupancy, because urban forms of displacement such as gentrification and slum clearance affect people who are not private property owners. They are the occupants of public housing projects, informal settlements, and apartments and do not have legally recognized private property rights of exclusive use and alienation.

The literature on indigenous land rights identified three main harms caused by removal: coercion, disruption of spatially embedded life plans, and the destruction of place-dependent goods. In order to see how these processes manifest themselves in cities, I focus on two examples: the demolition of Cabrini-Green and the Henry Horner Homes in Chicago.

Cabrini-Green was built in an industrial area near the Chicago River. Originally conceived as housing for returning World War II veterans, the project was soon expanded to accommodate blacks who were arriving in large numbers from the South. The location of public housing had to be approved by the city council; white aldermen blocked the construction of such housing in their wards, which meant that the only solution was the construction of high-density public housing in industrial or minority areas.[15] Federal guidelines also mandated very low construction costs and eligibility rules that excluded all but the poorest residents; together, these had the effect of concentrating poverty. After completion, 15,000 very low income people lived in 24 high-rise towers and low-rise townhouses. Although located in close proximity to Michigan Avenue's Magnificent Mile and Lincoln Park, Cabrini-Green was a separate world. It was not well maintained by the Chicago Housing Authority (CHA), and eventually became a symbol of crime, crisis, and urban decay. Observers have suggested that it was targeted for redevelopment not because of its irreversible deterioration but because of its proximity to the wealth of the city's Near North Side. According to Brittany Scott, Cabrini residents "did better on most indicators of economic and social well-being compared to residents in public housing further from the jobs and schools on the city's Near North Side."[16]

The last of the Cabrini-Green towers was demolished in 2011. This was part of a decade-long plan to restructure public housing in Chicago by razing the most dilapidated housing stock, renovating other units, expanding the availability of vouchers for private rentals, and creating new mixed-income developments with integrated social housing. Funding came in part from a federal program called Hope VI. CHA's "Plan for Transformation" aimed to replace 48,000 deteriorating units with 25,000 new or renovated units, including 9,000 designated for senior citizens.[17] The demolitions have been completed, but the construction of replace-ment housing slowed in the aftermath of the financial crisis. In response to litigation by tenants, the CHA signed a consent decree promising a "right of return" to all families displaced by the demolitions, but this right of return only guaranteed that the registered tenants of "lease compliant" units would have priority consideration for spots in the new buildings. Given the stringent screening requirements for residence in the mixed-income buildings, only 1,000–2,000 families qualified, and most "return-ees" have ended up in rehabilitated CHA buildings or subsidized market housing in poor, racially segregated, and peripheral areas of Chicago.[18] Only 400 former Cabrini-Green residents have been allocated apartments in the new mixed-income townhouses built on the site.[19]

Public housing residents had mixed reactions to the Plan for Transformation. Initially 90 percent of the displaced residents expressed a desire to return to their buildings or neighborhoods, but this did not hap-pen for many reasons: some families did not qualify for the new restric-tive leases, and others did not want to move again after spending years in temporary housing. For the former residents of Cabrini-Green, however, there was little public housing to return to. Members of the tenant board claimed that the construction of "mixed-income" housing was a nice way of describing a land grab. They argued that the plan amounted to evicting poor people from their homes and relocating them to more remote parts of the city, destroying the existing social networks and decreasing their access to city services. The land would then be used to house wealthier and whiter residents who worked downtown. Critics warned that the new, middle-class residents would become an interest group pressuring planners and politicians to completely exclude public housing from the site. This prediction was accurate: the plan was modified to decrease the number of affordable units and the remaining low-rises were demolished rather than renovated, as originally planned. One public housing resident pointed to the similarity to the removal of Native Americans: "Once you see the dogs coming in, then you know the neighborhood is gone ... I don't know if it's going to get better. It's going to happen. It's a flow. It's like when the pioneers came to the West and moved the Indians out."[20] Another Chicago resident pointed to the differential racial impact of the evictions: "We feel like man, they trying to like take over our neighborhood ... Y'all moving these white folks over here. We've been here for like 25 years and now you going to tell us we have to leave because you're moving these white folks here?"[21]

In order to counter the "discourse of disaster" that was used to pathologize public housing projects, the residents asserted a counter-narrative that emphasized home, community, and human rights.[22] Throughout the negotiations with the CHA, tenant leaders asserted a right to occupancy. Their claims differed somewhat from the arguments advanced by indigenous communities. They did not describe Cabrini-Green as a sacred place, nor did their connection to the site stem from a long history or a distinctive set of cultural practices. Unlike NIMBYs, they were not trying to prevent outsiders from gaining access to high-quality amenities; maintenance was so bad that at one point the garbage chute backed up to the 15th floor. But it was still home to many people, and they wanted to defend it. Raymond "Shaq" McDonald, a young resident of Cabrini-Green, described his relationship to the neighborhood like this: "It's my playground because I play in it. And I live in it. And it's home to me. And it's precious from right here" (pointing to the heart).[23] For McDonald, the playground and the neighborhood were important social spaces; forced relocation entailed a loss of social relations and also the stability and security of familiar places and routines.[24]

The response of the Cabrini-Green residents to forced relocation illustrates how attachment to place is solidified through networks of mutual aid. Some residents of Cabrini-Green described their attachment in language that is consistent with the idea of an "embedded life plan."[25] They emphasized that the social network of neighbors and relatives provided a safety net; neighbors would watch each other's children and this made it easier for single parents to work or do errands.

There are also affective and psychic dimensions of attachment to place. Bonnie Honig has drawn on Winnicott's theory of transitional objects to explain the power and importance of public space,[26] and this theory can also illuminate the Cabrini-Green residents' attachment to familiar features of their neighborhood. According to Winnicott, comforting objects are essential to human development. They provide stability and form, and humans invest them with meaning and power. Attachment to an object—something like a blanket or stuffed animal—helps smooth the child's transition from dependence on the mother to increasingly independent play. This attachment to enchanted objects, however, is not a temporary phase of childhood development.[27] Our affective investment in public things may be a way to smooth the transition between practices of independence and participation in social life. They help bring together the outer and the inner worlds.

The story of Cabrini-Green suggests that the displacement of public housing residents reassembles the forced removal of indigenous peoples in some ways. It was coercive, destroyed place-specific goods that were important to people, and also disrupted place-specific routines. But we must consider two possible objections. The first objection is that it is wrong to view this type of relocation as a form of coercion. The second objection is that these factors (coercion and harm), while present, might be minimal, or might be outweighed by other factors that were not present in the case of the removal of First Nations.

COERCION

According to the classic liberal approach, the harm of displacement stems from its coercive character.[28] Coercion is wrong because it violates the individual's autonomy. Coercion prevents a person from determining his own actions and achieving his purposes. Yet this definition seems too broad. There are many things that prevent people from achieving their purposes: natural disasters, broad social conditions, affective dispositions, laws, the consequences of past actions, including one's own actions and the actions of others. Coercion is a constant feature of modern life. In North America, drivers are forced to drive in the right side of the road. In Britain they are forced to drive on the left. In my city I face a steep fine for parking in my own driveway. How do we distinguish coercion from the limits on individual freedom that are a necessary feature of social life? Can someone be coerced even if her actions are not intentionally manipulated by someone else?

When a neighborhood gentrifies, the potential rent exceeds the actual rent, and the landlord is able to raise the rent and evict a tenant if the tenant is not able to pay; we might describe this as coercion in so far as the landlord's action prevents the tenant from realizing his goal of staying in his home. It meets the classic definition of coercion: "compelling someone to do something against his will." But if this is true, then we are all coerced everyday by the forces of the market. A single mother with a middle-income job might prefer to buy a home in a sought-after neighborhood with highly rated schools, but she does not do so because she cannot afford to pay the mortgage. In this case, no specific agent is intentionally preventing her from achieving her purposes, but there are a number of structures that effectively thwart her goals. These include the school assignment process, the real estate market, and the bargaining power of workers within firms.[29] Are these structural constraints coercive?

The paradigmatic example of coercion is the robber's threat, "Your money or your life." The victim is given a choice, but it is a choice in which there is really only one reasonable alternative, and therefore the victim cannot determine his own actions. According to Alan Wertheimer, this scenario can be formalized in the following terms: A proposes to do Y unless B agrees to do X or waives his right not to do X, where B has no prior obligation to do X.[30] The robber (A) proposes to kill the victim unless the victim gives the robber his money even though the victim (B) has no obligation to do so. There are two dominant approaches to the concept of coercion, the empirical and the moral. According to the empirical approach, the key issue is whether declining the offer actually makes B worse off. Assessing the coerciveness of a proposal involves comparing the proposed arrangement with the baseline. In other words, would B be rendered worse off by refusing A's offer? Being shot to death is a clear example of this, but most scenarios are not as dramatic. If an employer tells her employee that she will be fired if she does not work unpaid overtime, then the employee is rendered worse off by refusing the offer. In this case, the baseline is continued employment; employment is preferable to unemployment.

The moral theory of coercion, on the other hand, asks whether the proposal is legitimate. In order to clarify the difference between the empirical and the moral theories, consider the following case. A man's young son is very sick and he cannot afford to pay for the necessary medicine. A offers to buy the medicine in exchange for sex, and the father has no choice but to agree. This is not coercive from the empirical approach. A has no obligation to pay for the child's medicine and the father's baseline (the inability to pay for the medicine) is not worsened by refusing the offer. From the moral perspective, however, the offer is coercive. The key issue is whether A has a right to make his proposal.[31] The medicine-for-sex proposal seems immoral for at least two reasons. First, there are legal prohibitions against selling sex, which are based on the principle that sex is not a commodity. Second, benefitting from someone's extreme vulnerability is exploitation.

Even the supposedly empirical theory of coercion, however, cannot really avoid moral judgments. Consider a slight variation on the employment example mentioned above. Imagine that the employer does not demand unpaid labor but instead offers an employee a lower hourly wage. If the employee does not accept the new terms of the contract, she will be fired. In this case, her baseline is indeed worsened if she does not accept the offer, but this is not usually viewed as coercion. There are two ways that the empirical theory of coercion can distinguish these two cases. One is to modify the definition of coercion as follows: A proposes to do Y unless B agrees to do X or waives his right not to do X, where A has no prior obligation not to do Y. Since A (the employer) does have an obligation to follow employment law, he cannot fire his workers for refusing to do unpaid work. According to this new definition, it is coercive to do anything illegal or that violates some prior commitment. This modification, however, has the effect of bringing moral considerations back in, because we will be forced to assess what A is or is not obligated to do. In some cases this is easy—for example, when the law clearly prohibits certain conduct—but if coercion just tracks illegality then it is not really a useful or interesting concept.

The second way for the empirical theory to account for these cases is to distinguish between the baselines in the two cases. When I introduced the examples, I assumed that the baseline should be "continued employment," and therefore losing one's job entails a loss or harm. It would be possible, however, to assert the contrary. The baseline could be that workers have no expectation of continued employment and their wages can be renegotiated at any time. If this is true, then the second example (continued employment contingent on a wage cut) is not coercion, but the unpaid labor scenario is, since it is structured so that the employer *adds* additional work to the amount agreed to.

The upshot of this discussion is that the moral theory of coercion rests entirely on normative arguments about whether A has a *right* to make his proposal and even the empirical version of the theory is crypto-normative. By this I mean that it depends on how we evaluate the baseline, which is a term that describes what two parties owe to each other prior to the threat/offer. What does this mean for how we think about the displacement of indigenous peoples and people who do not have the ability to secure private property on the housing market?

First, this discussion shows that it is tautological to say that displacement is harmful because it is coercive. In characterizing it in this way, we are really saying that it is coercive because it is harmful, which forces us to delve more deeply into the issue of harm. To say that coercion is harmful because it violates a person's autonomy is also problematic because it is overbroad. Almost everything done by others either enables or prevents the individual's successful pursuit of his or her purposes. The second and more important implication is that it complicates the naïve sense of what is coercive. The displacement of indigenous peoples seems obviously coercive because it violates the normative prohibition on ethnic cleansing and, with hindsight, it is obvious that it was very harmful to the individuals who suffered and died and to entire cultures that were damaged, dispossessed, and destroyed. The baseline here is non-interference, and from this perspective, "your land or your life" is obviously coercive. In contemporary capitalist cities, the baseline is that each family must provide for itself on a housing market, where all property is privately owned. When a public housing authority or nonprofit provides a place to live, this is understood as a privilege, not an entitlement, and therefore the decision to withdraw this privilege, or to replace it with another less attractive unit, is not a threat or coercive offer but simply a less appealing gift.

This critical analysis of the concept of coercion is similar to Marx's broader critique of justice. For Marx, the definitions of right and wrong, justice and injustice, are determined by the broader system of right, which renders some processes visible and others invisible, and which defines some things as natural and other things as subject to individual or collective control. This is best captured by Marx's famous depiction of the labor market in chapter 6 of *Capital*: "There alone rule Freedom, Equality, Property . . . Freedom, because both buyer and seller of a commodity, say of labor-power, are constrained only by their own free will. Equality, because each enters into relation with the other, as with a simple owner of commodities, and they exchange equivalent for equivalent."[32] Marx's tone is sardonic, but the position expressed is one that he defends in other writings: moral arguments are not universal abstract theories but rather the idealized formulation of class interests that have a certain functional role within the dominant mode of production. The equality of the marketplace is real equality in the bourgeois sense of the term (all parties respond only to market pressures), but at the same time it mystifies the way that inequality forces some people into the market and gives them different levels of power within it. The issue of coercion and the implicit baseline function in a similar way. From the dominant perspective (housing as private responsibility filled on a commodity market), there is no right to public housing, therefore relocating or even evicting residents is not a harm and not coercion. The key step is to recognize the baseline and its regulative effects in order to subject it to examination and critique.

There has been a heated scholarly debate about whether Marx had a conception of justice. Allen Wood famously defended the position that a Marxian theory of justice is both incompatible with the Marxist method and unsupported by Marx's own writings.[33] I disagree with this interpretation of Marx, but my argument does not rest on this interpretive point, and assessing the textual evidence would digress from the main thrust of the chapter. Instead, I want to emphasize the way that a comparison between the indigenous and urban cases helps us see the unacknowledged and undefended baseline, which underpins the judgment of "coercion." This baseline is legitimate title. In the case of indigenous land, the basis of legitimate title is territorial right, the right of a political community to control a geographical area that it justly occupies. The baseline for public housing residents is the subject of contestation, but in the United States it is almost impossible to imagine a property right to public housing. In a system of private property, non-owners have limited control over the places that they occupy. This is true of tenants on the private rental market and in public housing. In the latter case, the state plays the role of landlord and exercises similar property rights. At best, homeless people might have a limited subsistence right to shelter. The baseline is private property and market allocation; therefore the way in which this structure constrains autonomy and choice is not something that is recognized as coercion. From the perspective of the theory of the urban commonwealth, however, the baseline looks very different.

The argument that I have made so far and will develop throughout the book is that neighborhoods and cities are a form of common-wealth. While this does not mean that tenants have exclusive control over a particular apartment, it does mean that they have a right of occupancy, which has both political and normative implications. Politically, it entails a strong claim to exercise collective control but not veto power over neighborhood change; from a normative perspective it means that the non-commodifiable values of home, situated life plans, proximity to the urban commonwealth, and social networks should be taken into account when deciding how to site, design, and allocate public housing.

The solidarist concept of "social property" helps us rethink the baseline against which we assess the coerciveness of a policy. It is not considered coercion when someone is asked to repay a debt; we do not consider it coercion when someone is forced to uphold his or her contracts. The solidarists introduced the concept of social property to justify the introduction of a progressive income tax to fund social programs, and they did this by making social property analogous to the enforcement of debts and contracts; to preserve social property was, in this view, simply upholding a voluntary agreement. The theory of social property was a rhetorical device intended to challenge the view that an income tax was an illegitimate form of compulsion. From the perspective that was dominant in the belle epoque, taxation for redistribution was considered coercive, because it was not voluntary and rendered the individual worse off financially. If the baseline is social rather than private property, however, then directing some of the value of this social property toward public goods is justified.[34]

When "coercion" is invoked today, it is against the backdrop of a baseline that naturalizes some constraints (especially the market) and problematizes others, without justifying the difference. The theory of the urban commonwealth suggests that the normative baseline should be social property rather than private property. Following the solidarists, social property here does not mean the abolition of private property, but rather the view that the social product is composed of collective and private shares, and that the division should be the product of democratic deliberation, guided by normative principles.

We can also use the solidarist theory of social property to think about cities by asking how best to allocate the benefits and burdens of cooperation. The framework of "benefits and burdens of cooperation" provides a promising way of distinguishing between the displacement of indigenous peoples and residents of cities. In the case of the colonization of the Americas, there existed no system of cooperation and no real benefits for the indigenous peoples. The burden of relocating was also enormous: loss of life, loss of possessions, and resettlement on new, unfamiliar lands that were less suited to farming and hunting. The harm caused by forcing a person to move down the street is much smaller than the harm caused by deporting him to a foreign country.[35] Moving within a locality does bring about some disruption but usually it is possible to pursue the same profession and see the same people. Relocating to a foreign country or remote area is very different. Often it entails significant losses: the ability to earn a living, see friends and family, participate in familiar cultural activities, possibly even the opportunity to speak one's native language. This undermines and sometimes destroys the individual's ability to pursue his goals and interests in a much more profound way. For theorists of territorial rights like Moore, eviction or displacement from public housing is not a violation of the right to occupancy, because this right is meant to protect access to collective, social, and institutional spaces—to a situated way of life—rather than to a particular place.

Urban forms of displacement initially seem to resemble the more limited burden of eviction from a specific unit. The displaced tenant can still take the bus across town to work or to visit friends. One moving scene from the film *Voices of Cabrini* showed a street festival that drew together displaced residents from all over the city. They were able, at least sporadically, to see friends and former neighbors, but the former residents of Cabrini-Green also lamented the loss of community and complained of the isolation of their new neighborhoods. One former resident of Cabrini-Green, Mark Pratt, described his experience in a way that highlights the social effects of dislocation. Pratt was one of first wave of residents to be relocated from Cabrini-Green. He recalls that he was happy to move to a safer community and a nicer house. But in the new neighborhood his 11-year-old son didn't have supervision after school, and started to get into trouble with drugs and gangs. In retrospect, he thought that this wouldn't have happened at Cabrini, because his son's grandparents, cousins, uncles, and aunts would have looked out for him. This reminds us that the scale of what should count as a "particular area" for the purposes of the right to occupancy varies according to population density, porosity of borders, social relations, mobility, and norms.

ALTERNATIVES TO DISPLACEMENT

Does urban displacement—including slum clearance, gentrification, and destruction of public housing—destroy a way of life and disrupt embedded life plans? The answer is "yes and no." It depends on how these projects are implemented and how these processes are regulated. Gentrification can occur without significant displacement of current residents if there are laws that limit rent increases during an individual's tenancy. The composition of the neighborhood still changes, but it does so gradually as residents move for a range of different reasons and are replaced with more affluent newcomers.

The restructuring of public housing can also be carried out in ways that minimize displacement. For example, in Toronto, Regent Park, the largest public housing project in Canada, was reconstructed on lines that initially seem to resemble the plan for Cabrini-Green. Like Cabrini-Green, Regent Park is located in close proximity to downtown, and therefore was a potentially profitable site for market-based real estate development. Regent Park had also suffered from neglect, and was in a state of disrepair. The plan involved demolishing the low-rise townhouses and replacing them with a mix of public and private high-rise housing alongside new commercial spaces as well as recreational and cultural infrastructure. The Toronto Community Housing Corporation (TCHC), unlike the CHA, committed to replacing all 2,083 of the public housing units on site. All of the Regent Park residents had a right to a new unit on site, and most were housed nearby during the construction. The new, denser Regent Park neighborhood included 3,000 market-rate condos. The public housing units are in separate but adjacent buildings and the rules and eligibility are consistent with citywide policies. This is very different from Cabrini, where the public housing families were subject to heightened screening criteria and strict rules; in mixed-income buildings, the returnees were required to provide records of their children's school attendance and had to follow rules about parties and guests that did not apply to their market-rate neighbors. Both redevelopment projects resulted in a more mixed community, but in the case of Regent Park, this was accomplished without permanently displacing the original residents.

As Jason Hackworth demonstrated in his book *The Neoliberal City*, the Hope VI project was used by local housing authorities to decrease the amount of public housing in a period when homelessness and waiting lists were at record highs.[36] In places like New Brunswick, New Jersey, downtown regimes used public money to remove public housing that was located near potentially profitable sites for commercial investment. The effect was to displace poor people to more peripheral parts of the city, or to force them to leave the city altogether. This entails switching schools, losing informal social networks, being cut off from institutional support systems, and possibly losing access to employment. While it might initially seem that displacement from one neighborhood to another is only a trivial harm, this reflects the perspective of someone who owns a car or lives in one of the few American cities that have a comprehensive public transit system. Even in the latter case, the cost of a transit pass is often prohibitively high for someone who is unemployed or disabled.

This chapter has argued that urban displacement entails the loss of place-specific goods and disrupts embedded life plans. Sometimes this is a violent process. Slums are cleared by the police who come in and raze the dwellings, driving away residents and arresting those residents who resist. More frequently, however, people make "voluntary" choices under circumstances of considerable constraint. Before public housing projects are demolished, the residents leave the city, move in with relatives, or accept a subsidized unit in a different part of town. In comparing colonial and urban practices of displacement, my intent is not to diminish the significance or specificity of the former, but rather to take something that is generally recognized as wrong to help reassess a practice that is treated as acceptable. This comparative framing, however, suggests that the two histories are unrelated, when in fact they are intertwined. The historic and on-going practices of dispossession drive indigenous people and African Americans into cities where their lack of access to private property makes them dependent on inadequate public housing.

The classic republican concept of non-domination provides an alternative framework for thinking about the issues associated with coercion.[37] Based on the paradigmatic example of master and slave, the theory of non-domination emphasizes freedom from the potential or actual exercise of arbitrary power. Private property played an important role in traditional republican theory, where it was seen as a way of securing a space free from the arbitrary power of others. Some republican theorists also emphasize productive property, because it can guarantee independence by providing the material basis for self-reliance. The French republican and forerunner of solidarism, Charles Renouvier, justified both private property and political association as forms self-defense against domination.

These classic republican ideas, however, are difficult to transpose into urban, industrial societies, places where no one is really independent. Private property secures power for some and new forms of dependence for others; moreover, these new power relations are mediated through the market, which makes the arbitrary character of power more difficult to recognize. In *Republicanism*, Philip Pettit emphasizes both public domination (*imperium*) and private domination (*dominium*), but he doesn't account for the experience of arbitrary control that comes about through the structuring effect of market forces. The radical republicans in late-19th-century France were keenly aware that the right to property could be understood both as a source of domination and, potentially, as protection against it. The theory of social property was a way to resolve the tension between freedom and property in Hegel's theory of property.

PROPERTY AND DEMOCRACY

Standing on the bank of the Mississippi River, Tocqueville was moved by the intuition that it is wrong to expel a people from the land where they have made their lives. But why exactly is it wrong? According to Oliver Wendell Holmes, people are shaped by places: "man, like a tree in the cleft of a rock, gradually shapes his roots to his surroundings, and when the roots have grown to a certain size, can't be displaced without cutting at his life."[38] To be forcibly uprooted—or to lack the means to control one's immediate environment—is to be subject to domination.[39] The acquisition of property is not the only way to sustain life, as Locke originally suggested. Hegel provides an alternative way of thinking about the justification of property. In *Philosophy of Right*, Hegel notes that in order to be free, a human being must be able to express his will externally. Freedom is not something which just occurs in thought.[40] It requires some domain outside the person's own mind where he can actualize his will by carrying out his purposes. To be free, the will must be made concrete through its expression in the material world. Hegel's formulation is notoriously abstract; one way to think about this is through an analogy with art. In order to make art, the artist must materialize her aesthetic vision through some medium. An artwork is not just a subjective thought in someone's mind. It must take an objective, sensible form through sound, shape, or language. For Hegel, property works in a similar way because it is the will made into an object. The body is the paradigmatic form of property, because controlling one's own body is the most immediate expression of one's will. This approach to property places special emphasis on land or space because, for Hegel, the right to property protects a physical space in which the arbitrary will of another person does not prevail.

Jeremy Waldron's essay "Homelessness and Freedom" helps explain how property secures freedom.[41] According to Waldron, humans are embodied beings, and as such they need to have a place in which to be. They need a place where they can perform basic life functions such as sleeping, eating, and expelling bodily waste. From this perspective, the right to property is a way to describe the right to be, which entails a right of access to a place in which no one can prevent us from performing necessary functions. If we are to be free, this access cannot depend on the arbitrary will of another person. Private property is appealing because it seems to carve out a domain in which the individual can secure his existence and pursue his goals without the arbitrary interference of others. Private property is often understood as "the right to exclude," because physical exclusion seems like a particularly robust way to create a space where others cannot interfere with an individual and control his actions. But it is not logically necessary to conclude that private property is the only way to secure this right to be. Another way to secure it would be through a right to occupy and use shared spaces that are regulated through consensus or negotiation to help ensure that the projects and purposes of some group members are fairly balanced with the projects and purposes of others. In a common property regime, the individual will is limited, but the limitations are ones we have agreed to, rather than restrictions that are forced upon us. Of course, this is an idealized account that serves more as a constitutive ideal than an empirical account of actual practices.

Hegel famously denied the viability of shared property, which he felt rested on the unstable and precarious foundation of contingent relations among men.[42] Paradoxically, he also treated shared property as the foundation of the political order described in *The Philosophy of Right*. According to Hegel, the family is the basis of the social order, and the family home is both private and shared property.[43] The head of the household may imagine the home as private property, as the archetypical domain of individual freedom which is secured by limiting the interference of outsiders. But this is not really the case. It is actually communal property: a shared place where the family members must find a way to both exercise and limit their freedom within the context of their social roles and their obligations to others. The family also needs a communal space in which to carry out the activities of family life such as education, love, and social interaction. If this is correct, then it must be true of other collectivities. For groups to fulfill their purposes, they need to have spaces where they can carry out their shared activities. Usually this entails shared control over a physical space. Building a church is often the first act of a religious congregation. There isn't even a commonly used word to describe a group of learners and teachers; instead we simply use the term for the physical space: "school."

The solidarist theory of common-wealth builds on Hegel's argument that property is "an external sphere" that is a necessary feature of human freedom,[44] but reworks it to include a collective dimension. Solidarists like Alfred Fouillée agreed that the individual flourishes when he can express his freedom in the material world. They departed from Hegel, however, in claiming that freedom can also be secured through access to shared property that is governed by consensual rules rather than solely through the despotic control of private property. The purpose of property—actualizing freedom—can be realized through a combination of different mechanisms including private property, collective property, usufruct, an individual right to occupancy, and a collective right to self-determination. The solidarists argued that the best solution was one that combined private and common property. Much like having a room of one's own in the family home, this allows space for both autonomy and solidarity. It also ensures that the freedom of some does not rest on the domination of others who have no access to or control over a place to be. In the context of a highly unequal distribution of private property, this requires considerable redistribution, but it also requires innovative ways of imagining property rights. Workers' cooperatives and mutual aid societies were the important innovations in the late 19th century. Both created an individual right to shared property and this right was intended to prevent members from becoming dependent on an employer or charity. The right to public housing could be understood as an extension of this logic. The final section of this chapter turns back to the story of public housing in Chicago to show how democratic associations can leverage the power of rights to transform public property into something that enhances rather than restricts freedom.

BACK TO CHICAGO: THE HENRY HORNER HOMES

Chicago's Plan for Transformation was the result of a process of negotiation between the local public housing authority, city leaders, tenants, the
courts, and HUD (the federal agency Housing and Urban Development).
Since it ultimately resulted in considerable displacement, draconian
new rules for residents of public housing, and a decrease in public housing stock, it may seem like a plan that was simply imposed on powerless
recipients of public beneficence. Yet this is not exactly true. Public housing tenants' associations used the courts to protect their right to housing,
and in some cases they gained considerable influence over the process of
renewal, the design of the new communities, and the rules that would govern how they lived together.[45]

There is a long history of organized opposition to the policies of the
CHA. In 1966, black residents of public housing filed a class action suit
accusing the CHA of intentionally promoting segregation through its
selection of sites and its process of assigning applicants to units in public housing. The court agreed; the resulting *Gautreaux* decision forced the
CHA to build new, smaller housing projects in more diverse neighborhoods and to provide families with vouchers that enabled the recipients
to relocate to the white, middle-class suburbs of Chicago.[46] Research on
this program, the Gautreaux Assisted-Housing Program (GAHP), found
that the families who relocated had somewhat better quality of life as
well as superior academic and employment outcomes. This research was
mobilized to justify the new housing policies of the late 1990s that tried to
"de-concentrate poverty" by replacing public housing with mixed-income
communities.[47]

Along with Cabrini-Green, the Henry Horner Homes was considered
one of Chicago's most dangerous and blighted public housing projects,
but the residents succeeded in regaining control over their homes. In 1991
the Henry Horner Mothers Guild filed a class action suit claiming that
the CHA was violating federal law by demolishing public housing units
and failing to replace them.[48] Their lawsuit forced the CHA to consult
and bargain with residents about the future of the project. They claimed

that extreme neglect over an extended period of time had rendered half of the units uninhabitable. The Horner project consisted of 1,775 units located on the West Side of Chicago. In November 1981 the vacancy rate at Horner was 2.3 percent, but, despite a long waiting list for public housing in Chicago, it climbed steadily, peaking, in 1991, at 868 vacant units, just under 50 percent of the total number.[49] Why were so many units empty? The lawsuit claimed that under the pressure of budget constraints, the CHA stopped maintaining and repairing their buildings.

According to District Judge Zagel, there was little dispute about the conditions at Horner, which included the following:

> non-functioning elevators, darkened hallways, lobbies and stair-wells, broken, boarded-up and leaking windows, broken trash chutes and common areas cluttered with refuse, missing exit, stair-way and fire escape signs, broken or missing stairwell doors, defective stairwell handrails, treads and landings, presence of human and animal waste in public areas and open, vacant apartments, broken screen doors and windows, numerous vacant units and abandoned laundry rooms with open or missing doors.

In 1991, city of Chicago officials inspected simply the Horner Homes and found serious violations in all 21 buildings, including 570 "dangerous and hazardous" violations of the building code. Only the violations that pose an immediate danger of life and limb to employees or tenants are designated as "dangerous and hazardous." Similar conditions existed across the city. In 1991, the CHA was designated a troubled housing authority by HUD and received a failing grade in 11 of the 20 assessment categories.[50]

It would be wrong, however, to see the horrible conditions as the result of bureaucratic incompetence or corruption. The CHA was operating under structural constraints. During the period from 1981 to 1991 there was a dramatic decrease in the level of financial support for redistributive policies in the United States, and public housing was particularly hard hit. This was the era of the Reagan Revolution. In 1978, 14.4 percent of the total federal budget for federal discretionary spending went to HUD. In 1983, after the cuts implemented by the Reagan administration, it was 4.1 percent, and in 2012 it was just 3 percent.[51] The reason for the deteriorating conditions was that there was very little money. The federal government had invested large sums in the construction of public housing projects and then withdrawn the funds necessary to maintain them. The consequences are well known. Everyone except the poorest moved out, creating high concentrations of extreme poverty. Crime and drug dealing increased and an ever-growing share of the limited maintenance budget went to pay for security measures, leading to a spiral of decay.[52]

One important difference between traditional public housing and the voucher system that has largely replaced it (Section 8 Housing Choice Vouchers) is the degree of control by residents and the way that control is exercised. Under Regulation 964, tenants in public housing are encouraged to form residents' councils that enable them to deliberate about policies and to participate in the management of developments.[53] The guidelines mandate regular elections, and councils receive funding in proportion to the number of units. Regulation 964 does not apply in private buildings, even ones that are entirely supported through public monies in the form of Section 8 vouchers. In these places, the rights of residents are protected through administrative review of rules governing residential leases and what A. O. Hirschman called "exit."[54] While residents don't participate in the management of the buildings, they can vote with their feet by moving out. In theory, vouchers increase choice because families can use them to rent any unit that accepts the vouchers. In practice, however, discrimination against voucher holders and lack of affordable rental housing have the effect of concentrating recipients in the same neighborhoods that contain public housing projects.[55] Regulation 964 and Section 8 are two different ways of addressing the goal of ensuring that the beneficiaries of public housing are not subject to arbitrary domination by the public housing authorities.

The struggle over the Chicago Plan for Transformation provides a window into the role that public housing tenants' organizations can play in protecting the interests of tenants. In many projects, the official local area councils were coopted by building management, but other groups played an important role in advocating for the renovation of public housing and against demolition and dispersion. The Cabrini-Green Local Area Council (LAC) sued the CHA on the grounds that the revitalization plans violated the Fair Housing Act and the *Gautreaux* decision.[56] They claimed that the process violated the statutory requirements to consult residents and that the outcome of the plan would be to increase racial segregation. Although the CHA denied these claims, it did accept a series of measures intended to end litigation. The consent decree included provisions to build additional public housing, to find alternative housing for all displaced residents, to involve the LAC in the planning process, and to provide some public and affordable units in the new market-rate developments on the Cabrini-Green site.

The Henry Horner Mothers Guild was considerably more successful at renewing the project for the benefit of its residents. The Henry Horner Mothers Guild is a not-for-profit corporation established to improve living conditions at the Henry Horner Annex.[57] Together with residents in the Henry Horner towers, the group became the lead plaintiff in a class action suit that forced the CHA to the bargaining table. The Mothers Guild proposed a plan that involved demolishing the decrepit high-rise towers, renovating the mid-rises, and building new housing on site to ensure no net loss of public housing. The plan, which was approved, was to be completed in phases to minimize displacement. It also provided residents with a choice of returning to the new project or using Section 8 vouchers to relocate to other parts of the city. Fifty percent of "Phase I" residents and 75 percent of "Phase II" residents chose to stay. Phase II, however, was completed after Congress changed the law which required that renewal projects not cause a net loss of public housing. This transformed the legal and political context, and enabled the CHA to proceed with its plan for mixed-income housing. In Phase II, only 32.5 percent of the new units were designated for public housing residents, but the residents' association successfully fought to prevent the CHA from using excessively stringent screening criteria to keep former residents from returning.

After the reconstruction was completed in 2005, half of the leaseholders were former Henry Horner Home residents. Overall, the development benefitted the community rather than displacing it. Residents and other local people were hired to work on project construction and maintenance. The prizewinning design was also developed in collaboration with residents who reviewed and approved the designs of the buildings. At the Horner Annex, the architects had weekly meetings with residents and incorporated their suggestions about the configuration of the apartments.[58] According to William Wilen, the lawyer for the Henry Horner

Homes Mothers Guild, this was not simply a matter of pro forma consultation. For over ten years the seven members of the Horner Residents Committee met at least monthly with stakeholders to work out conflicts over a wide range of issues including screening of applicants, maintenance and behavior standards, and reviewing the performance of the management company. Eighty percent of the original residents agreed that the tenants themselves played the leading role in the redevelopment.

Despite this considerable success, it is not possible to draw simple lessons about democracy from this case. Unlike participatory budgeting in Porto Alegre, a favorite example used by urban theorists, this is not an edifying story in which grassroots mobilization, institutional innovation, participation, equality, and city building fit nicely together. Instead, a mobilized group working outside of designated institutional channels used a lawsuit to force a local bureaucracy to follow existing federal law. Under the threat of legal sanctions, the CHA and residents worked out a plan to turn their decaying shelter back into a community and home, but then Congress changed the law, which allowed the CHA to permanently decrease the supply of public housing.

Political theorists emphasize that even though elections and majoritarianism are important institutional mechanisms of contemporary democracy, democracy and majoritarianism are not synonyms. Democracy should be a way for the people who are most affected by the exercise of power to gain some control or influence over it and to prevent power from becoming arbitrary domination. These two sides of democracy often come into tension with one another, and this gives democracy its paradoxical character. The theory of the urban commonwealth does not provide a solution to the paradox. Citizens will still have to decide how to allocate the resources that are designated as belonging to the pubic share, and they will still have disagreements about which public goods to prioritize and how to distribute them. One thing that seems to have been missing from this debate about the right to public housing—and the competing visions of a right to stay and a right to choose—is this more basic premise of solidarity. The repeal of a law requiring the replacement of public housing is not as dramatic as the destruction of dozens of high-rise towers, especially when the latter are detonated by the people who built them. Both are signs of the death of the urban commonwealth and the theory that sustains it: the view that society has produced an enormous amount of wealth, that part of this wealth is a collective inheritance that belongs to everyone, and that this inheritance should sustain public things and redress unfair shares.

CONCLUSION

The analysis presented in this chapter draws on the right to occupancy, but it also points to the limits of the analogy between the displacement of public housing residents and the displacement of indigenous peoples from their lands. The crucial difference is sovereignty. The forced removal of the Navajos, the case considered by Stilz, violates the indigenous peoples' right to occupancy because they did not consent to the territorial jurisdiction of the United States. This does not mean that the right to occupancy and the right to self-government are the same, but without legitimate, shared political institutions there was no reason to consent and no way to do so. The indigenous peoples were not part of the public considered in evaluating the public good. They were forced to bear all of the costs without receiving any of the benefits of inclusion in the polity. They had no voice in negotiating the terms of coexistence. The Hegelian-inspired discussion of property explains why this is wrong. For members of the Navajo nation, displacement not only disrupted their way of life and situated life plans, but it also rendered them completely subject to the arbitrary will of another.

This chapter has treated indigenous and urban dispossession as two distinct experiences and drawn on theoretical insights from the former to illuminate the later, but in reality they are intertwined. In some parts of Canada, more than half of the people identifying as Aboriginal[59] live in cities and they are disproportionately affected by homelessness. In a legal brief submitted on behalf of plaintiffs who were evicted from a tent city in a public park in Abbotsford, BC, Dr. Yale Belanger linked historic and contemporary dispossession. He suggested that the separation from traditional land and the destruction of kinship networks were factors that contributed to homelessness in cities.[60] Dispossession is not something that happens at one moment that is fixed in time; it makes life more precarious in a way that renders people subject to ongoing practices of dispossession.

Legal rights can be a way to resist these practices and they provide tools to citizens that colonial subjects don't have. The right to occupancy developed in this chapter helps explain why the Cabrini-Green LAC was right to challenge the displacement process and why members of the general public should be persuaded by their arguments. It its broadest sense, the right to property is meant to protect freedom, to secure some ability to be-in-the-world without the arbitrary interference of others. For people without private property, a right to public or common property provides an alternative, one that depends not on the power to exclude but on proportionate influence over the terms of coexistence.

By demolishing Cabrini-Green, the CHA was acting both as a landlord and as an agent of the public interest. In its role as landlord it asserted a property right and interpreted this to include the right to exclude and to control its investment. This set the stage for the clash between the residents' rights to occupancy and the CHA's right to control its property. When rights conflict, as they do in this instance, how do we decide what is to be done?

I will return to this question in the final chapters of the book. In the first half of the book, I draw on a series of arguments about "the right to the city" to highlight and criticize injustice in cities. At the same time, however, we see that problems of urban injustice cannot be fully resolved from the perspective of normative theory. The limits of a rights-based approach force us to turn to political institutions in order to weigh competing and incompatible claims to occupy, control, and create the city. Chapters 7 and 8 examine more explicitly political concepts such as civil disobedience, democracy, and the public good. Chapter 9 introduces the concept of hetero-rights, a concept which is meant to bring out the political and agonistic dimension of rights. Rights claims are not only abstract theories. They are also rhetorical and political tools that shield people from domination by the strong; they invoke a way of thinking and acting that is not simply reducible to self-interest or power. They provide reasons for favoring one set of claims over another. Rights must always be interpreted and balanced against other rights and the public good. Moreover, rights are effective when they are institutionalized either through legal decisions, norms, or statutes, and this means that political procedures are critical sites in the struggle for the right to the city.

[5]

WHAT IS WRONG
WITH GENTRIFICATION?

In 1875 Karl Marx wrote a scathing critique of the proposed platform of the German Social Democratic Party—the famous Gotha Program. He rejected the "ideological nonsense about right(s) and other trash so common among the democrats and French socialists." The *Critique of the Gotha Program*, of course, was not directly an attack on solidarism. Many solidarist ideas and proposals were already circulating in this period, but it wasn't until the 1890s that solidarism crystalized into a distinctive program. Nevertheless, Marx's forceful critique of concepts such as social property, social rights, and fair distribution is relevant to my attempt to reappropriate these ideas.

Marx noted the paradox that capitalism created an immense increase in productivity, but this social wealth did not benefit the workers and even decreased their power vis-à-vis the owners of capital. This view was shared by reformers and revolutionaries alike. Marx departed from the reformers by rejecting the assumption that the solution is for the state to redistribute wealth more fairly among citizens. He raised three objections to the idea that the dark side of capitalism can be mitigated by applying the principle of "equal right." First, he noted that the concept of equality is indeterminate. Given that people have different abilities, inclinations to labor, and needs, how can there be equal distribution? Second, Marx argued that "right" is a legal concept and as such it is context dependent. A contract that pays subsistence wages is fair according to bourgeois right, the only possible standard of right in capitalist societies. Finally, he insisted that "fair distribution" of social property is a fundamentally misguided goal because it focuses on the rectification of inequalities and ignores the production of inequalities.

Solidarism provides responses to the latter two arguments. Léon Bourgeois's notion of quasi-contractual debt was an attempt to reconfigure the meaning of right, transforming bourgeois right into social right. Marx, of course, was skeptical of this move because of his view that right, which can mean both justice and law, is super-structural. It reflects economic structures rather than transforming them. The solidarists shared this materialist view up to a certain point. Their normative theory of debt repayment rested on the empirical claim that the division of labor created an increasingly socialized process of production. According to Gide, the role of the capitalist-entrepreneur was declining and the worker-manager was becoming more important. Urbanization also created greater interconnectedness and a social product—urban infrastructure—that was naturally collective. The solidarists concluded that these circumstances created the material preconditions for new "social rights" that could solve some of the problems of capitalism. The "redistribution" critique can also be addressed in solidarist terms. Wage earner funds (see chapter 2) are one way of reallocating the social product by restructuring the ownership of the capital rather than through redistribution of profits.[1]

The third critique—indeterminacy—is the hardest to refute. Marx was correct to point out that there is no certain way to resolve the question "what is a fair share?" The difference between the market value of inputs (labor plus materials) and the value of the product—what Marx called surplus value—does not naturally belong to any one, and therefore the allocation of this value is the subject of negotiation. Minimum wage laws, collective bargaining rights, public finance, taxes on capital, and progressive taxation all affect the way it is allocated and, as the democratic state plays a larger role, ideas about fair and unfair come to shape the distribution of things.

In *Critique of the Gotha Program*, Marx presented his own views about how to distribute the value produced by social property. After mocking the idea that a socialist state would distribute the "undiminished proceeds of labor," Marx suggests that the social product should be allocated first to maintain the "administration;" second to subsidize "the common satisfaction of needs, such as schools, health services"; third to support "those unable to work," and only after that to provide a basic income to workers. Marx also points out that even among socialists there is a great deal of disagreement about which public goods to prioritize and how to share them.

It is correct to see the concept of "fair share" as one that is open to contestation rather than determined in a deductive or logical fashion. It is precisely for this reason that the solidarists treated contextual or applied normative theory as a supplement to structural analysis. By supplement I mean that it is a necessary addition but also one that is a source of tension and contradiction.[2] The key idea of solidarism is that social property is naturally composed of private and public shares and that the public share should provide for the needs of the whole society. This is a persuasive explanation of why the laissez-faire/libertarian approach to social problems is incorrect, but it doesn't tell us which needs are most important or how they should be met; nor does it tell us which public goods are most vital and how they should be distributed. We need additional concepts and arguments to help answer these questions.

The focus of this book is the urban commonwealth and the public goods that are related to the city. These include housing, public transport, and public space. The previous two chapters both focused on housing. The destruction of informal settlements and public housing are visible, often large-scale forms of dislocation and dispossession. Gentrification is a more gradual, complex, piecemeal transformation of urban space, but it raises similar issues about access to the urban commonwealth. This chapter draws on egalitarian theory to examine the harms of gentrification.

Few people openly celebrate gentrification. The term itself hints at the logic of class struggle; it highlights the way that cities are sites of struggle over inclusion and exclusion. Increasingly, however, the critical concept of gentrification is being replaced by alternatives such as "inclusion," "livability," or "smart cities," concepts that describe the shift in class composition and power in more positive terms. While the concept of gentrification implies a negative assessment of neighborhood change, the reasons for opposing it are often assumed rather than defended. This chapter takes implicit assumptions about gentrification and reformulates them as explicit arguments in order to explain the case against gentrification.[3]

The key argument I present draws on the work of the philosopher Gerry Cohen, who used luck egalitarianism to challenge the assumption that exchange value is a fair basis for distribution.

WHAT IS GENTRIFICATION?

In his pathbreaking book *The New Urban Frontier*, Neil Smith described gentrification as "the process by which poor and working class neighborhoods in the inner city are refurbished by an influx of private capital and middle class home buyers and renters."[4] Smith emphasized the importance of structural economic factors in understanding gentrification. For Smith, the key factor is the "rent-gap," a cycle of disinvestment that ultimately renders poor neighborhoods potentially profitable sites of reinvestment. This is an important force driving gentrification, but other commentators have emphasized the cultural dimension of the phenomenon.[5] The term "gentrification" also points toward a link between demographic, economic, cultural, and spatial change and depicts this process in a negative light. City officials may promote mixed-income neighborhoods, livable cities, urban renaissance, revitalization, and renewal, but almost no one defends gentrification.

The multifaceted character of gentrification was apparent even in the earliest use of the term.[6] Ruth Glass coined the term "gentrification" to link together a demographic process (the replacement of working-class residents by middle- and upper-class residents) and a spatial transformation (conversion of rental units and rooming houses into larger single-family homes) and to make empirical claims about the trajectory of this process. Crucially, she argued that once this process has started, it continues until almost all of the original residents have been replaced. The result is the radical cultural transformation of a neighborhood. While the built environment may be modified only slightly, the character of the neighborhood is destroyed and replaced by something different. Some scholars describe gentrification as a three-step process that begins with an influx of new residents with low financial capital but high cultural capital (artists, bohemians); they are followed by middle-class people who are drawn to the bohemian atmosphere and low prices; finally, the neighborhood is transformed to the point where it becomes attractive to developers and upper-middle-class professionals. Jason Hackworth captured the core meaning succinctly when he defined gentrification as "the production of space for progressively more affluent users."[7]

Critics have identified five primary harms of gentrification: residential displacement; exclusion; transformation of public, social, and commercial space; polarization; and homogenization.[8] The normative assessment of gentrification is distinct from the debate about the causes of gentrification. The scholarly debate about gentrification has largely focused on structural versus cultural (e.g., consumption-driven) explanations of neighborhood change. Scholars may agree that polarization and displacement are harmful, even if they disagree about whether surplus capital is the main factor driving gentrification.

Residential displacement and exclusion are terms that explain the decline in the number of poor and working-class residents. Displacement happens when landlords increase rents in order to profit from demand for units in the area. If there are no laws stabilizing rent and regulating tenancy, then high-income earners simply outbid the original residents. Scholars have also pointed out that even in places like Ontario where rent increases are capped for the duration of the tenancy, market pressures can drive out the poor. In a gentrifying neighborhood, landlords have no incentive to negotiate with tenants who fall behind on their rent payments. It is in the landlords' economic interest to pursue eviction rather than negotiation since they can lease empty units at a higher rent.[9]

Another mechanism for displacing longtime residents is the conversion of rental units into condos or single-family dwellings. In California, this is enabled by the Ellis Act, a state law that allows landlords to evict tenants without cause if they do not plan to return the units to the rental market. In San Francisco, the tech-sector boom has placed upward pressure on rents, and the number of Ellis Act evictions has increased 170 percent from 2010 to 2013.[10] In a hot property market, landlords have an incentive to cash out, forcing their low-income tenants, who cannot afford to purchase a home, to move out of the neighborhood. Gentrification also entails the transformation of social space. This occurs through commercial displacement as well as political activity that changes the physical environment and the rules governing public space. Commercial displacement can happen in two different ways. Either businesses close because they cannot afford the increasing cost of rent in a gentrified neighborhood, or they lose their traditional customer base and are no longer profitable.

The term "exclusion" reminds us that gentrification not only affects the current residents of a neighborhood but also harms potential residents who are prevented from moving into a neighborhood because of rising costs. For example, in Little Portugal, a gentrifying neighborhood in West Toronto, 66.4 percent of the longstanding Portuguese residents are home-owners, and therefore less vulnerable to displacement.[11] Nevertheless, rising home prices in the area make it difficult for the children of these residents to establish their own households and prevent new immigrants from moving into the neighborhood. Conversion to single-family homes can also decrease the total stock of rental units, thereby excluding renters from an area.

Many people assume that gentrification must involve residential displacement, given that gentrification is sometimes defined as the replacement of low-income residents by high-income residents. But replacement and displacement are conceptually distinct, and there has been a great deal of debate about whether displacement does indeed take place and if so, whether the phenomenon is widespread.[12] The empirical record seems to be mixed. In one study of two neighborhoods in New York City, Lance Freeman found that displacement is not a significant force driving change in gentrifying neighborhoods.[13] By comparing the mobility of poor people who live in gentrifying neighborhoods with those who do not, he found a difference of just 1 percent. On the other hand, Rowland Atkinson's longitudinal study of residential patterns in London concluded that there is reason to believe that some displacement is driven by gentrification.[14] It is beyond the scope of this book to resolve this debate; moreover, the degree of displacement varies dramatically depending on factors such as existence of public housing, rent control, tenant-landlord regulations, enforcement of regulation, and overall market pressures. Given this controversy, I will examine the normative arguments about displacement and exclusion separately.

Even if gentrification is driven by replacement rather than displacement, the outcome may still be construed as harmful to the polity. The terms "homogenization" and "polarization" highlight negative aspects of gentrified neighborhoods.[15] The term "homogenization" points to the way that diverse neighborhoods turn into elite enclaves and the adjacent commercial districts come to resemble upscale malls. Polarization describes the opposite phenomenon. In neighborhoods where rent-controlled housing and expensive residences are in close proximity, the result may be what Robson and Butler describe as "tectonic": social groups in these neighborhoods come into contact with one another like tectonic plates, contact which takes the form of disruptive collisions.[16]

THE LIBERTARIAN APPROACH TO GENTRIFICATION

Before I examine these critiques of gentrification, I would like to consider the opposite view: that housing should be allocated on the free market, a claim that rests on the normative judgment that this is both efficient and fair. In "Housing and Town Planning" Friedrich Hayek defends this argument,[17] but the more extreme libertarian version is just a clearer and more forceful version of ideas that are widely shared on both the right and the left. To give just one example, Battery Park City, a neighborhood built on waterfront land created by the excavation of the Twin Towers, was initially intended to be mostly low- and middle-income housing. After a long series of delays and financial crises, the stakeholders decided to use revenue from the development to renovate existing public housing in Harlem and the Bronx and to build a small amount of new public housing in those lower-cost neighborhoods. According to the logic of the market, this is a rational decision. Waterfront real estate is a luxury, an expensive taste, and therefore siting public housing on the waterfront would be wasteful.

Hayek extended this logic and applied it to public housing in general. He was writing in the 1950s and gentrification was not his focus, but, as we will see, his analysis also applies to policies like rent control that stabilize housing prices. Hayek was concerned about the ways that public housing would distort urban property markets and exacerbate housing shortages. According to Hayek, urban land is desirable because of its commercial and industrial uses; it can therefore command a higher purchase price and rent. In a free market, each individual decides whether the benefits of urban living outweigh other preferences such as working fewer hours, having more space, transportation time, and so on. If the government tries to lower the cost of housing, either directly through subsidy or indirectly through regulation, it makes the true cost less transparent, rendering it impossible for individuals to calculate their preferred trade-offs. It also does nothing to alleviate the problem of excess demand and provides no fair alternative way of allocating housing. According to Hayek,

> [Public housing] amounts to a stimulation of the growth of cities beyond the point where it is economically justifiable and to a deliberate creation of a class dependent on the community for the provision of what they are presumed to need. . . . Providing them with much better quarters at an equally low cost will attract a great many more. The solution of the problem would be either to let the economic deterrents act or to control directly that influx of population; those who believe in liberty will regard the former as the lesser evil.[18]

Versions of this argument are still popular and not only on the right. The core intuition is that middle-class people often move to the suburbs and endure long commutes because it is the only way to afford enough space for a family. Why then should public housing residents have access to the most expensive real estate downtown when they could be rehoused at lower cost in cheaper areas such as the inner suburbs?

Hayek's analysis in "Housing and Town Planning" is relevant to the issue of gentrification for at least two reasons. First, following Hayek's logic, gentrification is not a problem, but rather a morally neutral and perhaps even desirable consequence of market principles. Paying higher rents in the city is a rational investment for those workers who will benefit from access to highly paid jobs; for workers who are unable to command a higher salary, it makes more sense to live in lower-cost areas. According to the economist Charles Tiebout, people sort themselves into neighborhoods based on their ability to pay, which reflects the productivity of their labor.[19] For Hayek, this is no injustice, because city living is a luxury rather than a basic need. He assumes that poor people could remain in rural areas, where the lower cost of living makes it easier to be self-supporting. If companies want to attract workers to the central city, they will be forced to pay correspondingly higher wages.

Hayek's argument rests on two assumptions, one empirical and one normative. The empirical assumption is that people can meet their basic needs in rural areas. He treats the countryside the way Locke treated "the Americas," as a place where land is plentiful and subsistence can be guaranteed through labor. This is a fantasy. In fact, in most of the world, the levels of extreme poverty, malnutrition, and inadequate basic health care are much higher in rural areas than they are in cities.[20] People need cities because cities are where they can best meet their needs. This empirical assumption is also the basis of Hayek's normative argument. He assumes that slum dwellers move to cities because their disposable income (wages minus rent) is higher in cities. This is a kind of reverse surplus value argument. The surplus is the value of the higher productivity of labor in the city. According to Hayek, there is nothing wrong with individuals seeking this surplus, but there is no positive obligation on others to create the conditions to help them do so. This is why he opposed public housing, rent control, and public transit. But is this argument persuasive? The concept of the urban commonwealth explains why it is false. The greater productivity of urban labor is a social product, which was created by a vast array of direct and indirect contributions to technology, social networks, and infrastructure. The built environment of the city and the dense networks of production and exchange are social products and do not naturally belong to the middle or upper classes. On the contrary, there is a positive obligation to ensure that these collective resources are not privatized and enclosed for the benefit of the few when they were created by the many.

In "Housing and Town Planning," Hayek also admits that the free market mode of allocation may have disadvantages, but he insists that it is impossible to come up with a fair alternative. Subsidizing housing in the city increases demand. If housing is not allocated through market mechanisms, then it must be allocated in some other way. The ten-year-long waitlist for access to subsidized housing in many cities, including Toronto, is one manifestation of this challenge. Hayek is correct that a fair alternative is difficult to formulate, because it involves balancing efficiency with various dimensions of justice and rights, and doing so under conditions of unequal power, path dependency, and bureaucratic structures is even more difficult. This book aims to contribute to the process by deepening and clarifying some of the implicit and explicit claims about justice, fairness, and rights.

It might be tempting to dismiss Hayek as a libertarian with no interest in social justice, but there is also a similar concern that emerges from left-wing egalitarian theory, where it is called the problem of expensive tastes. The term "expensive tastes" is likely to be somewhat distasteful to urbanists who are unfamiliar with this debate. It seems to rest on the view that structural transformations are driven by consumer preference and choice, but in fact, the upshot of the argument is exactly the reverse. As we will see, this concept explains why choices are not free, in the sense that they are made against the backdrop of structural forces that the individual does not control.

The theoretical debate about expensive tastes is useful in unpacking opposing views about the harms of gentrification. The core question is whether people should receive extra resources in order to enable them to live in neighborhoods that have become expensive due to gentrification. Drawing on the work of philosopher Gerry Cohen, I will argue that longtime residents of gentrifying neighborhoods did not *choose* to develop their "expensive taste" for downtown living, and therefore they deserve the extra resources that would enable them to satisfy this preference. In order to support this claim, however, I will need to make a fairly long detour through some debates about egalitarianism in political philosophy. The intuition that equality is a basic principle of justice informs a range of different political theories, but there are different views about what this means. I start with the solidarist argument that public share of the common-wealth should enhance equality, because the value created collectively by past generations is the inheritance of the whole society. In order to work out what this means, I begin by discussing the concept of equality, and then provide an account of how this theory could inform debates about urban issues.

LUCK EGALITARIANISM

Equality can be interpreted in many different ways: equality of opportunity, resources, welfare, basic needs, rights, or democratic citizenship.[21]

For the purposes of this chapter, I approach the concept of equality from the perspective of "luck egalitarianism," which holds that inequalities caused by bad luck are morally problematic in a way that inequalities produced by choice are not. It is a widely shared moral intuition that we are responsible only for those actions that we caused (our choices) and not for outcomes that are beyond our control (luck). In *Solidarité*, Léon Bourgois argued that this idea justified government insurance schemes against unemployment and disability.

Unlike Bourgeois, who was directly concerned with social policy, contemporary moral philosophers tend to focus on principles of justice, even when such principles are not widely recognized and/or are difficult to transpose into practical measures. Ronald Dworkin has argued that a just society is one in which the initial distribution of resources is equal and is supplemented by an insurance system designed to compensate people for disadvantages due to bad luck. Through the insurance scheme, someone born with a physical disability would receive extra resources, but an able-bodied artist, who choses creativity over paid labor, would not. Welfare egalitarians, on the other hand, support a transfer of resources until no further redistribution would leave anyone more equal in well-being.[22] Between these two poles are a number of positions that try to equalize capabilities[23] or opportunity for welfare rather than outcomes.

In "Equality and Welfare," Ronald Dworkin explains that he cannot accept a theory of equality that aspires to equalize welfare, because such a theory would be indeterminate and could not solve the problem of expensive tastes. A person with expensive tastes "needs more income than others simply to achieve the same level of welfare as those with less expensive tastes." It is important to note that some object A is not an expensive taste if everyone prefers A to B. An expensive taste is relational. Some people love French fries and others adore plover's eggs; some drink Budweiser and others need an ancient claret.[24] Some people adore the central city and others have built satisfying lives in places like Scarsdale or Scarborough. In order to achieve equal welfare, society would have to provide more resources to people with expensive tastes. Initially this seems like an absurd suggestion. Not only would the artist need extra resources to live like a banker but the skier-banker would need more resources than the basketball-playing banker. How could one defend this view?

In "On the Currency of Egalitarian Justice," Cohen does just that. He argues that individuals should receive extra resources in order to satisfy expensive tastes as long as these tastes were not acquired intentionally.[25] This could be understood as a reworking of the socialist principle "to each according to his needs" transposed into the language of Anglo-American normative philosophy. For Cohen, it is a matter of "bad luck" to have expensive tastes and therefore a consistent application of luck egalitarianism requires that people be compensated for them. In order to make this more plausible, Cohen notes that it is difficult to distinguish between a disability and an expensive taste. Cohen introduces the example of Percy, a man who finds the taste of tap water unbearably sour and therefore chooses to drink bottled water.[26] Given the cost of bottled water, Percy would need extra resources in order to have the same well-being as people with normal taste buds. In a certain sense, the purchase of bottled water is a choice, but it also has much in common with other disabilities that justify special compensation to overcome disadvantages.

Dworkin responds to Cohen by distinguishing between two types of tastes: tastes that the individual affirms and tastes that the individual would disavow. Percy would prefer that water were not so distasteful, but most people's attitudes to their expensive tastes do not fall into this category. The wine enthusiast, the exotic traveler, the foodie, and the skier would not voluntarily swallow a magic pill which would make them indifferent to their preferred activities. According to Dworkin, people who subjectively identify with their expensive tastes are exercising a choice and are therefore responsible for the costs that this choice entails.

In an essay entitled "Expensive Taste Rides Again," Cohen addresses this objection.[27] He insists that Dworkin overlooks the way that both choice and chance play a role in determining expensive tastes. People may affirm their tastes (choice) but they are still victims of bad luck in so far as they would obviously prefer that these tastes were not expensive. In other words, they are victims of "bad price luck" not "bad preference luck." For example, I enjoy serial dramas with high production values and complex plotting, but would prefer not to have to pay the extra cost of a subscription to HBO. If given the opportunity to take a pill that would transform me into a fan of the fireplace channel, I would not take it—but I would certainly use my magical wand to make other people into HBO fans, if this would drive down the cost. The point is that the market determines whether a taste is expensive or inexpensive and the individual is not able to control the market. Dworkin disagrees, and maintains that without a market there is no fair way to set prices. The market expresses the opportunity cost of satisfying one preference over another and, assuming that the initial distribution of resources is fair, it is the best way to give equal weight to everyone's preferences.

Dworkin is right to point out that it is nearly impossible to imagine that any government could equalize something as complex as the opportunity for welfare, but that does not mean it is wholly useless as a thought experiment that helps us understand conflicts over redistribution in new ways. I see Cohen's defense of expensive tastes as a way of approaching the very real dilemmas that governments face when they have to decide whether to intervene in the market. The defense of expensive tastes is a provocative way of reminding us that market prices do not correspond to value. Cohen helps explain why it is legitimate to distort market prices in order to achieve a different distribution of goods. Dworkin insists that the normative theory behind this position is flawed and the practical implications are absurd,[28] but gentrification is a real-world issue that demonstrates the plausibility of Cohen's position.

Poor people who wish to remain in their gentrifying neighborhoods are classic victims of "bad price luck." These residents could not reasonably be held responsible for the expensiveness of their taste. After all, they are the ones that moved into a low-cost neighborhood. These original residents acquired an attachment to a working-class neighborhood, which, due to the structural incentives for investors or the locational preferences of the creative class,[29] subsequently became expensive. Recall that an expensive taste is not merely a luxury that everyone desires but rather something that certain people need more than others in order to have the same level of well-being. This describes the preferences of current residents of transitional neighborhoods. Many people may desire to live in a certain neighborhood, but as we saw in the previous chapter, residents often develop a particularly intense emotional attachment or sense of place that would be painful to disrupt.[30]

How does this attachment to place come about? One possibility is that humans are by nature territorial and feel a greater level of security on their home turf. A more cultural account was developed by Yi-Fu Tuan, who coined the term "topophilia" to describe the affective bond between people and place.[31] Topophilia has multiple sources, including visual pleasure and sensual delight; people feel fondness for home because it is familiar, incarnates the past, and expresses pride of ownership or creation. Residents of a neighborhood also become attached to a place because they benefit from informal community support. All people, but especially poor people, rely on the support and aid of others.[32] People who live in proximity to one another create networks of mutual support. Physical proximity makes it efficient for neighbors to collaborate on mutually beneficial projects such as looking after each other's children, sharing tools, or fostering safety through "eyes on the street." These projects require trust and social capital, which take time to build. If tenants are forced to relocate to another neighborhood, these networks of mutual aid are disrupted, which entails financial costs and emotional hardship.

The following hypothetical example illustrates how the debate about expensive tastes applies to gentrification. In the town of Commontopia, there is a guaranteed minimum income that makes it possible for all residents to pay the average cost of rent for an appropriately sized apartment in the city. Should people who currently live in gentrifying neighborhoods (places where market rents were recently below average but are now above average) receive a supplement that enables them to pay the new higher-than-average rent? Following the logic of Cohen's argument, residents of gentrifying neighborhoods (including adult children of residents) should receive extra resources in order to fulfill their preference to continue living in their increasingly expensive neighborhood, but non-residents should not. For the residents, the price increase was a matter of bad luck, and therefore, according to luck egalitarian principles, the victims should be compensated.

This is a hypothetical scenario, but one that illuminates real issues in contemporary urban housing policy. For example, a few years ago Toronto city councillor Case Ootes proposed that the Toronto Community Housing Corporation (TCHC) should sell dozens of high-value properties in order to raise revenue to pay for the backlog of repairs needed in high-rise dwellings. These houses were located in neighborhoods such as Riverdale and Leslieville that had undergone gentrification; the houses had been purchased at low cost, but gentrification had driven up the value of these properties to over half a million dollars each. From Dworkin's perspective, it is hard to explain what is wrong with evicting the poor residents and relocating them to less costly neighborhoods. After all, he dismisses the idea that "bad price luck"[33] is a legitimate concern of justice, and treats market prices as objective, neutral facts about the world.[34]

Drawing on debates from egalitarian theory, this section has shown that there are good reasons to worry about the displacement of current residents, but a further implication is that there is less cause to be concerned about the exclusion of non-residents. This is because the two groups are affected by gentrification in different ways. Non-residents do not rely on existing place-specific networks of mutual aid. Moreover, they do not have the same attachments and loyalties that are produced through histories, routines, and experiences connected with a particular place. They did not participate in the creation of the *oeuvre* of the neighborhood. But attachment to place is not the only thing to consider. Many non-resident immigrants may have strong preferences to live in enclaves where a dense network of ethnic businesses facilitates work, socializing, and the logistics of everyday life. And what about other people who share the taste for downtown living? Immigrants, both domestic and international, may also desire access to the cultural, economic, and architectural commons of the city. The fact that affluent people are bidding up the price of homes in gentrifying neighborhoods is itself a sign of these preferences. This brings us back to Hayek's point that demand will outpace supply, and some authoritative form of allocation will be necessary. For Hayek, the market ensures that freedom rather than force prevails.

The theory of the common-wealth explains why this is wrong. For the solidarists, the social product is composed of private and public shares; the private part is justified because it supports freedom, fosters productivity, and legitimately but imperfectly reflects the value of labor. The public part reflects the value of the collective contribution (past and present), and secures freedom for everyone through collective control. It would be wrong to allow the ability to acquire private wealth to also secure privileged and disproportionate access to public goods like the city, or what Italians call *il comune*.[35] This is what happens when gentrification raises housing prices to the point where longtime residents must leave and non-elites are excluded.

Hayek is correct to warn that there is no simple solution to sharing a much-desired but limited good, but we cannot simply abdicate responsibility for this decision by relying exclusively on market forces. Democratic institutions are the sites where we can consciously decide how to weigh competing priorities. There are no philosophical principles or mathematical formulas or invisible hands that will solve this for us. As citizens, we will have to provide reasons to explain why certain needs should have priority, rather than simply deferring to the market, which allocates all goods on the basis of economic power.[36] In the case of housing, we should decide to give priority to the needs of current residents by adopting measures to promote neighborhood stability (rent control, regulation of tenancy, public housing). To expand access to the city, we can also build more affordable housing through inclusionary zoning, cooperative housing, and infill public housing. We might also promote arrangements that help people to live near their workplaces in order to decrease traffic congestion and help the environment. Another way to approach the issue is to ask why non-residents desire to move into certain neighborhoods, and see whether their features can be replicated elsewhere. If the attraction is proximity to public transportation and recreational amenities, then another remedy would be to expand the public infrastructure so that all residents have reasonable access.

Hayek may also be wrong when he worries that de-commodifying housing would lead to excess demand and limited supply. He assumes that supply is fixed and lowering prices will increase demand, but he fails to consider how commodification increases the demand for investment properties, which decreases the supply of residential space available for use. In many countries, including Canada and the United States, the tax structure gives people an incentive to overinvest in housing. In addition to the large number of units left completely empty by investors, many "owner-occupied" homes are actually homes and investment properties in one. By this I mean that owner-occupiers purchase a larger home than necessary in order to benefit from the lower taxes on this type of capital gain. This points to another set of tools for slowing the pace and diminishing the extent of gentrification: eliminating tax incentives to overinvest in housing and introducing excise taxes on empty units.

DEMOCRACY, TERRITORIALITY, AND PLACE

So far, this chapter has treated the harm resulting from gentrification in individualistic terms. Even values like community and "loyalty to place" have been described as the preferences or needs of particular individuals. Yet anyone who has studied gentrification knows that this does not exactly capture the complexity of the phenomenon. Often what is lost through gentrification is not the individual's home or apartment, but rather the neighborhood itself. Some long-term residents may stay, but they increasingly feel like aliens or outsiders in "their" neighborhoods. One aspect of this process is commercial displacement. In Ontario, commercial tenants are not protected by the same law that limits rent increases for residential tenants. This means that commercial areas can change much more quickly than the surrounding residential neighborhoods. Unable to compete with new commercial tenants, nonprofit cultural centers, mutual aid societies, and other community institutions may lose their leases.

Gentrifiers also use political as well as economic power to transform the character of public spaces.[37] Near my neighborhood in West Toronto, a conflict emerged when new residents wanted to turn an abandoned lot into a community garden; newcomers saw this as beautification, but old-timers were angered by the loss of a makeshift soccer field. Gentrifiers redesign parks to make families, tourists, or professionals feel welcome and homeless people unwelcome;[38] they mobilize to ensure that certain bars do not get their liquor licenses renewed.[39] They try to prevent social service providers from expanding their activities. Gentrifiers remake the public realm in order to fulfill their needs and desires, and through this process a neighborhood's social system is changed and its history is effaced. In this section I consider the issue of gentrification from a collective rather than an individual perspective. In what way might groups have a collective right to a certain kind of shared public space?

From the perspective of liberal theory, it is very hard to even conceptualize group rights. Liberal theory treats individuals as the bearers of rights, and foremost among these is the right to private property. Liberal theory also assumes that property is a commodity that is bought and sold on a market, albeit a market which is regulated and sometimes limited in order to promote the public good. This framework is so hegemonic that it is sometimes hard to recognize it as a historical and cultural product; it is deeply embedded in the legal system, the popular imagination, and dominant strands of normative theory. Yet there are alternatives such as feudal property, native reservations, Waqf property (Islamic charitable trusts), and *eijdo* land. In *Land, Conflict, and Justice*, Avery Kolers argues that liberal political theory is ill suited to illuminating conflicts over space and place because it rests on an unacknowledged ethnogeography, in particular, a culturally specific conception of land.[40]

In *Sovereign Virtue*, Ronald Dworkin provides a striking illustration of the liberal-capitalist ethnogeography. In order to explain the basic idea of equality of resources, he asks the reader to imagine castaways on an uninhabited desert island. With no hope of rescue, the castaways must decide how to distribute the land and resources equally. Each person receives an equal number of clamshells that she can use to bid on parcels in an auction. According to Dworkin, this would result in an equal distribution of resources that satisfied each person's preferences and left no one with any legitimate reason to envy anyone else. But, as previous commentators have pointed out, this schema is premised on the assumption of a shared set of values, namely a preference for individual, alienable property.[41] Dworkin states at the outset, "I shall assume, for this purpose, that equality of resources is a matter of equality in whatever resources are owned privately by individuals."[42] Dworkin suggests that this premise is "arbitrary," but it seems far from arbitrary since it is actually a culturally specific assumption that benefits some people over others. Early modern thinkers such as John Locke felt the need to justify private property, but contemporary liberal theorists mostly take its legitimacy for granted. Dworkin does not consider that the decision to adopt alienable private property might itself be a matter of justice.

By treating this liberal ethnogeography as a premise, Dworkin is unable to consider how private property might itself result in the unequal treatment of different people. What if some of the castaways prefer collective property and a lifestyle based on hunting and herding rather than sedentary agriculture? This preference could not be easily accommodated on an island divided into a patchwork of parcels. In a similar vein, Kolers points out that in the real world, an auction would not lead to the fair treatment of groups that see the land as the basis of a traditional lifestyle rather than a resource to be exploited. He uses the example of the Bedouins (*badawiyyīn*, from the desert) bidding for ownership of Arabia. He suggests that even if they controlled equal resources, they could not compete fairly with would-be oil barons. The oil barons could bid up the price of this land because their profit from future oil sales would enable them to purchase other goods. The Bedouins, on the other hand, would be forced to overspend for the land, leaving them with no other resources to purchase goats for herding or tents for shelter. Either they would be unable to purchase their land or they would be forced to become oil producers rather than pastoralists.[43]

Dworkin argues that the auction is fair because the resulting distribution would meet "the envy test": no one would have any reason to prefer someone else's bundle to his own.[44] Since everyone started with the same resources and could bid on any parcel, the resulting distribution should satisfy all preferences. The inequity stems from the fact that the distribution achieved by the auction might be less desirable to some people than a distribution based on another conception of the value of the land. There is no neutral, universal criterion for privileging a certain schema for distribution. Given that there are multiple, culturally specific conceptions of land, Kolers thinks that we need a robust conception of territorial rights. A territorial right, according to Kolers, is an ethnogeographic community's overriding interest in manifesting its ethnogeography.[45]

This conception of territorial rights is most useful in understanding disputes over land in postcolonial contexts, but it can also be brought to bear on theoretical debates about the harms of gentrification. I do not mean to suggest that working-class and poor neighborhoods in North America are ethnogeographic communities that possess territorial rights. They are diverse communities that include many people who are strong supporters of the free market. Empirical accounts of gentrification confirm that owner-occupiers are often enthusiastic about gentrification because it increases the value of their investment.[46] Nevertheless, the concept of ethnogeography helps illuminate the claims made by opponents of gentrification. After moving into derelict neighborhoods, bohemians, squatters, recent immigrants, the working poor, and the not-working poor create a world that has value to them. I don't mean to suggest that these groups all value the same things or that these values are completely outside the market, but these derelict spaces provide some room to experiment with living differently.[47] Yet as soon as wealthier groups need more *Lebensraum*, then the space for these alternatives immediately diminishes. Squats are cleared to make room for lofts, and the social clubs where old Greek men played cards are displaced to make room for winebars. There is very little that poor people can do to stop these changes.

The loss of a shared public world is a real harm, but it is one that is particularly difficult to remedy. Urban neighborhoods are too porous and too integrated into the broader urban framework to be true ethnogeographic communities. One possibility would be to think of neighborhood communities as micro-ethnogeographic communities and grant them some limited territorial rights that would allow them to control the pace and direction of change. For example, neighborhood councils could have powers to veto new developments, modify existing bylaws, or direct public monies to local projects, but these powers could easily be used to create exclusive communities rather than to promote access to public goods. For example, in 2012, Craig Cobb began purchasing cheap properties in Leith, North Dakota, in order to create a white enclave.[48] A white-supremacist heterotopia may be an extreme example, but I think that this type of decentralization would do more harm than good. These neighborhood councils would easily be captured by gentrifiers and used to accelerate rather than slow the pace of change. These powers would also be used by elite or homogeneous neighborhoods to keep out poor people, immigrants, and public housing. Exclusion is problematic even when it is not motivated by racial or socioeconomic exclusion. If the city is a form of common-wealth, then we need to find ways to increase rather than restrict access to it, and this involves infill and density in all neighborhoods.

Nevertheless, the concept of micro-ethnogeographic communities helps us understand why members of countercultural groups oppose gentrification. They live in neighborhoods that were abandoned by capital through disinvestment and turned them into heterotopias, places for living differently.[49] Squatters, for example, affirm the use value of buildings that have lost their exchange value. Activities and lifestyles that are not oriented toward profit and efficiency find a place to flourish. When real estate capital returns to reclaim these neighborhoods, the space for living differently diminishes. One example is the transformation of Times Square, from an informal red-light district to a hub of tourism and commerce. Even if one sees this as an example of the benefits of gentrification, it is clear that it made Times Square look and feel more like the rest of Manhattan.[50] Even if it is unwise to give ethnogeographic communities strong powers to exclude, it still makes sense to include neighborhood character, history, and local needs in policymaking. Giving local councils the power to set funding priorities through participatory budgeting is one way to do this.

POLARIZATION AND HOMOGENEITY

Critics of gentrification see the process as a colonization of working-class and immigrant neighborhoods that creates a uniformly middle-class environment. Proponents of downtown revitalization, however, take a somewhat different view. They think that far from displacing beloved neighborhood institutions, new retailers contribute to the vitality of declining neighborhoods by renting space in buildings that have been empty for months or years. The rise of shopping malls, automobiles, and supermarkets rendered mom-and-pop stores obsolete and entire commercial streets were abandoned and boarded up. These upscale boutiques and galleries are a way of recycling the built environment and adapting it for new uses. Gentrification is also sometimes promoted as a way of creating mixed-income, diverse neighborhoods. When upper-middle-class residents move into working-class neighborhoods, they increase rather than decrease the diversity.

What does the empirical literature say about these conflicting claims? In a study of Vancouver, Toronto, and Montreal, Alan Walks and Richard Maaranen examined whether gentrification increased or decreased socioeconomic and ethnic diversity.[51] While there were some

differences among the cities, this study found that completely gentrified neighborhoods tended to have greater levels of income polarization
and economic inequality than they did before the influx of high-income
residents. The increase, however, was not as great as the increase in
inequality in the city as a whole during the same period. Most gentrified
neighborhoods became more ethnically diverse over the period studied (1971–2001), but this reflected the changing demographics of the
metropolitan area, and these neighborhoods still ended up less diverse
than the city as a whole. Walks and Maaranen conclude that gentrification results in greater levels of income polarization and declining levels
of social mixing, ethnic diversity, and immigrant concentration within
affected neighborhoods.[52]

This rigorous research provides important insights into patterns of
demographic change within neighborhoods, but we should be very careful before drawing normative conclusions about gentrification in general.
This is because the study identifies two different categories of neighborhood change: "gentrification" and "incomplete gentrification." Both types
of neighborhoods experienced an increase in the average personal income,
but in the neighborhoods which experienced "incomplete gentrification"
income did not rise above the Census Metropolitan Area (CMA) average.
In both Toronto and Montreal, more neighborhoods experienced incomplete than complete gentrification. This seems to contradict the conventional wisdom that once gentrification begins, it does not stop until all
of the poorer residents have been displaced.[53] Walks and Maaranen show
that many neighborhoods that gained high-income residents in the 1970s
or 1980s were still socioeconomically diverse in 2001. Between 18 and
25 percent of residents in "incompletely gentrified" neighborhoods still
had household incomes below $20,000. The authors still worry that these
mixed neighborhoods will become more economically polarized and ethnically homogeneous, but their evidence shows that, so far, many of the
gentrifying neighborhoods in Toronto and Montreal have not become
elite enclaves, but instead have stabilized as mixed-income neighborhoods. This longitudinal study shows us two trajectories, one that results
in neighborhoods that are more homogeneous than the city as a whole
and one that creates neighborhoods that are more economically diverse
(but also more polarized) than the rest of the city.

Should "social mix" be construed as a harm or a benefit? The academics, policymakers, and planners who celebrate the idea of social mix do so for a number of different reasons. Some see it as a way to promote democratic citizenship by fostering informal social relationships and mutual understanding between different types of people.[54] Others promote it as a way to help the poor by de-concentrating poverty. When middle-class and poor people live side-by-side, the poor benefit from the amenities and the public services that the rich are able to secure: good schools, responsive policing, competitively priced shopping, recreational facilities, and regular street maintenance. Some go even farther and suggest that the informal interaction between the poor and the rich may help inculcate more appropriate norms of behavior and build social connections that will lead to better jobs or academic success. The empirical evidence in favor of these claims is fairly thin. Recent qualitative work on gentrification has pointed out that gentrifiers tend to build social networks with other people from the same social class even though, in theory, they enthusiastically endorse the diversity of the neighborhood.[55]

The term "diversity" tends to have a positive connotation, but a neighborhood with economic diversity could also be described as polarized. In their study, Walks and Maaranen showed that income polarization increased in both types of gentrifying neighborhoods. When higher earners move into fairly homogeneous working-class neighborhoods, economic diversity and polarization increase. The score for income polarization is particularly sensitive to the presence of extremely high and low incomes. In incompletely gentrified neighborhoods poor people and rich people live in close proximity. High levels of owner occupancy, rent control, tenant protection laws, and public housing all tend to create neighborhoods that change very slowly, but the new high-income residents increase the level of economic polarization.

Polarization can occur in many different ways. Imagine a society that initially has an equal distribution of wealth that, over time, becomes polarized. Our normative judgment depends on both our theory of equality and the empirical account of how polarization emerged. Consider the following three scenarios:

A) Due to greater skill and hard work, half of the citizens become more prosperous while the others maintain the same income.

This would increase polarization but would also be preferable from a utilitarian perspective because some are better off and no one is worse off.

B) A group of the original residents band together and use their economic and political power to redistribute resources rendering some poor and others rich. In this scenario there is a zero-sum game where the enrichment of some people comes directly at the expense of others.

C) A group of citizens introduces a division of labor and a set of material incentives which make some people more prosperous than others, but everyone is better off than they were under a system of equality. This is just according to Rawls's difference principle (inequalities are justified if they benefit those who are the worst off) but not Cohen's more demanding form of luck egalitarianism.

Egalitarians condemn B but they are split about scenarios A and C. The empirical question is also subject to intense dispute, and a great deal depends on whether the growing income polarization in wealthy countries follows pattern A, B, or C.

Another important factor to consider is the significance of inequality in general and to distinguish it from the way inequality is expressed in physical space. Income polarization is the unequal distribution of incomes among people within a polity. Neighborhood income polarization, on the other hand, describes the arrangement of people within space. It is possible to have neighborhoods with no income polarization, yet still have a very polarized society. Imagine a metropolitan area in which elite enclaves and poor ghettos are geographically separate from one another. As an egalitarian, I would like to see a decrease in income polarization in the polity, but until this happens, we must consider whether class segregation (e.g., homogeneity) or integration (e.g., polarization) is preferable. Based on the theory of the urban commonwealth, I think that there are good reasons for preferring integration. The main reason is that residents of wealthy neighborhoods are usually more effective at securing public goods. These are the neighborhoods that have high-performing schools, recreational amenities, public transportation, and fewer environmental hazards, and we should try to equalize access to these neighborhoods. The premise of this argument is that elites tend to use territory in order to maximize power;[56] they erect barriers in order to prevent non-elites from gaining access to desired goods. Egalitarians should promote a policy of porosity across boundaries and maintain a critical attitude toward urban policies that lead to exclusion.

My primary concern is not promoting diversity as an end in itself, but rather preventing exclusion. In the abstract, it is hard to assess whether increasing social mix is a good or a bad thing. A useful starting point is Iris Marion Young's nuanced analysis of debates about segregation and polarization.[57] She argued that racial segregation has been a source of injustice because it systematically prevents certain people from enjoying the infrastructure and amenities available in other parts of town. Nevertheless, the ideal of integration isn't the solution, because there are also real advantages that come from living clustered together with people who share the same language, culture, or lifestyle.[58] These benefits range from supporting a viable market for culturally specific projects and services to creating a safe space for counter-hegemonic practices. As an alternative, she advocates an approach which she calls "together in difference," a way of organizing urban space that sustains distinctive enclaves while linking them together through public forums and institutions. The goal is to combat segregation when it limits choice, undermines equality, and mystifies the real level of social inequality. I take this to be a defense of a mosaic vision of cultural pluralism, one that recognizes the value of distinctive enclaves that enable diverse urban dwellers to feel at home while still emphasizing the importance of building links and alliances that cut across entrenched identities.

I don't think that the normative ideal of "together in difference" provides strong theoretical reasons for either defending or criticizing gentrification. Gentrification increases social mix in some cases and decreases it in others. Furthermore, it is unclear whether social mix is beneficial to subaltern groups and whether the benefits outweigh possible harms. I suspect that critics of neo-liberalism are correct in arguing that the ideal of social mix sometimes functions ideologically to legitimize projects that take land currently used for public housing and make it available for private development.[59] The right to share the urban commonwealth is a more powerful argument against removing poor people from downtown and housing them in less expensive areas on the urban periphery. The key concern of Young's writing on "together in difference" is a desire to understand the spatial dimension of the ideal of equality. In order to achieve equality, subaltern groups need more power. Sometimes living together in enclaves can be a source of power, either by facilitating political mobilization or by exercising informal control over a small area. At the same time, increased social mix can ensure access to desired public goods. Instead of focusing on social mix per se, we should think about how particular urban policies strengthen or weaken the position of the most vulnerable residents.

CONCLUSION

In this chapter I have considered five primary harms of gentrification: residential displacement; exclusion; transformation of public, social, and commercial space; polarization; and homogenization. Residential displacement is the most serious harm since it distributes the costs of neighborhood transition to people who are not responsible for the change. For these residents, gentrification is a form of bad luck and an egalitarian society should try to socialize the costs of experiencing this bad luck. This could take the form of rent control, public housing, or the expansion of limited equity co-operative housing. The exclusion of non-residents is a lesser but still serious harm; non-residents are usually not attached to the neighborhood in the same way, but exclusion still unfairly magnifies the impact of economic inequality by transforming the most dynamic cities into de facto gated communities. The gates of gated communities ensure that the aesthetic and recreational amenities are reserved for the benefit of wealthy homeowners; the prices of houses in cities like San Francisco, New York, Vancouver, and London have the same effect, but many of the amenities that they effectively privatize include natural and cultural heritage and public goods. In some cities, the harm of exclusion could be addressed by ensuring that all neighborhoods have access to comparable public amenities, including good schools, public transportation, and recreational facilities. A more radical solution would be to distribute housing using non-market mechanisms. Given the predominance of free market ideology and practices in North America, this solution probably sounds undesirable or impractical to most people, but it is worth noting that cities such as Vienna, Singapore, and Amsterdam have been successful at de-commodifying housing.[60]

The transformation of public/social space, polarization, and homogenization all describe harms to communities and to the city itself rather than to just the individual. As I suggested above, these changes may be harmful or beneficial depending on the composition of the city as a whole and the power dynamics involved in the transformations. It is easy to overlook the way that the loss of certain distinctive neighborhoods and spaces may be accompanied by the creation of new ones located in parts of the city that are unfamiliar to the gentrifying class. Scarborough, an inner suburb of Toronto, provides many examples. There are few stately historic brick homes or quaint narrow commercial streets, but there are lots of dynamic strip malls filled with ethnic entrepreneurs and "third spaces" that meet the needs of immigrants living in the nearby high-rises.

If the gentrification of downtown is harmful, should we view de-gentrification or proletarianization as a benefit? Not exactly. In places like Detroit, the exodus of private capital has the reverse but equally harmful effect. Like a house of cards, the flight of private capital destabilizes the public and small-scale private components of the common-wealth, sometimes leading to collapse. This question helps us focus on the core harm of gentrification, which isn't gentrification itself but rather inequality. Gentrification makes the increase in inequality and income polarization into something visible, vivid, and concrete. Moreover, it reminds us that the wealthy get to take what they want and leave everyone else with what they discard. Urban policy by itself cannot solve this problem.[61]

[6]

TRANSIT JUSTICE

On December 9, 2013, a group of San Francisco Bay Area activists obstructed a Google shuttle bus as it picked up passengers in San Francisco's Mission District.[1] During the protest, a window on another bus was broken, and graffiti was scrawled on the sidewalk that read: "Trendy Google Professionals Help Raise Housing Costs." For protesters, the Google buses were visible symbols of growing economic inequality in the Bay Area and also contributed to two harmful phenomena: gentrification and the privatization of public transit. The private shuttles revealed the inadequacy of public transit and a lack of viable solutions to the problem.

Debates about public transit are contentious in part because the grounds for distributing public goods are unclear. Normative arguments about the distribution of public goods have received surprisingly little attention in political theory.[2] Economists, however, have offered an account of public goods that is both parsimonious and clear: public goods are things like clean air, which cannot be provided by the market because it is impossible or inefficient to make them available to some people without providing them to everyone.

Many of the things we call "public goods" fall outside of the economists' definition, which emphasizes non-rival, non-excludable goods. Schools, housing, and transit are excludable; indeed, there were boarding schools, houses, and carriages long before the state began to subsidize any of these things. These goods become public when the state decides it is morally necessary or efficient to subsidize them. Sometimes almost everyone benefits, and then these are described as universal public goods—things like education and, in most wealthy countries, healthcare. Public housing, on the other hand, is usually described as a non-universal good, since it is subsidized by the state but allocated based on need.

What kind of good is public transit? According to a 2009 report by the U.S. Department of Transportation, private vehicles were used for 83.4 percent of all trips; only 1.9 percent of all trips relied on public transit,[3] so transit is not a universal public good. Mark Garrett and Brian Taylor have argued that public transit in the United States is a social service.[4] Outside of a few major cities like New York, Boston, and Washington, DC, most middle- and high-income people drive cars; the overwhelming majority of public transit users are children, the elderly, and the poor. Racial minorities are also overrepresented among riders. Garrett and Taylor use the term "transit dependents" to describe people who have no choice but to use public transit to meet their fundamental needs, including education, work, healthcare, and shopping.

The politics of public transit is complicated by the fact that transit dependents are only one constituency. The other main constituency—discretionary rather than dependent users—is commuters, and many of them drive to commuter rail stations that are linked to downtowns. The forms of transit used by wealthy whites (commuter rail) are much more likely to receive large government subsidies than the forms used by poor people and minorities (buses).[5] In *Seeking Spatial Justice*,[6] Edward Soja focused on this inequity. He recounted the struggle of the Los Angeles Bus Riders Union and its historic legal victory, which forced the Los Angeles County Metropolitan Transit Authority to provide better service in poor, minority neighborhoods. Soja shows how inequalities are spatialized and describes the innovative social movements that seek to dismantle the geographical barriers that prevent equal access to the city. In order to prevail in democratic deliberation, particular interests must be recognized as general interests or values. The theory of the urban commonwealth helps explain why the mobility of transit-dependent people is a matter of general concern.

Public transit is necessary to ensure fair access to the urban commonwealth, especially for transit dependents. In a city without income inequality, transit would cease to be a matter of justice, because everyone could decide how to balance their desires for private space, proximity, accessibility, and time. The goal of this book, however, is to think about the cities we live in rather than to imagine an ideal alternative. Under conditions of inequality, we must ask whether decisions about the funding and expansion of transit infrastructure have a negative impact on those who are already disadvantaged.

There are two ways to share the urban commonwealth. One is through direct proximity. Living in an amenity-rich area makes it easy to enjoy its benefits and contribute to its ongoing construction. The other possibility is to increase mobility through transportation. Following Thad Williamson, I define mobility as "the capacity to access and participate in the economic, civic, and social life of one's community, without respect to social class or personal economic circumstances."[7] This chapter proceeds in four steps. In the first section I pose a very basic question: Is there a right to mobility? Drawing on Kant, I argue that mobility is a condition of freedom and a matter of public right. This is a useful starting point, but one that doesn't go far enough in guiding debates about transit justice. The problem is that transit cannot be distributed equally, in the narrow sense of providing the same access to all people regardless of dispersion in space. Most normative issues are complex, but transit is particularly challenging because it involves technical issues; competing norms and interests (commuters vs. transit dependents, separation vs. integration); and huge, fixed investments. The second and third sections consider the right to mobility in two very different contemporary struggles over public transit, which took place in Richmond and Toronto. In the final section, I propose a set of guidelines based on the legal theory of equal protection that can be used to assess whether differential treatment is unfair.

THE RIGHT TO MOBILITY

The "right to mobility" might seem like exactly the kind of expansive term that effectively renders the concept of "right" meaningless. In an essay in the *New York Review of Books*, Ronald Dworkin uses traffic rules as an example of something that does *not* involve rights. In his essay, traffic rules are a counterexample that serves to illustrate his broader point about the distinctiveness of rights. According to Dworkin, traffic rules and rights such as free speech fall into different categories:

> [T]hough the New York City government needs a justification for forbidding motorists to drive up Lexington Avenue, it is sufficient justification if the proper officials believe, on sound evidence, that the gain to the many will outweigh the inconvenience to the few. When individual citizens are said to have rights against the government, however, like the right of free speech, that must mean that this sort of justification is not enough.[8]

What exactly is the difference between driving down a road and publicly expressing one's political views? According to Dworkin, basic liberties such as free speech protect something other than the arbitrary freedom to do as one pleases; they protect "human dignity," a term that is meant to identify the most fundamental aspects of human personhood. While perhaps somewhat imprecise, the concept of human dignity does seem intuitively plausible. There must be some way to distinguish between trivial limitations on freedom, which the government may regulate to promote the common good, and fundamental freedoms that transcend this calculus. While scholars may differ on where to draw the line and even how precisely to justify it, it seems obvious that transit belongs on the side of pragmatic balancing rather than rights.

This chapter challenges this view and presents arguments in favor of a right to mobility.[9] Although I start with a discussion of rights, I think it is more appropriate to describe my position as a defense of transit justice.[10] Public transit is something that is naturally shared, and therefore it is particularly problematic to treat it as an individual right. The starting point of my argument is that government regulation limits freedom, and it can only do so to decrease inequality and not to increase it. This argument draws on the political philosophy of Immanuel Kant, and is especially indebted to Arthur Ripstein's interpretation of Kant. Strong social democrats and progressives already believe in the decommodification of basic goods; in order to persuade a broader audience, I show how a defense of transit justice can also rest on liberal principles.

In his book *Force and Freedom*, Arthur Ripstein makes a Kantian argument in favor of a principled approach to traffic rules.[11] I will begin by explaining and assessing this argument and then consider how it provides reasons in favor of *public* transportation and access to the city. Ripstein is not primarily concerned with mobility or the right to the city. Instead, his goal is to challenge the dominant view that the concept of "police powers" describes a domain in which the government can legitimately make decisions based on its pragmatic assessment of the best way to balance benefits and burdens. Traffic regulation is introduced as part of a rhetorical strategy that is the reverse of the straw man argument; by examining the issue that seems intuitively most suited to pragmatic balancing, he can make the strongest possible case for a principled approach to government regulation.

Ripstein argues that the state's entitlement to make traffic rules is derived from its obligation to provide the conditions of equal freedom.[12] This argument draws on Kant's political philosophy. In *The Metaphysics of Morals*, Kant insists that the state is a legitimate form of mandatory cooperation.[13] The underlying idea is a spatial one. People live together on a shared earth and will inevitably come into contact with one another, and therefore there must be some non-arbitrary way of resolving conflicts. Proximity is not the source of constant strife, but the potential for conflict is omnipresent, and it can be resolved in two ways: might or right. According to Kant, rational agents are purposive and seek to pursue their own ends. Might, or arbitrary rule, is a unilateral limit on our freedom to pursue our ends; therefore reason teaches that we must bring about right, or non-arbitrary rule. For Kant, the state is not the product of individual consent, but rather a necessary feature of the rational order, and rational agents are obligated to bring it about and to support it.

Read in a certain way, this approach may sound individualistic, and indeed Kant did place the rational individual at the core of his moral philosophy, but it also has a collective dimension. In the *Metaphysics of Morals*, Kant asks, "Can the sovereign be regarded as the supreme proprietor of the land?" and answers in the affirmative. According to Kant, the state is not created through the aggregation of individual private properties but through the distribution or division of land.[14] Private property is not absolute, and is subject to general rules created by the state. For Kant, the power of mandatory taxation, including taxation for the purpose of redistribution, is derived from the sovereign's "basic right of ownership."[15] Kant insists, "the nature of the state thus justifies the government in compelling prosperous citizens to provide the means of preserving those who are unable to provide themselves with even the most rudimentary necessities of nature."[16]

Given Kant's emphasis on the state and political obligation, why does Ripstein emphasize freedom as the central Kantian category? Answering this question is necessary to understand the limits and extent of political obligation. Kant rejects the libertarian idea that all obligations are purely voluntary products of arbitrary choice or contract, but does that mean that the state can compel people to place the general interest above their own? Freedom is the primary category because it is the end or goal of human action, and a system of right (a state that is ruled by law and not arbitrary power) is the only way to secure this end. For Kant, what it means to be human is to have an idea of the good life and to try to secure it. This is not a radically individualist notion. This good could be service to God or family or country, but Kant's analysis does rest on two individualist premises: reason and will. Freedom is possible because I can understand different options, choose among them, and act on this choice. Freedom and obligation are not antithetical, because freedom involves the ability to understand and accept obligations. The state is able to compel certain actions such as paying taxes or serving in the military because these things are necessary to secure the freedom of all. Kant concludes that the sovereign is not institutionally limited by a system of checks and balances—like Hobbes, he worries that this will lead to anarchy and civil strife—but the sovereign is limited by this normative principle of equal freedom.

Ripstein argues that the public provision of roads and corresponding traffic regulations are necessary to secure private freedom, and this means that they are potentially matters of right. Initially, it might seem somewhat paradoxical to suggest that regulations are a way of securing rather than limiting freedom. If there is a traffic law that prohibits me from driving more than 65 miles an hour, then my reason (my decision that speeding is worth the risk) and my will are subject to the purposes of another. These other purposes may be laudatory, such as preventing harm to pedestrians or decreasing greenhouse gas emissions, but imposing them still limits my freedom. This objection, however, rests on a conflation of private and public right. For Kant, the state, acting on behalf of the citizens as a collectivity, has legitimate powers that are distinct from the powers of individuals or private groups.[17] This is true because mandatory coordination is necessary to secure freedom. Ripstein uses the example of roads to illustrate how this works.

Imagine a libertarian utopia where all property is privately owned and each person has the right to exclude others from her property and enjoy it as she sees fit. The overwhelming disadvantage of the system becomes apparent when you want to leave your land. Surrounded on all sides by other people's private property, you must secure your neighbor's permission to leave your property.[18] Rational agents may consent to mutually beneficial agreements, allowing others to cross their land in exchange for similar permission, but no one is required to do so, and anyone can arbitrarily decide to opt out. While you are traveling, your neighbor might sell his land and the new owner, not subject to the original agreement, could forbid access, thereby making it impossible for you to return to your own land. According to Kant, no person is obligated to help another attain his or her ends, and this means that a neighbor who prefers not to offer passage over his land is not acting wrongly in preventing your passage; nevertheless, the outcome is that you could become a prisoner on your own property, subject to a de facto house arrest.

Private property in land is a structural condition that has an enormous effect on human freedom. Without public roads, the exercise of the most basic human functions—the ability to communicate and act collectively with others—is subject to the arbitrary will of another. Even if private companies acquired land to use for toll roads, there would be no entitlement to access them, and therefore independence would always be in jeopardy. In order to exercise freedom, in the most literal sense of physical motion in pursuit of basic interests, roads are necessary. A Kantian perspective helps us see why these must be public roads. Sociability and commerce are never more than insecure privileges if the provision of such roads is not subject to right.[19]

The concept of "subject to right," however, requires further clarification. For Kant, humans have an innate capacity for reason but are also governed by desires, and some may even have pathological desires.

Perfectly reasonable creatures would not need a state, and totally irrational ones would not be capable of sustaining one, but humans can recognize and fulfill the obligation to create an authority capable of restricting wild or excessive freedom so that the freedom of each would be compatible with all. The best form of government for Kant is a republican one, because it is structured to serve the public interest; but he also recognizes the legitimacy of authoritarian forms of government. This may have been partially due to the fact that he was writing under the threat of censorship by his own authoritarian government. He argued that such governments, while imperfect, create social order, which makes improvement possible. "Subject to right" means that an arrangement is structured to protect the equal freedom of all rather than the particular interests of some.

Public right exists when all of us will the rules that bind each of us, and this would entail public roads that preserve mobility and freedom. Private property only works in connection with its opposite: public property. By itself, the right to mobility does not tell us anything about the quality, design, or financing of roads or, by extension, of other forms of public transportation. It does, however, provide us with reasons for prioritizing equal freedom and recognizing the state's role in securing public right. Below I will describe these two ideas as "classic liberalism." With these principles in mind, I turn to two examples that help us think about the politics of public transit.

RICHMOND, VIRGINIA

Richmond has a population of just over 200,000. It is a majority black city, situated in a majority white metropolitan area with a population of 1.3 million.[20] According to Thad Williamson, the municipalities in the greater Richmond area blocked state funding for intra-urban public transportation, which made it difficult for inner-city residents to access suburban amenities and jobs. The spatial mismatch between job seekers and job opportunities and the lack of public transit to correct this has been documented in other metropolitan areas.[21] Through the lens of critical urban

theory, what initially appears like a natural relationship between municipal boundaries and municipal services comes to seem like a mechanism of
exclusion and racial segregation. Without public transit, it is difficult for
poor, inner-city residents to access suburban jobs and amenities.

A skeptic could argue that the absence of regional public transit is
not exactly the same as a world without public roads. In Richmond there
are roads, and residents could walk or bike to work, or pool resources
to cover the cost of sharing a car, but these options are not realistic for
all people. For many people it is simply too far to walk; the elderly and
infirm cannot bike, and lack of bicycling infrastructure makes this option
dangerous. The result is that people cannot access things that they need
to flourish, mostly jobs, but sometimes also grocery stores, schools, or
doctors. According to Williamson, "to lack the ability to access physical
spaces beyond one's most immediate environment is to be a second-class
citizen and also to face living a sharply constricted life."[22] Mobility is necessary for equal freedom; in small-scale communities this need may be
fulfilled by footpaths, but in large-scale urban environments it requires
regional public transit.

Richmond mayor Roy West explicitly rejected the suggestion that
there is a right to public transit: "Lack of transportation is just an excuse.
People have a personal obligation to get to their jobs. Society doesn't owe
anybody a right to transportation."[23] The people living in the suburbs did
not think that they had an obligation to contribute to a regional public transit system. Racial anxieties probably played some role in legitimizing this
position. In her book *How Americans Make Race*, Clarissa Hayward explains
that "the systematic channeling of public and private investment away
from black ghettos and toward white suburbs layered material inequalities atop identitarian distinctions, thus helping produce, not just racial
identities, but also a (white) racial *interest* in . . . residential exclusivity."[24]
Opposition to public transit is one way of securing such exclusivity, but it
was defended using the coded language of localism. This does not mean
that all opposition to regional transit was motivated by racism and, in
fact, West himself is black. The problem is that once racially motivated
differences are materialized in space, it becomes difficult to dismantle
them, both because of the direct costs involved and because of the way
that citizens use the political system to defend their financial interests,

especially property values. Hayward and Swanstrom have used the term "thick injustice" to describe the way that inequalities, once embedded in physical space, are particularly hard to rectify.[25]

In Richmond, opponents drew on theories of limited government, efficiency, and local autonomy to explain their opposition to regional transit.[26] The theory of limited government holds that the role of government is primarily to ensure public safety. In fact, the principle of limited government was applied inconsistently. The neighboring counties spent considerable tax revenue on road maintenance and education. Officials felt that these public goods were both desired and necessary; public transit, which required immediate costs and promised uncertain benefits, was perceived as neither necessary nor particularly desirable to suburbanites. Basically, city residents wanted regional transit but suburbanites did not. This is where localism comes in. Despite a clear need for regional public transit, the immediate demand came primarily from city residents, and the surrounding counties were under no obligation to take these preferences into account.

A Kantian-inspired framework provides reasons for rejecting this way of avoiding responsibility. When suburban municipalities or counties block transit, they are similar to the hostile neighbor who refuses access to a right of way over his land. In a system of private right, the neighbor's private preferences are not subject to review, and this means that his arbitrary will determines the range of actions of those living adjacent. Public right is necessary to prevent this from happening. If suburban governments are able to pursue their narrow interests and city residents and officials have no way to prevent this, then it begins to look a lot like arbitrary rule. This is why a regional structure is necessary. In fact, the state government does have the power to implement regional transit, and the state legislature has taken tentative steps in that direction, but the political will was weak in the face of opposition from suburban constituencies. One reason for framing the issue in terms of *Recht* (right) is that this is a way to challenge majoritarian preferences. The current allocation of public resources enhances the mobility of car owners at the expense of less affluent, less mobile pedestrians. Even though this may reflect voter preferences, especially the preference of the majority of the population who can afford a car, government action should minimize rather than reinforce inequality.

TORONTO

Scarborough is an area on the urban periphery of Toronto with distinctive demographic and spatial characteristics (high levels of poverty and a high percentage of recent immigrants, many of whom live in concrete-slab high-rise towers).[27] The transit infrastructure in this area is significantly worse than in other parts of the city. In Toronto, the affluent central city is well served by two fast, efficient subway lines. The poorer, non-white inner suburbs are served by buses rather than subways. A study done by the Martin Prosperity Institute of the University of Toronto looked at the provision of public transit in high-, middle-, and low-income parts of Toronto, and found that high-income areas have 3.2 times better service than low-income areas.[28] Only part of the difference is explained by the fact that low-income families are increasingly concentrated in the lower-density inner suburbs.

Furthermore, residential density, by itself, is an imperfect proxy for demand for public transit. It is also important to take into account whether other forms of transit, including walking, biking, and driving, are available. A recent survey showed that 23 percent of households in the city of Toronto do not have a car, but car ownership is lower in the poor, high-rise neighborhoods of the inner suburbs. According to a report on "walkability in Toronto's high-rise neighbourhoods," 41 percent of households in these mostly inner-suburban neighborhoods do not have access to a car.[29] This means that there is a mismatch between transportation and transit-dependent people. Low-income people who cannot afford car ownership are priced out of walkable, transit-oriented neighborhoods and forced to live in less dense, peripheral neighborhoods. The result is decreased access to employment and several hours of unpaid para-labor every day, the auxiliary labor time it takes to commute to and from work using slow, poorly connected bus services.[30]

The "equal freedom" approach to mobility, however, does not provide too much insight into this issue. Unlike the greater Richmond area, where non-drivers lack a viable way of reaching most jobs in the suburbs, Toronto has a functional public transit system. Residents of Scarborough are poorly served compared to people living in more affluent and central parts of the city, but mobility is possible, and so minimal freedom is ensured.

The challenge is to unpack the meaning of "equal freedom." Equal freedom makes sense when it is understood as a negative right. For example, all people, rich and poor, black and white have the same "right to remain silent" and cannot be compelled to testify against themselves. Equal mobility, in a literal sense, is impossible. In any system some people will live closer to transit hubs and others further away, and different modes of transportation are appropriate for different spatial configurations. One could object that the government is not permitted to treat people unequally, and that it does so by providing better public transit to wealthy neighborhoods. The problem is that unequal access to transit infrastructure is often produced by the market rather than the state. Even if the initial allocation of transit investment is fair, what happens when people with vastly unequal resources bid in an auction for desirable (e.g., transit-accessible) locations? A recent study showed a positive and statistically significant relationship between gentrification and the presence of urban rail transit stations. An earlier study found a high correlation between property values and proximity to the subway network in Toronto. These studies suggest that people are willing to pay a premium for public transit access, and the spatial inequality reflects underlying patterns of economic inequality.[31] Is the state obliged to equalize the transit infrastructure in poor and wealthy parts of the city?

Classic liberalism does not require the government to counteract inequalities that result from general circumstances, the actions of others, or individual choices. The classic liberal theory of freedom provides strong reasons for a system of public right, but does not require a politics of redistribution. As long as the Toronto subway was originally sited in way that did not confer greater benefits on more affluent neighborhoods, it met the requirement that benefits and burdens of cooperation be distributed equally. Since people value access to public transit, the prices of transit-accessible housing increased and, over time, the more affluent people who were able to afford these higher prices came to predominate in these neighborhoods. From a classic liberal perspective, it isn't the responsibility of the government to redistribute an allocation that resulted from individual choices, even though those choices were constrained by unequal access to private resources.

Solidarism provides a different way of approaching this issue. If we see transit infrastructure as part of the common-wealth, then it is problematic if it does not remain common but is instead effectively monopolized by privileged groups. This infrastructure is a collective good and a shared inheritance bequeathed by the previous generation, and no group naturally deserves disproportionate access. Once we identify this spatial pattern of exclusion/displacement as a kind of dispossession, then it is possible to ask what kind of compensation or redistribution is justified. Given the structural character of the process, the state is the appropriate agent of redistribution. The concept of dispossession serves to justify the principle of equalization that should guide transit and urban planning.[32] Of course, this does not mean that every person and every neighborhood can have the same access to public transit or subways. There are legitimate reasons that some areas will have better service than others—a point which will be addressed below—but these differences must be justified. This principle of equalization can be realized in two ways: by providing greater access to neighborhoods with high concentrations of the common-wealth and by investing in public goods across the city.[33]

Roads are a classic example of a public good both in the narrow sense of the term (something that must be provided to everyone in order to fulfill its purpose) and in the broader sense (something that is fundamental to human flourishing). But transit infrastructure is extremely costly, and this is why many politicians and taxpayers prioritize controlling costs over equalizing service. What is surprising is that many progressives have been opposed to the proposed extension of the subway into Scarborough. A typical example of the anti-subway position is the following quote from Royson James, a columnist in the left-leaning *Toronto Star*. He explained his opposition to the city council's close vote to support subway expansion:

Another reason, emotional and disquieting: The buildup of the narrative of the aggrieved and downtrodden Scarborough, a community that must find redemption in this subway or become the city's outcast, a wasteland abandoned to the damnable second-class LRT [light rapid transit]. The mayor and several city counsellors are responsible for feeding this beast. Shame.[34]

In this quote, opposition to spatialized inequality is pathologized as not only illegitimate but also animalistic and beastly. The main substantive arguments advanced by the anti-subway camp, however, are that there are less costly alternatives and that support for subway expansion is "political." According to critics, key politicians support subway expansion because they hope to win votes by pandering to the selfish or ignorant preferences of people living in the inner suburbs. They define "the political" as action that is motivated by partisan electoral considerations rather than the public good. The problem with the definition is that it treats the "public good" as something that is self-evident rather than the subject of ethical and political deliberation and struggle. The opposite of politics is often assumed to be "efficiency," which is treated as a neutral criterion for resolving conflicts over how to distribute resources. A properly political approach, however, helps us see how efficiency can naturalize and reinforce inequality. Equalizing infrastructure is always costly; therefore it seems more cost-efficient to maintain an unequal system.

A political question is a conflict that exposes different understandings of the public good. It is both agonistic *and* normative. Politics makes different interests, perspectives, powers, and desires visible and then forces a decision between them. An effective political argument does not assert "this is good for me" but rather "this is right for us." It helps people see their interests in new ways, or to prioritize the needs of others. Politics is also normative in the sense of deciding which procedural and substantive standards apply in particular cases.

Politics, in this sense, can help us recognize inequality and injustice in practices that would otherwise seem neutral, familiar, or inevitable. Both the built environment and the distribution of social classes across the built environment are usually perceived as natural phenomena rather than products of power relations. The political process is also a way of expressing the view that inadequate transit infrastructure causes harms that locationally privileged people do not even recognize.

The most common objection to the politicization of transit planning is that policy decisions must be based on empirical evidence such as ridership and population density. Solid research *is* important, but what is often overlooked is the way that the selection and use of evidence rests on a point of view that is not acknowledged or examined. For example, critics of the subway expansion argue that the overall population density is lower in areas without subway service. This is correct, but the density of neighborhoods whose growth has been stimulated by proximity to high-quality transit cannot fairly be compared with the density of poorly connected, peripheral neighborhoods that are interspersed with deindustrialized lands with enormous, yet unrealized potential for growth. The economic feasibility of transit infrastructure depends on high population density, but transit also facilitates densification, and densification is a way of meeting the need for housing. The use of evidence is a dimension of political judgment, not an alternative to it.

EQUAL PROTECTION

It is difficult to decide what portion of collective resources should be devoted to meeting the needs of city residents who are both worse off in absolute terms and underserved by public goods. Voters are often torn between principles and self-interested motives such as the desire for lower taxes or for things that benefit them directly. Even if principles are not simply universalized versions of class interests, they are certainly intertwined with interests. Would it help if we examined this issue from the Rawlsian original position? Behind the veil of ignorance, in the "original position" where one does not know whether one is rich or poor—able to afford a renovated Edwardian on a leafy urban street or a deteriorating 1960s high-rise apartment on a busy corner of the inner suburbs—would Torontonians endorse the same transit plan?

Rawls himself emphasized that the heuristic device of the veil of ignorance was intended to generate general principles, not to resolve disputes over specific policy issues, because the latter would require balancing interests and detailed knowledge of relevant facts. Nevertheless, this thought experiment is a good place to start when trying to decide whether a policy would be acceptable from the perspective of those who are worse off. In transit planning, the resulting principle would be that places and people with similar needs and characteristics should have comparable levels of accessibility, and that equalization should take priority over improving access for those who already have greater accessibility.

The veil of ignorance is basically a way of asking what things look like from the other's point of view, which is both impossible to achieve and necessary to attempt.[35] It is also particularly difficult to use this device to figure out how to dismantle thick injustice—injustice that accumulates over time and is materialized in space.[36] Behind the veil of ignorance, people choose principles of justice and imagine that they are applying them to a kind of blank slate or Garden of Eden, a place not yet structured through generations of unjust practices and distributions. Under these circumstances, creating a just world does not entail the loss or transformation of things to which people are attached. In the world we live in—and particularly in the physical places we inhabit—people have affective attachments and routines that bind them to the structures of inequality. They may favor the principle of equality while still opposing measures that distribute public goods more equally.

The underlying reasons for this performative contradiction have to do with temporality (historical accumulation) and complexity. Rectifying spatial inequality is even more challenging than addressing economic inequality. If one person has too much money and another person has too little, it is possible to simply transfer money from one person to the other. If one family has a large home and another family has a tiny home, however, redistribution is more difficult. You cannot simply transfer children from one house to another, nor can you remove one story of the house and graft it onto the other. When certain areas have benefited from high levels of investment over several generations, it is even more difficult to equalize things in a short period of time. With financial transfers, it is possible to gradually diminish inequality over time, but the built environment cannot be gradually modified in the same way. Even measures that decrease the absolute level of spatial inequality may be problematic because they fix inequality in space. For example, building a light rail system at a cost of $1.5 billion would decrease the amount of inequality between Scarborough and the central city, but it would also make it impossible to build a $3 billion subway extension.

The second reason why the original position provides only limited insight is complexity. The original position explains why moral agents should select the principle of justice that secures the greatest benefits for those who are the worst off. In the debate about public transit, however, everyone accepts this principle, but they differ about who is worst off and how to distribute benefits in a way that balances different needs. This means that different views about how to secure justice are expressed as disputes about facts, and these factual claims are both contested and uncertain.

Cost-benefit analysis is meant to provide an objective way to answer these questions. According to cost-benefit analysis, we should consider whether the cost per rider is significantly higher than it is in other parts of the system, or if less costly alternatives result in only modest increases in transit times. If so, then subways might not be justified. It would not make sense to build subways in rural areas or to expect direct flights from small cities to all destinations.[37] There is a limit to the costs that the collective should assume to increase the convenience of a few.

Yet, while cost-benefit analysis surely must play a role in providing public services, it can never replace a more comprehensive discussion of the public good. We pay significantly more to educate students with special needs, even though this would seem inefficient if evaluated in terms of the cost per pupil. Similarly, we have invested in very costly modifications to the built environment in order to ensure that people with disabilities have access to the physical infrastructure of the city. Public transportation is precisely the type of public good that could mitigate other forms of inequity. Improved public transit could diminish rather than exacerbate other forms of inequality, by making the common-wealth more accessible. It could also lessen the physical distance that separates less costly residential areas from the amenities and opportunities located in other parts of the city.

Another objection to the concept of transit justice is that a rigidly moralistic approach to transit planning can lead to worse decisions. According to the anti-subway camp in Toronto, a less costly form of transit would free up resources to invest in a more comprehensive transit network. Proponents of this approach argue that it would improve mobility for a larger number of underserved people. If both sides agree that the primary concern should be equity and the decision about mode should be evaluated based on the best information available, in light of that end, how do we do this? How do we compare a transit plan that makes a limited budget go the farthest with alternatives that will create greater benefit but at a much higher cost?

The legal theory of equal protection provides some useful tools for answering this question. In order to clarify the meaning of the principle of equal protection, the Supreme Court of Canada introduced a legal test that provides a set of guidelines. The Law Test (named after the 1999 case *Law v. Canada*) instructs courts to examine whether state action *either* explicitly imposes differential treatment *or* fails to account for a group's disadvantaged position. The two-part criteria is important because it recognizes that a statute or policy may be neutral on its face while still either intentionally or unintentionally harming members of particular groups. For example, the infamous grandfather clauses, which limited black suffrage without identifying a target group, had a systematically differential impact. According to the Law Test, legislation must meet a higher standard of justification when the differential treatment of such a group imposes a burden or withholds a benefit from its members. This does not mean that groups may never be treated differently, only that reasons must be exceptionally strong and well supported. This is similar to the strict scrutiny standard, which is used in the United States to examine the way that laws affect protected categories, such as racial and religious minorities. The distinctive feature of the Canadian approach, however, is that it emphasizes the disadvantaged position rather than specific protected categories.

The underlying principle of equal protection or equal benefit should also guide politicians, planners, and citizens as they think about the debate on transit. If public investment in different parts of the city is uneven, or if it produces differential impacts on a disadvantaged part of the city, then the reasons and the supporting evidence must be exceptionally strong. For example, if a certain type of transit infrastructure would damage the environment or endanger health or pedestrian safety, then it might be legitimate to use another form, even if this failed to provide comparable service to a disadvantaged area. The upshot is not that everyone must be treated the same, or have identical access to public goods, but that differential treatment must meet a higher standard of justification.

The debate over the expansion of public transit in Toronto—and indeed in most places—is contentious because of the costs involved. Transit is publicly financed, so everyone has to contribute even though not everyone directly benefits. Advocates of public transit rightly point out that there are huge indirect benefits for drivers or pedestrians, including less congested roadways, cultural/social/economic dynamism, and better circulation of goods, but to many people these benefits seem vague and the costs are substantial.

The solidarist theory of social property provides a new way of thinking about these costs and a better way of justifying promising financing tools. For example, tax increment financing is best understood as an application of the classic theory of rent. Rent here refers to the difference in value commanded by two similar parcels of land. Tax increment financing calculates the additional property tax revenue generated by a public investment and uses this revenue to reimburse the cost of building the infrastructure. The problem with tax increment financing is that it strongly links public spending and commodification. By this I mean that it provides an incentive to invest in areas that are likely to command the highest returns, and this can serve to exacerbate rather than mitigate inequalities.

Another approach would be to implement value capture across a broader geographic area. One source of the common-wealth is the city itself. Through real estate markets, the value that people place on urban amenities, proximity, and economic concentration is transformed into exchange value, and some of this value can be captured by the state and used to fund public goods across a city or metropolitan area. In urban planning and policy this is called "value capture." Activists in San Francisco employed this principle to justify two novel mechanisms for funding public transit.[38] First, they proposed the creation of a Transit Assessment District to administer a property tax on downtown commercial businesses that would provide a dedicated revenue stream for the entire Muni system (San Francisco's public transit agency). Second, they called for a transit impact development fee on new downtown office buildings to pay for expanding the fleet of buses and trains. The business community mobilized against these proposals, and advocates failed to convince the board of supervisors to adopt them, but the proposals are interesting because of the way that they draw on the idea of the common-wealth. The proponents argued that the high value of downtown land depended on Muni. Given the extreme concentration of high-density office buildings and lack of parking, the success and prosperity of the downtown business community depended on the way that Muni connected different parts of the city. Transit activists argued that the value of downtown high-rises and the commercial rents they command is sustained by a nexus of public-private inputs, but the profit is appropriated entirely by the private sector. The proposed transit tax is a way to recapture this value for the public.

The transit activists were unsuccessful in San Francisco, but in France, the birthplace of solidarism, the right to mobility has gained more traction. Free public transit is part of an "alternatives to austerity" campaign, and its supporters include both environmentalists and populists.[39] In 2008, the midsized town of Aubagne decided to make the public transit system free. A report commissioned by the city found, unsurprisingly, that use of the bus system increased by 173 percent. The majority of trips are to work or school, so the program helps the local economy. It also facilitates the social and cultural integration of youth, the poor, and elderly people who cannot drive. Since the city abolished transit fares, there has been less vandalism and less tension between fare collectors and poor youth who tried to evade paying bus fare. Twenty-three towns in France also have free public transit.[40]

CONCLUSION

This chapter has presented two arguments in favor of a right to mobility.[41] The Kantian one provides a justification that is consistent with the liberal approach to politics. It identifies the limited circumstances under which state intervention is necessary to secure individual freedom. The ability to move in physical space and interact with other people is among the most basic freedoms; therefore, this approach requires that mobility should not be subject to the arbitrary control of another. This is why roads and transit should be public. The examples presented in this chapter, however, remind us how difficult it is to know what this means in practice. When we move from a negative right not to be prevented from leaving home to a positive obligation to facilitate the circulation of people, then the scope of this obligation becomes a subject of political debate rather than moral necessity. This is why we need a concept like the right to the city or the urban commonwealth. Instead of imagining people isolated on their private properties, potentially deprived of the good of sociability and the freedom to pursue their purposes, we could imagine moving around to discover the world that we have created together, by improving and expanding what we have inherited from the past. Some places would be suited for individual activities or intimate groups and reflect the resources and vision of their inhabitants, and others would require greater collaboration and be open to all. This second version of the right to mobility is no better able to provide a perfect formula for siting or financing transit infrastructure, but it does help us see transit in a new way, as a mechanism for sharing what belongs to all.

[7]

OCCUPYING THE COMMONS
The Populist and the
Sovereigntist Public

The normative arguments described in the previous chapters—in favor of the expansion of public transit and against displacement through slum clearance, gentrification, and demolition of public housing—have had mixed success at convincing citizens, judges, and policymakers. There have been some victories for people who see the city as something other than a luxury good. By using the courts, mobilized public housing tenants in Chicago received help finding subsidized accommodation, and families with children in South Africa have gained a justiciable right to shelter. In India, the courts have been ambivalent about the right to housing, but local politicians have exerted influence to prevent some informal settlements from being destroyed. These wars of position are not unimportant and can make a positive difference in the everyday lives of people whose lives are already very difficult. At the same time, however, structural forces unleashed by neo-liberal political strategies have continued to transform cities.[1] For example, in the past 40 years, Toronto has undergone a profound socio-spatial transformation. In 1970, 66 percent of neighborhoods were middle class and 19 percent were poor.[2] In 2005, after a long period of economic growth, only 29 percent were middle class and 53 percent poor. Professionals live in the historic, transit-oriented center city and immigrants and service workers are concentrated in the periphery. This sorting process, or what more critical scholars have called economic apartheid, is occurring to varying degrees in most prosperous world cities.[3] There is a glaring disconnect between the ideal of equality endorsed in normative theory and the reality of growing inequality.

In "Justice or Legitimacy, Barricades or Public Reason?" Simone Chambers points to this tension between ideal theory and politics in the work of John Rawls. Rawls famously argued that in a just society, the only acceptable inequalities are ones that benefit the least well-off.[4] He advocated a constitutional right to a minimum income and called for the democratization of ownership and control of property. At the same time, however, Rawls rejected the kind of contentious politics that would be necessary to bring about his just society. He advocated institutional arrangements that reproduce existing distributions of power. What do we do when the politics necessary to bring about a more just world seem to violate principles of justice? The broader relationship between ideal theory, applied normative theory, and political practice is too big an issue to address systematically in this book, but it is also too important to simply ignore. In this chapter and the next one I try to address it indirectly by looking at struggles over the right to the city that are staged in public space rather than negotiated through political institutions. This chapter focuses on Occupy Toronto and Occupy Wall Street. This movement, while short-lived, drew attention to the rapid rise of economic inequality and the effects of the great recession: the foreclosure of four million homes in the United States alone, the loss of housing wealth, decreased funding of public goods, and high unemployment.

In this chapter, I consider the tactic of occupation rather than the ideology of the movement or the outcomes it achieved. As Gregory Smithsimon and Sharon Zukin put it, "public space is the city's commons, where dissident views find a voice."[5] In *Notes Toward a Performative Theory of Assembly*, Judith Butler emphasizes the performative dimension of assembly, a practice through which a political demand is both "enacted and made, exemplified and communicated."[6] The occupation of public space is a form of political communication and political action with a long history that runs from republican Rome through the Paris Commune to Gezi Park. In ancient Rome, farmers, veterans, freed slaves, and artisans used the politics of the street to compensate for their exclusion from the Senate. Through demonstrations, they pressured the government to reform the food supply, restore the power of the tribunes of the people, obtain debt relief, and redistribute land.[7] The right to public space is a claim to a share of recreational and cultural amenities provided by the state, such as parks and libraries, but it is more than that. Public space is also an essential site of the popular public sphere, a forum that is not fully controlled by government, corporate, media, or academic elites, where people congregate, communicate through both actions and words, and engage in extra-parliamentary politics. The occupation of public *space* is the part which stands for the more inchoate whole: popular control of the common-wealth. According to Judith Butler, "the very platform for politics becomes the object around which political mobilization rallies."[8]

In this chapter, I challenge the view that occupying parks and plazas was an illegitimate privatization of public space, a view endorsed by US and Canadian courts.[9] As we saw in chapter 3, the Indian Supreme Court described pavement dwellers in similar terms, as privatizers and pickpockets who were illegally appropriating public space. While my focus is public *space*, I suggest that appropriating space was the most visible aspect of collectives asserting control of the common-wealth of society. In other words, we should understand the occupations synecdochally as struggles over the meaning and power of public and private. The first section of the chapter introduces the case of Occupy Toronto—one especially interesting site of the broader "Occupy" movement sparked by Occupy Wall Street—and explains why critics of the occupation described it as a privatization of public space. The next section of the chapter introduces two different theories of the public, which I call the sovereigntist and populist models. This distinction helps explain the polarized reaction to OWS, and provides an alternative way of theorizing the public. In the final section, I identify some problems with the populist theory and consider how they illuminate the challenges faced by the post-eviction OWS movement.

The terms "public" and "private" are difficult to define not only because they are contested but also because they are used to describe a series of related but inconsistent distinctions.[10] The contrast between public and private helps distinguish between the state and the economy or the state and the family.[11] Private can mean the intimate and corporeal as opposed to the visible and accessible. More generally, the public encompasses things that are relevant to everyone and excludes private issues which are relevant only to the individual or a limited group.[12] Yet the tension is obvious when we consider that the economy ("private") is public in the sense that it affects the entire society. The deeply contested character of the terms public and private is apparent in the debates about whether to remove the Occupy encampments. In cities across North America, occupiers and their supporters challenged evictions in court, and the resulting legal decisions rely on theories of public and private that require more thorough examination. This chapter focuses on a Canadian court case, *Batty v. Toronto*, because the case provides a particularly detailed defense of the view that the tactic of occupation should be treated as a privatization of public space. By focusing on this case, I hope to uncover and critique some of the tacit assumptions about control of the common-wealth in a liberal democracy such as the United States or Canada. Drawing on public discourse, legal theory, and social movement theories, my argument is best viewed as a contribution to "the political theory of occupation."

OCCUPY TORONTO

On October 15, 2011, about 2,000 participants responded to calls to march in solidarity with OWS and to occupy Bay Street, the financial center of Toronto. That night about 100 people camped out in St. James Park, a small park jointly owned by the city of Toronto and the neighboring Anglican Cathedral. Similar occupations were taking place around the world. Local labor unions supported the initiative by donating 19 portable toilets and three yurts to provide sheltered communal space. Following the model set up a month earlier in Zuccotti Park, there was an elaborate outdoor kitchen, a General Assembly, an active media tent, drumming circles, teach-ins, an extensive library, and a "free store." The site became a nodal point for marches and demonstrations against economic injustice and, at the height, there were up to 300 campers, including an estimated 100 homeless people.

The occupation was met with immediate opposition from local business owners. On the first day of the occupation, a member of the Business Improvement District told reporters that reservations at his restaurant were down. Two weeks after the start of the occupation, Toronto mayor

Rob Ford stated that he had received many calls from concerned taxpayers and business owners and was trying to find a way to remove the encampments. On November 14, Toronto police officers accompanied bylaw officers as they posted eviction notices on tents in the park. The eviction was temporarily stayed in order to wait for the outcome of the court hearing on the constitutionality of the issue. The Superior Court of Ontario rejected the claim that the right to free speech and protest entailed a right to camp in public space. After 39 days in the park, most of the occupiers left voluntarily rather than face arrest.

"How do we live together in a community? How do we share public space?"[13] In his decision to evict Occupy Toronto, Justice Brown of the Superior Court of Ontario posed these questions. He agreed that the protesters had a right to express their political ideas in public, but not to occupy public space. The rationale for evicting the protesters in Toronto was similar to the rationale used in cities across the United States.[14] The core claim was that the occupation of public or quasi-public spaces amounted to a privatization of public space. According to Justice Brown, the protesters "did not practice what they were preaching when they decided to occupy the park."[15] Although the protesters proclaimed a message of participatory democracy, "they did not ask those who live and work around the Park or those who use the Park—or their civic representatives—what they would think if the Park was turned into a tent city."[16] Justice Brown concluded that the occupation was anti-democratic at its very core because it denied the city government's authority to regulate the use of public space.

This court decision forces us to ask a series of related questions. One set of questions has to do with public space: what is public space and how should it be regulated? Underlying these queries, however, lurks one of the perennial questions of political theory: how can democracy be both a way of legitimizing the state and a practice of dissent and critique? The traditional response is that the constitutional state and the principles of liberal democracy enable both dimensions of democracy to flourish simultaneously. The decisions of the majority are legitimate because the liberal principles of free speech, petition, association, and individual rights ensure that the minority is neither oppressed nor prevented from becoming the majority. The Occupy movement was a response to the perceived shortcomings of this model. It was neither democratic nor liberal in the conventional sense of these terms.[17] It was not democratic in so far as it used tactics that used to be called "extra-parliamentary." It questioned whether existing democratic institutions enable citizens to exert equal influence over politics. It worked from outside the political system rather than within. The occupation was a form of political speech addressed to decisionmakers and citizens, but it was more than that. It was also a practice that tried to challenge the values of individualism, self-interest, and autonomy that underpin liberal theory and practice.

This chapter examines the legal and normative debates about Occupy Toronto and treats these debates as emblematic of issues raised by the international Occupy movement.[18] I use the term "Occupy Wall Street" (OWS) not only to refer to the Zuccotti Park encampment but also to refer to the movement in general. In other words, I am not interested in whether the decision to evict the protesters in *Batty v. the City of Toronto* was a plausible application of legal precedent.[19] Instead, I read the carefully constructed arguments as an expression of the dominant view that treats public space as space owned by the state. By making the dominant assumptions explicit, it is possible to analyze and challenge them. The public/private framework is so hegemonic that it is hard to even imagine an alternative; one possibility is that we see public space as a commons and the state as a trustee that manages this common-wealth on behalf of the people. One advantage of this approach is that the concept of trusteeship makes it possible to distinguish the government and the people and this distinction is a necessary precondition of the principle that the government is accountable to the people.

In *Batty v. the City of Toronto*, the Superior Court of Ontario decided that the Canadian Charter did not prevent the city administration from evicting the protesters who were occupying St. James Park. According to Justice Brown, the rights to free speech, assembly, and association do not entail a right to appropriate public land. It is interesting that the decision does not depend on the principle of "law and order." The occupiers were depicted initially as "privatizers" rather than subversives. The court decision endorsed an argument that had become increasingly prominent in media accounts in the weeks prior to the eviction. Drawing on interviews with neighboring business owners, these articles concluded that the protesters were anti-democratic because they were not deferring to the will of the majority, which is expressed through the city ordinances that ban tent camping without a permit. According to Justice Brown, "The Charter does not permit the Protesters to take over public space without asking, [and] exclude the rest of the public from enjoying the traditional use of that space."[20]

This is an interesting reversal of the "traditional public forum doctrine," which is a staple of American free speech jurisprudence.[21] The traditional public forum doctrine comes from a landmark US Supreme Court case, *Hague v. CIO*.[22] In the opinion for the majority, Justice Owen Roberts wrote, "Wherever the title of streets and parks may rest, they have immemorially been held in trust for the use of the public and, time out of mind, have been for the purposes of assembly, communicating thoughts between citizens, and discussing public questions. Such use of the streets and public places has, from ancient times, been part of the privileges, immunities, rights and liberties of citizens." In *Batty v. the City of Toronto*, Justice Brown relies on a shorter history and identifies the traditional use of public space as recreation. He criticizes the occupation as a form of privatization that prevents local residents from accessing public space. The court decision relies on depositions from dozens of local residents living in the neighborhood surrounding St. James Park. Some neighbors complained of noise and odors, and others insisted that their ability to play Frisbee or stroll was curtailed. Much of the outrage came from dog walkers. Opponents of the occupation came to interpret it as a struggle between traditional, legitimate uses of public space (dog walking, strolling, and enjoyment of nature) and illegitimate, private uses such as camping, preparing food, protesting, and subcultural community building. Francis Dupuis-Déri has described this fear of the political use of public space as agoraphobia.[23]

TWO APPROACHES TO THE PUBLIC

The parties in the court case advanced two different views of the concept "public." These are not primarily legal conceptions; they circulate in scholarly, popular, and political discourses as well. I will call one approach the sovereigntist and the other the populist. The sovereigntist understanding of the public is based on the Hobbesian theory of sovereignty. Something is public if it is authorized by legitimate state institutions. This variation of the public/private distinction draws on Hobbes's use of the terms "political" and "private."[24] According to Hobbes, "private are those [systems] which are constituted by subjects amongst themselves, or by authority from a stranger."[25] He defines a system as "any numbers of men joined in one interest or business." Hobbes contrasts private systems with political systems, which are authorized by the sovereign power. These include municipal or provincial governments as well as other corporate bodies (universities, churches, trade associations) that are legally instituted under state authority. Hobbes is very clear that these subordinate political systems do not have any independent authority.[26] They may legitimately govern the conduct of their members, but the sovereign retains the right to judge disputes and revoke their authority.

This understanding of the public is similar to the one that Habermas labeled "German Hobbesianism."[27] Habermas introduced the concept in his analysis of another occupation of contested space. In the 1980s, German peace activists tried to prevent the deployment of nuclear weapons by blocking the entrance to American and German military bases.[28] The protest shared some features with OWS; 700 protesters lived for a week in nearby communal "tent villages" that served as a base for people manning the blockades. Habermas used the term "German Hobbesianism" to describe the theoretical grounds for conservative opposition to the blockades, which was based on the assumption that legitimacy stems from sovereignty. Habermas challenged this view and argued that legitimacy is not guaranteed by legality, but rather through right itself. He concluded that even in a democracy there are times when law and right diverge, and in these situations the citizens may have to disobey the law in order to draw attention to their cause.[29]

Habermas interprets Hobbesianism as a distinctively German trauma produced by the misinterpretation of history, notably the view that extra-parliamentary protests in the Weimar period created the preconditions for Nazism. Just as Hobbes worried about the anarchy of the English Civil War, postwar German conservatives worried about the anarchy of Weimar. In fact, the sovereigntist model of the political is also hegemonic in Canada and the United States today. According to this approach, the public is synonymous with sovereignty, and refers to a centralized, unified state apparatus that governs society by enacting and administering laws.[30] This model has two key features. First, it takes for granted the separation between the rulers and the ruled. Even when sovereignty is vested in a representative assembly rather than a monarch, there is still a sense that public power is something distinct from the aggregate of citizen-subjects. The second feature is a consequence of the first. The state has a monopoly over legislating and enforcing the law, and citizens have a responsibility to comply.

The democratic variant emphasizes dissent as a crucial component of this model. By dissent I mean nonviolent expressions of political disagreement such as political speech, petition, and assembly. Although dissent was not a prominent feature of Hobbes's original formulation, it plays a decisive role in legitimizing the state today. Dissent is what makes sovereignty legitimate. The protection of nonviolent dissent within the bounds of the law is supposed to guarantee that the law reflects the will of the people, which is the source of legitimacy. As Habermas points out, however, this rests on an unrealistic view of democratic procedures. In practice, a range of factors, including the impact of money on politics and the structure of the mass media, distort the process of political representation. Nevertheless, the right to dissent is consistent with key sovereigntist assumptions. First, dissent is justified in terms of the need to prevent internal violence, which is the primary goal of the state. Second, dissent is acceptable only in so far as it functions "within the bounds of the law"; this caveat reinforces sovereignty in so far as government officials decide what constitutes legitimate dissent and what constitutes disobedience.

The populist model of the public is different. I choose the term "populist" because it signals the political mobilization of the people outside the institutional structures of the state. One vivid expression of this idea is found in Machiavelli's *Discourses*, where he describes the perennial conflict between the *grandi* and the people.[31] Based on his reading of the history of ancient Rome and Renaissance Italy, Machiavelli concludes that elites seek power and domination, which make them a threat to a republic. The common people, on the other hand, only want to avoid being dominated; therefore, their interests naturally promote a free way of life (*vivero libero*). Thus, Machiavelli's analysis rests on a deep appreciation of class conflict as something endemic to political life. Instead of describing sovereignty as coherent and unified, Machiavelli enables us to see the state as something produced and reconstructed through the struggle between conflicting groups.

This populist reading of Machiavelli differs from the influential republican reading of Machiavelli, which emphasizes three features of his analysis in the *Discourses*: the importance of balancing the interests of the people and the elite; the rule of law; and the prudential benefits of promoting the common good.[32] I want to draw attention to a different feature: the extralegal expression of popular dissent.[33] It is worth quoting the key passage at length because it so fully captures the populist approach to the public. In the passage, Machiavelli defends his controversial claim that the clashes between the nobility and the elite helped preserve Rome's freedom. He writes:

> And if someone were to argue the methods employed were extralegal and almost bestial—the people in a mob shouting abuse at the senate, the senate replying in kind, mobs running through the streets, shops boarded up, the entire populace of Rome leaving the city—I would reply such things only frighten those who read about them. Every city ought to have practices that enable the populace to give expressions to its aspirations. . . . The city of Rome had a number of practices of this kind. For example, when the populace wanted a law passed, either they demonstrated, as I have described, or they refused to enroll for military service, so that in order to pacify them it was necessary to give them at least part of what they wanted. The demands of a free people are rarely harmful to the cause of liberty, for they are a response either to oppression or to the prospect of oppression.[34]

The scene described by Machiavelli does not involve the exchange of public reasons that is envisioned in theories of deliberative democracy. Nor does he seem particularly concerned with harmony and the rule of law. It is interesting that Machiavelli describes the people as "almost bestial." Just as Machiavelli urged the prince to be both a fox and lion, he implies that the people are not doing anything wrong when they stampede like a herd of wild animals. It is precisely this bestial quality that is the source of their strength. It is the expression of power, unity, and resolution that wins concessions from the government.

Although Machiavelli does not use the term "public," this passage describes the key features of the populist theory of the public. First, Machiavelli notes that the rule of law itself requires the extralegal as a kind of supplement. A supplement works in paradoxical ways, because it is both an addition and a substitution. The extralegal is a substitute for the legal in the sense that it asserts the legitimacy of collective power outside the state. It involves the claim that the people assembled on the plaza or marching down the street are a more legitimate expression of the *demos* than the government enacting laws in the Senate. At the same time, however, it is an addition that supports and facilitates the operation of the law. Because aggrieved citizens can express the intensity of their discontent through protest and non-compliance, the government is forced to negotiate and compromise, thereby incorporating the people's desires into the law. In stark contrast to the sovereigntist approach, the extralegal is not defined as private or unjust. From the populist perspective, this public sphere of contentious politics is an important way of ensuring a free way of life.

Machiavelli's account justifies dissent as a matter of power and interest rather than individual rights. Machiavelli does not argue that the plebeians of Rome have a right to run through the streets. Instead, he suggests that the elites should recognize "the good effects that derive from them."[35] This is a prudential argument, one that is based on a certain conception of self-interest. According to Machiavelli, a republican government unleashes the productive and martial energies of the population because the people feel that they will benefit from their efforts.[36] This in turn provides a compelling reason for the elite to support a republic: this vitality makes it more likely that society as a whole will prosper. The danger is that the personal ambition and greed of elites may sometimes jeopardize this greater good. The way to prevent this from happening is to promote institutional mechanisms and norms that ensure that the people, the natural custodians of liberty, can limit the corruption of the elites.[37] Machiavelli's analysis points to two additional features of the populist approach to the public. It is collective rather than individualistic, and it makes claims based on power and interest rather than petitioning for the recognition of rights.

What does this mean for OWS? I think that the polarized response to the OWS movement reflects these two very different understandings of the term "public." The first is the sovereigntist model, which identifies the public with the state. A public space is one that is owned, authorized, or regulated by the state. From this perspective, erecting a tent in a park is a form of privatization because it violates ordinances that prohibit camping. This is true even if the tent is a large yurt that houses a library and has a sign inviting anyone to come in, read a book, and talk about political issues. The second approach to the concept "public" is the populist model, which sees the public as a force that emerges outside of state institutions in order to challenge policies and publicize issues that do not make it onto the government's agenda. The populist model defends contentious politics as a necessary means of persuasion;[38] it justifies the extralegal as a way of ensuring that the law does not protect the interests of the elite at the expense of the common people.

OWS tried to create a space for discussion about questions of freedom and justice, instead of simply petitioning government for specific reforms, and it was this aspect of OWS that many commentators found so perplexing and irritating. The first newspaper articles on Occupy Toronto already posed the questions "What do they want? What can they accomplish if they ask for nothing?" These commentators were dismissive of the movement because it issued no demands and thus departed from the familiar script of contentious politics. Groups are supposed to demonstrate in order to pressure leaders to take specific steps, such as removing Pershing missiles, divesting from South Africa, or ending the war in Iraq. According to Machiavelli, this script actually dates back to Roman times when the plebes would demonstrate in order to force the *grandi* to pass a law. Machiavelli also noted that the people tend to promote a free way of life because the people, unlike the *grandi*, do not wish to rule others but simply desire not to be ruled. OWS took seriously this ideal of "no-rule."[39] This strand of the populist theory of the public inspired many of the features of the encampments: the free stores, general assemblies, communal kitchens, and decentralized decisionmaking. This idea of "no-rule" also informed the assumption that the state should not have the authority to prohibit people from engaging in peaceful activities like camping or distributing food in public space. Of course some uses are incompatible with others, but this means that the different users should work together directly to decide on the terms of their shared coexistence.

THE DEATH AND LIFE OF THE URBAN COMMONWEALTH

For example, Occupy Toronto made sure to respond to the needs of other users by not erecting tents on the ornamental gardens and the pathways through the park.

PRIVATIZATION AND PROTEST

The sovereigntist definition of the "public" grounds the decision of the court in *Batty v. the City of Toronto*, which evicted occupiers from St. James Park. Similarly, in *Waller v. New York*, Justice Michael Stallman agreed that evicting the protesters from Zuccotti Park constituted a reasonable time, place, and manner restriction that did not place an excessive burden on free speech.[40] Justice Stallman acknowledged that the rules prohibiting camping in Zuccotti Park were adopted after the start of the protest with the express purpose of removing the protesters, but he endorsed the New York Police Department's view that the encampment posed a general threat to hygiene and fire safety. In other words, the NYPD is authorized to draw the line between peaceful protest and unlawful disruption. Justice Stallman also emphasized that the protesters' right to free speech should not trump "public access by those who live and work in the area . . . the intended beneficiaries of this zoning bonus."[41] The "zoning bonus" refers to the statute that allowed real estate developers to build taller buildings in New York City in exchange for the creation and maintenance of privately owned public spaces.[42] Stallman's statement hints that public space is not really intended to be used by all of the people. It is there for people who "live and work in the area." It is a place for office workers to eat their lunches. Similarly, the Ontario court made it clear that St. James Park in Toronto was intended to be a place where condo dwellers could stroll with their children or walk their dogs, rather than a place for homeless people to sleep or political activists to organize. This reminds us that the legal discourse about public space also draws on an underlying set of cultural assumptions about what the public should look like. The term "public" refers both to places that are legitimately regulated by the government and to people who use this space in legitimate ways, "the people who live and work in the area." Interestingly, this phrase describes the public in terms of their private identities as workers and the occupants of private dwellings.

The public are private individuals who use public space for recreation and leisure rather than disruptive political activity.

The *Waller v. New York* decision was not surprising, given the legal precedents. The most important precedent is a US Supreme Court case, *Clark v. Community for Creative Non-violence*.[43] Activists wanted to publicize the plight of the homeless by camping on the grounds of the Mall and Lafayette Park, two prominent public spaces in Washington, DC. The Supreme Court upheld the National Park Service's decision to deny a permit on the grounds that such a demonstration would damage the lawns.[44]

Batty v. the City of Toronto draws an even starker opposition between the public (the government and the community of law-abiding citizens) and the occupiers who "exclude the rest of the public" through "unilateral occupation" that appropriates the common public space for their own use. Participants in the Occupy Toronto movement objected to this way of thinking about public and private. The disagreement extends to both the accuracy of the description of their tactics and the values that underpin them. They did not concede that the occupation excluded other people and other uses of the park. Although tents did cover about half of the small park, the pathways through the park and a large ornamental garden were free of any kind of obstruction. This enabled people to stroll through the park and to sit on benches in the garden. Furthermore, some of the structures were explicitly designed to be welcoming to people who did not reside at the camp. These included the library yurt, a free university tent, a free "store," and the gazebo where the assemblies took place. The occupied park was not exclusive like a country club or a high-priced amusement park; it was an open, evolving assemblage of different initiatives. There was also a large area with paints, markers, cardboard, and paper where people could make their own signs and display them alongside hundreds of others. This area was a mix between public art and the Hyde Park Speakers' Corner. The signs became a kind of mosaic of political expression. The encampment "disrupted the familiar phenomenology of the street."[45]

In their affidavits to the court, the Occupy protesters also described a distinctive understanding of the public, one that flourished outside of the state and therefore could serve as a site of critique. According to Lana Goldberg and Bryan Batty, the encampment had a threefold purpose. It served as real shelter for homeless people in the community; it was a symbolic expression of the dispossession caused by the financial crisis; it was also a place to enact new forms of community and practice the values that inspired the protest. One of the prominent signs at the camp featured a quote from Gandhi: "Be the change that you want to see in the world." They tried to do this by including the local homeless population and meeting participants' basic needs without the mediation of state or market. Another key idea was that values must be lived before they could be espoused. This is a particularly striking departure from academic ethics and political theory. Theories of deliberative democracy and discourse ethics identify truth and sincerity as underlying preconditions of successful communicative action.[46] Many of the occupiers, however, took the idea of sincerity and placed it at the core of their approach. They insisted that before you preach against inequality and injustice you must practice non-domination in your relationships with others. This practice not only deepens your understanding of your values, but it also transforms the relationship between the citizen and the state. It positions the citizen as an agent rather than a supplicant who is asking the state to provide some good or service.

The city of Toronto's authority to evict the protesters from the park was based on the Trespass to Property Act, an act designed to protect the rights of private property owners. In invoking this act, the city of Toronto asserted a private property right over public space. The court had to decide whether this property right should have priority over the rights to free speech and assembly. The court recognized that the occupation was clearly a form of political expression and therefore the eviction required judicial review.[47] The legal issue that the courts had to settle was whether the erection of tents and the occupation itself could be construed as a kind of symbolic expression that should be protected as a form of free speech. Other Canadian courts had already decided that the creation of structures was a form of protected speech. These included a tent on Parliament Hill and a hut used for a peace vigil. Given these legal precedents, Justice Brown accepted the claim that the encampment itself was a legitimate "part of the manner of expressing the political message."[48] The central question was whether the government's right to regulate the park like private property could be construed as a reasonable limit "prescribed by law" that "could be demonstrably justified in a free and democratic society."[49] The court affirmed that the ban on camping was a reasonable restriction.

Given the legal framework of liberal constitutionalism, it was almost impossible for the courts to recognize the claims made by the protesters. The key terms that the court used to adjudicate the dispute between the government and the protesters were "law," "democracy," and "reasonable." Yet these words turned out to be almost synonymous. The law is democratic because it is enacted under the oversight of representatives who are selected by the citizens through near-universal suffrage. The term "reasonable" seems to function as the glue that holds the law and the *demos* together. In his analysis, Justice Brown asks whether a rational citizen would choose to have parks where anarchy reigns. His description of such a place recalls Hobbes's famous depiction of the state of nature. According to Brown,

> without some balancing of what people can and cannot do in parks chaos would reign; parks would be battlegrounds of competing uses, rather than oases of tranquility in the concrete jungle. Our parks would become places where the stronger, by use of occupation and intimidation, could exclude the weaker or those who are not prepared to resort to confrontation to carve out a piece of the park for their own use.[50]

Despite the testimony of city officials that the occupation was peaceful, Justice Brown paints a picture of St. James Park that resembles the war of all against all.[51] The rational citizen must choose the Leviathan. Law, democracy, and reason are all linked together. While this constellation is explicit in the language of the Canadian Charter, it is implicit in the decisions of the courts in the United States as well.

THE POPULIST CONCEPTION RECONSIDERED

Studying OWS and the evictions enables us to see the powerful legitimation that comes from this confluence of law, democracy, and reason. OWS challenged this account of democracy in the name of a public outside of the state. The effective use of the phrase "We are the 99 percent" was an artful populist move; it both signaled a fundamental antagonism and tried to constitute a new universal.[52] Of course, the occupiers and their supporters realized that they were not embraced by the overwhelming majority of the people, but they were asserting that they should be. As Jason Frank put it in his study of post-revolutionary America, "the people are a political claim . . . not a pre-given, unified, or naturally bounded empirical entity."[53] In a similar vein, Judith Butler argued that we should view popular sovereignty as a performative practice of self-constitution, a perpetual act of separating from state sovereignty.[54] The people is not meant to be an empirical description synonymous with *demos*, but rather a claim to be the force advancing the public good of non-domination.

Nevertheless, this gap between the constitutive and the descriptive public is important, and Machiavelli's theory is not too much help here. In the *Discourses*, Machiavelli was writing about ancient Rome, a society divided into slaves, plebeians, and patricians; here, it is easy to see that the people and the plebeians are one and the same. In both ancient Rome and Renaissance city-states such as Florence and Venice, political institutions were organized to promote the corporate interests of different social classes. Political theorists differed about whether the elites or the people were most likely to advance the public good, but there was an underlying shared assumption that the *demos*, the majority, and the poor were different names for the same group. The same chain of equivalence between these terms does not exist today. The phrase "We are the 99 percent" was an attempt to constitute the people through an act of political identification. One of the initiatives organized by OWS was a blog where people could post pictures of themselves with a cardboard sign recounting their struggles as part of the 99 percent. Featured on the blog were unemployed, indebted college graduates, but also older workers struggling with illness and immigrants supporting families.[55] The signs displayed in the photos evoked the cardboard signs that homeless people often use to solicit donations on the street. Like the tent cities, this served symbolically to link the struggling middle classes to the most dispossessed strata of society.

Representative democracy may be superior to the existing alternatives, but it also functions ideologically to erase the distinction between the people and the state. The existence of groups such as the poor, the people, and elites is obscured by the modern category of the sovereigntist public, which is made up of the majority that chooses the government through legitimate elections. Without a plausible sociopolitical category such as the proletariat or plebes to fall back on, there is no obvious alternative way to imagine the people. OWS was not only an occupation of public space but also an attempt to represent the people. At first this might sound like an odd claim, given the movement's strong emphasis on direct democracy and its critique of representative democracy. The word "representation," however, corresponds to two different German terms: *Vertretung* and *Darstellung*.[56] *Vertretung* signifies the type of political representation that is realized through elections and assemblies.[57] *Darstellung*, on the other hand, is more like an image or a portrait. This was the type of representation performed by the Occupy movement and other anti-statist movements like Taksim Square. It created an image of the public that was different from the famous illustration on the cover of Hobbes's *Leviathan* depicting a sovereign composed of the multitude. The people remained plural and unity was produced through the gathering itself.

The Occupy movement made visible the contradictory character of the term "people," which means both the marginalized (the excluded, the poor, the precariat) and the source of political legitimacy and power.[58] In what sense could a motley assortment of activists, street youth, students, homeless people, aging hippies, and leftist intellectuals claim to represent the public? Jacques Rancière helps answer this question. According to Rancière, the political is produced through "polemical scenes, paradoxical scenes that bring out the contradiction between two logics" or by positing existences that are at the same time nonexistences.[59] Rancière distinguishes between politics and "the police," a broader category which includes aggregating consent, regulating behavior, distributing resources, defining roles, and legitimizing these distributions.[60] He reserves the term "politics" for an activity that is disruptive and antagonistic to policing. Politics is whatever breaks the rules, patterns, assumptions, and habits that fix bodies into their place.[61] For Rancière, the political is the rupture produced when the excluded confront the regulatory order of the police.[62] This confrontation does not provide new answers, but it poses new questions, such as whether labor or maternity are public or private matters.[63]

OWS, perhaps unintentionally, was extremely effective at staging these polemical scenes. Occupiers, many of whom were not experienced political activists, organized alternative institutions to replace ineffective ones that were based on economic power rather than political equality. When citizens occupied public space they were called privatizers and accused of trespassing on public property. In Slovenia, the local Occupy movement tried to stage a teach-in on the property of the national bank. When a security guard said that they could not enter private property, one activist insisted that the bank was public property because it had originally been state property and had been illegitimately appropriated by private interests.[64] As the guard hesitated, the protesters were able to enter the bank. The occupation in London also focused attention on the way that non-democratic institutions and actors control ostensibly public spaces. After receiving an eviction notice, Occupy London challenged the authority of the City of London Corporation, a remnant of feudal autonomy that governs the city center but is exempt from national law.[65]

These incidents illustrate the way that the occupation functioned synecdochally. The occupation of physical space was one part of a broader attempt to reclaim and reconfigure the ideal of the public. By occupying a diverse range of public, quasi-public, and even private spaces and turning them into sites of deliberation, community, and political activity, the activists were trying to make a broader claim about the need to redistribute the common-wealth that has been appropriated or controlled by a narrow stratum of society.

CONCLUSION

After the encampments were dismantled, Occupy groups continued to organize demonstrations and engage in local struggles against foreclosures, privatization, and poverty. On March 18, 2015, 20,000 people took part in an anti-austerity protest in Frankfurt, organized by Blockupy, a German offshoot of Occupy. Yet the question quickly changed from "how did OWS generate such incredible enthusiasm?" to "why did it disappear so quickly?" Although this book does not directly address this question, the discussion of public and private may still provide some insight.

In his influential book *Power in Movement*, Sidney Tarrow argued that collective action is effective when marginalized groups build solidarity and create uncertainty, thereby challenging elites.[66] OWS created solidarity among disparate groups through the experience of sharing physical space and the rituals of living together. It challenged the state by claiming that the state acted to advance the interests of the *grandi* rather than the people. The most critical feature, however, was the ability to create uncertainty. Tarrow used Italo Calvino's story *The Baron in the Trees* in order to illustrate how this works. In the novel, a young nobleman defies his father's authority by going to live in the trees. Not only does he embody his challenge in physical space, but he performs a seemingly excessive and irrational act that creates uncertainty. Like the baron in the trees, the people in the plaza were engaging in what appeared to be an excessive and irrational act. People with homes were living outside among homeless people, and were willing to stay for weeks in spite of inclement weather. They tried to carry out the seemingly impossible task of collective self-rule. The success of OWS was at least partially due to the uncertainty that was created by linking an assertion of sovereignty outside the law with the practice of "no-rule." After the evictions, however, the main source of solidarity—physical co-presence—was gone. Moreover, the uncertainty created by the growth of an alternative in the heart of the city disappeared as well.

One lesson of OWS is the significance of public space. The political work of post-eviction Occupy activists is important and may even be successful at advancing social justice, but it has been much less effective at inspiring hope and stimulating a broader political debate. If this is correct, then it also reveals something very important about public space.[67] We need public space not only for recreation, consumption, and leisure but also for survival, communication, and dissent. But what exactly is public space? Spaces can be public in at least three ways: they are owned by the government; they are inclusive and accessible to everyone; they facilitate sociability among friends and encounters with strangers. This analysis of OWS has suggested a fourth dimension of public space. It is a place for staging polemical scenes, a site where the conflict between opposing interests is made visible and subject to dispute. The publicness of space is something that is claimed and produced through political action. This action, however, takes place against the backdrop of social conditions, norms of policing, and regulations that make certain spaces more or less possible to transform into spaces of appearance.

It may seem ironic that OWS took place in Zuccotti Park, a privately owned public space. Zuccotti Park was created under the "density bonus" provision of the planning code, which allowed real estate developers to build taller buildings if they created and maintained spaces that were accessible to the public. Since Zuccotti Park was not owned by New York City, it was not subject to parks department regulations, which mandated curfews in all city parks. Prior to the demonstration there were signs prohibiting skateboarding and bike riding, but no one had anticipated an extended occupation and so it was not explicitly forbidden. This regulatory uncertainty gave the protesters the opportunity to establish their presence and secure the media attention which made violent eviction more difficult. This element of surprise did not exist a month later when Occupy London protesters were prevented from setting up a satellite camp in Canary Wharf, London's second major financial center.[68] The Canary Wharf Group, the corporate owner of the 97-acre urban renewal project, got an injunction banning protesters from their massive property. In the case of Zuccotti Park, private ownership of the park provided an opportunity, but in many other cases private ownership prevented protesters from using space for political activity and protest. Public-private partnerships such as Canary Wharf have put entire neighborhoods under corporate control, but this control is only visible to those who are excluded.

The state, like the corporate owners of Canary Wharf, can function as a landlord who exercises the right to exclude, but this right is much more constrained. The landlord is also a politician who fears losing power. Furthermore, the state is limited by constitutional provisions requiring that regulations be reasonable and not excessively or arbitrarily burden citizens' right to free speech. These two factors explain why public (state-owned) space is the most likely setting for polemical scenes that start conversations about how to share the common-wealth.

Public space should not be viewed only as a site for leisure or recreation but also as a place where people can come together to meet as citizens rather than as consumers or clients.[69] Public space is a place where individuals can come together and unite in order to overcome the disempowering effect of isolation. Even in the age of social media, embodiment and visibility are still important features of publicity. The protesters camping in parks and plazas across North American made economic inequality visible in a way that it had not been before. This is because the populist public is made up of both spectators and actors.[70] A successful performance requires a stage.[71] Civil disobedience differs from conscientious objection because it is an activity performed by groups and oriented toward an audience of fellow citizens.[72] Words and deeds must be visible to others. These polemical scenes do not have to convince the spectators and elicit sympathy, but the actors must at least be able to confront them.

[8]

PARKS AND REFS
Democracy, Disobedience,
and Public Space

For years, the Mission Playground, located in a predominantly working-class Latino neighborhood in San Francisco, was the site of informal pickup soccer games. Locals knew the rules: seven on seven, first to score, and the winning team got to stay on and play against other rivals. In 2012, the run-down park underwent a $7.5 million renovation and concrete was replaced with artificial turf and new lighting. As part of a citywide initiative to recover costs through new user fees, the Parks Department introduced a reservation system and rented out some prime-time evening slots for $27. By providing a credit card, young urban professionals who had moved to the area to work in the booming tech industry[1] were able to jump the queue.

The stage was set for a showdown, which was captured on a video, and viewed by over 600,000 people. During the summer of 2014, local kids and teens were regularly asked to vacate the field to make way for exclusive games organized by adult permit holders. The kids had nowhere else to play. They decided to disobey the new rules and film the resulting confrontation. Their informal spokesperson was a college student who said his family had been displaced from the neighborhood. He did not think local kids who couldn't afford permits should be excluded from public space.[2]

Some of the permit holders were wearing "Dropbox" T-shirts, which helped turn a quotidian dispute over turf into synecdochal conflict.

A synecdochal conflict is one in which the part stands for the whole. It is both literal and emblematic, because the particular dispute over a soccer field is a dimension of a broader conflict over the right to the urban commonwealth. The temporary privatization of a sought-after piece of public space exposed a number of broader fault lines: gentrification, income inequality, and different views about how to allocate public goods. Edward Soja used the helpful term "zones of contention" to describe these places where the publicness of public space is negotiated.[3] In this chapter, I argue that this struggle cannot be resolved by invoking democracy because it was precisely the meaning of democracy that was contested. Should we privilege the *demos* (the people, "the community") or *kratos* (rule, "the state")? To answer this question, we need a theory of the public good.

It is tempting to read this conflict as a morality play. This reading is plausible because of the tone of some of the comments that were captured on the video. One of the "tech guys" says, "Who gives a shit? Who cares about the neighborhood?"[4] But, taken out of the structural context, the positions taken by each side are reasonable. The permit holders were following the rules. The permit system was adopted after a process of consultation; it provided a way of distributing a scarce good and covered the administrative cost of performing the gatekeeping function. The youths' position was also reasonable. They had developed a system of allocation that facilitated broad access to a public good without generating transaction costs. Not only was their system attractive from the standpoint of fairness, it was also more efficient than the bureaucratic alternative, in so far as it didn't create any administrative costs. Without a formal gatekeeper, there are no transaction costs. The "winner keeps the field system," however, does have some downsides. It makes it difficult for weaker or inexperienced players to participate and doesn't allow drilling or league play.

Comments on the video were divided. Some people described the mostly white tech guys as "douchebags" and others called the neighborhood teens "thugs."[5] The two sides also drew on different principles to explain their positions. One side invoked the sovereigntist conception of public space and the other drew on the populist conception. Defenders of the permit holders emphasized that rules should be followed because they are rules: "Keep it simple, stupid. If there is a rule to book the facility, book it and then play. No exceptions." This comment fails to consider that rules themselves may be unfair, or that certain groups may have greater ability to influence the process of rule-making.

There were two versions of the sovereigntist argument. The democratic-sovereigntist position emphasized that the rules were legitimate because they were the outcome of a democratic process. For example, David Vo wrote, "If you don't like the reservation system, fine, go complain to the Parks and Recs department or city government. Instead, these kids show up night after night (their words) and pick fights with people who follow the correct process and reserve the park to play their league games."[6] The neo-liberal variant of the sovereigntist argument defended the principle of "pay to play" on both procedural and substantive grounds. For example, Henri Cook wrote, "Places can choose not to implement a reservation model. But they do, because it's better business. These places need to be maintained and survive at the end of the day."[7] Here, sovereignty is not imagined as the will of the people expressed through majoritarian institutions, but rather as the rational action of the entrepreneur-state. This was one of a number of comments that treated public space as a commodity that should be sold in order to generate revenue to pay for maintenance and, in fact, several people compared parks to for-profit venues such as movie theaters.

Commentators defended the populist approach in even more forceful terms. What I call the populist view incorporated three main arguments: (1) legality must be distinguished from legitimacy; (2) civil disobedience is necessary because normal political processes are inadequate; (3) the community norm of open access is legitimate, in part because of its status as community norm and in part because it is objectively fairer.

This round of the fight over the public space went to the populists. On the day the video was filmed, the permit holders reluctantly agreed to share the field with the pickup players. A few months later, after the video was widely viewed, political activists organized a protest and the policy was changed. In the evenings, the soccer pitch at Mission Park would be available for pickup games without permits. The conflict provides an opportunity to evaluate the sovereigntist and the populist approaches in more depth and to consider the role of democracy as a way of resolving the conflict between them. Both sides claimed their actions were justified by democracy. The permit holders were following the rules adopted by the government agency responsible for regulating public parks. The pickup players insisted that their actions were justified by a non-statist form of rule that more accurately reflected the will of the people.

This conflict, like many conflicts over public space, reveals the paradoxical character of democracy. Democracy is both a way of legitimizing the state and also a way of challenging it. A conception of democracy that denies this paradox is inadequate,[8] therefore democracy should be understood in the terms Claude Lefort set out in his essay "The Question of Democracy." The key feature of Lefort's approach is that he defines democracy as an "empty place." Democracy does not achieve the impossible; it does not secure the equal distribution of power or rational agreement, but it does prevent the state from closing off contestation. The first half of this chapter introduces the agonistic approach to democracy and explains how it differs from the theories of civil disobedience endorsed by Habermas and Rawls.[9] Contestation, however, involves making arguments about how to structure the terms of living together, who to regulate and coerce, and what forms of freedom to protect.[10] If we reject the view that procedurally fair state policy is synonymous with the public good, then we must ask "what is the public good?" In the second half of the chapter I explore this question by looking at two forms of citizen mobilization about land use: NIMBYism (not-in-my-backyard) and environmental justice. In order to distinguish between them, we need the concept of the common-wealth.

DEMOCRACY AGAINST THE STATE

Claude Lefort's original reflections on democracy played an important role in the genesis of the anti-foundationalist approach to political theory. Lefort was an important figure in the anti-Stalinist left in France, and became well-known for his critique of totalitarianism. He also advanced an original analysis of democracy as a symbolic structure. In "The Question of Democracy," he emphasized the distinction between politics and the political, or what Lefort described as mis-en-scène and mis-en-forme.[11] For Lefort, politics is what most people associate with the term: the type of regime and the distribution of power and things. Drawing on phenomenology, he reworks the political and describes it as society's way of representing its wholeness to itself. Politics is the way that the social order is viewed as an object and the political is the sense people make of it, the meaning it has, and the way it is lived.

In premodern times, the king was the paradigmatic way of representing social unity. This is why kingship had a dual structure that incorporated the material body of the monarch and the symbolic body of society. According to Lefort, the French Revolution destroys this source of unity and unleashes two alternatives: a practice that aims at actual unity (totalitarianism) or one that rests on the impossibility of unity (democracy). In other words, democracy establishes a new, paradoxical symbolic order, one that leaves the source of unity empty.

For Lefort, modernity is characterized by deep pluralism, which includes both class conflict as well as other divisions. There are two ways of responding to deep pluralism. The totalitarian response is to try to transform symbolic unity into real unity by abolishing social divisions. It does this by denying the distinction between the state (or party) and society. Any lingering signs of division, such as bourgeois attitudes or the kulaks, are then pathologized as the products of foreign agents and treated as deviations that must be destroyed.[12] Political power circulates through the bureaucracy and secret police, dissolving preexisting forms of solidarity (family, labor union, religion), and substitutes a relationship between the individual and the leader.

Democracy is exactly the reverse. According to Lefort, "the legitimacy of power is based on the people, but the image of popular sovereignty is linked to the image of an empty place." Because it is impossible to occupy the site of power, political officials can never claim to appropriate it.[13] This is what Lefort means when he describes the heart of democracy as an empty place. Democracy is, in a sense, a contradictory form. On the one hand, it is the power of the people as a whole, but at the same time, it is the power of no-body. The people cannot be fully unified, and therefore they do not possess a body that is equivalent to the king's body, one that can be imagined as whole.

For Lefort, the vitality of democracy stems from this contradiction. The danger is that one of the two poles that sustains the tension will be weakened, leading to collapse. If the "unity of the people" becomes too dominant, then there is a slide toward fascism or totalitarianism. Given the experience of World War II and Stalinism, this was Lefort's primary concern. But he also recognized the possibility that the opposite phenomenon could predominate. There is a danger that the place of power could be treated as empty in a more radical sense. This happens when it becomes impossible to imagine the public good. Government is directed by individuals in service of private interests, and this in turn leads to a collapse of legitimacy. The result is a spiral of privatization, as groups and individuals pursue their corporatist interests and solidarity declines. This seems to describe the current situation in the United States, where trust in government is extremely low and private interest predominates.

Lefort's approach contains two insights for democratic theory. The first and better known insight is the one about the nature of democracy. Describing democracy as an empty place has consequences for the way that we see society, the state, and the relationship between them. Miguel Abensour explains that for Lefort, democracy is a way of coming to terms with the originary division of the social.[14] This implies that division is not something to be controlled or even legitimized; instead it should be treated as a source of liberty. Abensour calls this "savage democracy."

The echoes of Machiavelli are not a coincidence. The subtitle of Abensour's book is "Marx and the Machiavellian Moment."[15] The vision of politics endorsed by Lefort and Abensour is the inverse of Plato's *Republic*. In the *Republic*, Plato celebrates a stratified yet unified political order in which each person and group is fixed in its assigned place, doing one job. The rule of reason ensures that passion and self-interest will not generate conflict and instability. The Machiavellian approach explained in the previous chapter emphasizes that the public good is produced through conflict, which helps secure a balance of forces.

Lefort's own theory resembles Machiavelli's in crucial respects. He thinks that freedom is secured through the struggle between social forces which prevents domination from being consolidated in the state (law/bureaucracy/police). This formulation makes it clear how far Lefort is from the Marxist approach to class struggle. Lefort emphasizes social division and struggle but forcefully rejects communism as a resolution of class struggle. He also dismisses the Marxian utopia of "the withering away of the state" because he thinks this rests on the incorrect view that social antagonism can be definitely resolved. Not only is a withered state implausible in practice, it is also highly problematic as an ideal. For Lefort, critique is formulated from the standpoint of democracy rather than communism.[16]

From this perspective, democracy is not a way to legitimize the sovereignty of the state, as it was for the judges in the Occupy Toronto and Wall Street court cases. Instead, it is a way to unsettle the democracy/state nexus, or, as Miguel Abensour put it, to imagine democracy *against* the state. This perspective does not generate any specific lessons for institutional design, but it does make it possible to imagine the self-rule or self-organization of the people outside of the state. By self-rule, however, I do not mean anarchism or "no-rule."[17] Anarchism is best understood as a symbolic form and an alternative to both democracy and totalitarianism. Even if we reject Lefort's claim that the "withering away of the state" implies a potentially totalitarian erasure of social division, anarchism is quite different from democracy, as Lefort understands it. Most theories of anarchism assume either that non-distorted social relations will be harmonious or that pluralistic affinity communities diffuse conflict through decentralization. Lefort, on the other hand, treats conflict as irresolvable and defines democracy as an exercise of power that is subject to procedures of periodic redistribution.[18]

CIVIL DISOBEDIENCE AND THE PUBLIC SPHERE

How does this approach compare to more conventional theories of democracy such as the communicative theory of Jürgen Habermas? In order to answer this question, we need to provide a fuller account of Habermas's approach to civil disobedience. This chapter focuses on Habermas's later political theory as developed in *Between Facts and Norms*.[19] The problem addressed in the book is the relationship between facticity and validity. This is one of the perennial themes of political theory: how do normative ideals and the realities of power, interest, and desire fit together? Do we draw on universal, abstract truths to design political institutions or do we observe political reality in order to identify imperfectly realized possibilities of collective life? It is beyond the scope of this book to summarize Habermas's answer to these questions. For our purposes, the crucial section of *Between Facts and Norms* is the chapter "Civil Society and the Political Public Sphere." The key idea is that actual political institutions fail to realize the normative principles that serve as the basis for political legitimacy. For Habermas, this is not a reason for rejecting the normative approach, but rather a reason to be concerned with the mechanisms that help bring "facticity" closer to "validity." Social movements have an important role to play. According to Habermas, social problems that primarily affect people at the periphery can be transformed into broader political issues through the mediation of the public sphere.[20] The liberal public sphere has two dimensions. The first dimension is institutional and includes the networks of communication, such as the free press and mass media. The second dimension, which Habermas describes as "latent dependency," refers to the role of the public sphere in linking together civil society and political institutions. It is the normative ideal that is realized when the public sphere works the way it should.

According to Habermas, the liberal public sphere is able to incorporate much more than just rational arguments about the public good. It provides a way for "subinstitutional political movements" and peripheral groups to influence the political agenda through "sensational actions" and "mass protests."[21] Even civil disobedience has a role to play. As we saw in chapter 7, Habermas recognizes that "acts of nonviolent, symbolic rule violation" may be the only viable way for some groups to get decisionmakers to consider their claim that a particular law is illegitimate.[22]

The Mission Park conflict could be viewed in precisely these terms. Latino teens are a classic peripheral group. Too young to vote and usually excluded from informal modes of influence, they were nevertheless disproportionately and negatively impacted by a policy change. The video captured what looked like a spontaneous conflict, but it was actually part of a strategy of civil disobedience. The pickup soccer players engaged in a nonviolent, symbolic violation in order to protest against a rule they thought was illegitimate. Through the media, in this case the rhizomatic circulation of a viral video, they were able to inform and mobilize supporters. This publicity activated this "latent dependency"; government officials changed the policy in response to public opinion, which, in a left-leaning city like San Francisco, favored the pickup soccer players.

At first, this case seems to fit nicely with liberal theories of civil disobedience. Like Habermas, Rawls too agreed that civil disobedience is sometimes necessary as a "final device to maintain the stability of a just constitution."[23] But it is clear from Rawls's discussion that he also wants to limit civil disobedience, since his primary concern is the stability and legitimacy of the law. He insists that for civil disobedience to be justified, the injustice must be substantial and it should also be an injustice that makes it considerably more difficult to resolve other injustices fairly.[24] Political participation, access to education, and collective bargaining would meet these criteria. Rawls also insists that legal means of redress have been tried and failed and legal protests have had no success. The actions taken by the youth in Mission Park do not meet any of these criteria. Limited access to the soccer pitch during prime evening hours isn't a "substantial injustice"; access to a soccer field is not a precondition of other democratic rights; and there is no evidence that all legal channels had been tried without success.

The concept of a "synedochal conflict" is important to assess the legitimacy of the tactic of civil disobedience and to understand its effectiveness. Many people in the San Francisco Bay Area are concerned about income inequality, its impact on local real estate prices, and the resulting displacement or exclusion of poor and middle-income people.[25] Yet the process of gentrification, like structural injustice in general, is complex and difficult to solve, particularly at the local level. Rising real estate prices benefit some long-term residents and harm others, and neighborhood change is the outcome of thousands of individual decisions that are made against the backdrop of a range of structural constraints (availability of jobs, transportation, housing costs, access to public and community institutions, etc.) This means that civil disobedience may be effective *not* when the injustice is most substantial but when it is the most legible. This happens when the conflict simplifies important issues, makes them vivid, and fosters sympathy that breaks the habitual indifference to the fate of others. Does effectiveness also imply legitimacy? I want to argue that up to a certain point it does, and this is why it is important to evaluate civil disobedience in terms of the broader political context instead of just assessing the individual action from an abstract perspective. Confronting a little nugget of unfairness can be an occasion for stimulating a broader discussion about injustice.

Rawls's legitimacy-based approach does recognize a role for civil disobedience, but his account is still too abstract. His discussion of civil disobedience is unsatisfying because it treats legitimacy as a feature of the act itself rather than treating it as a tactic that must be assessed in light of the legitimacy of the broader political goals. Rawls also treats civil disobedience as a necessary evil, an extreme measure that is appropriate in the direst circumstances. It is akin to amputating a leg to make sure that gangrene doesn't spread to the rest of the body. For Rawls, civil disobedience entails considerable danger, since it can undermine the legitimacy of law itself.

In *Property Outlaws*, Sonia Katyal and Eduardo Peñalver propose a very different account of the relationship between law and disobedience.[26] They argue that lawbreaking is an important source of information that drives legal change.[27] Sometimes this takes the form of classic civil disobedience. Civil disobedience involves violation of the law that is open, loving, and aimed at persuading an audience of fellow citizens of the injustice of a law or a practice that disproportionately affects a minority. These are what they call "expressive outlaws." As we saw in chapter 3, they also recognize the role of "acquisitive outlaws."[28] These are lawbreakers who are primarily motivated by personal benefit. Unlike classic practitioners of civil disobedience, their conduct may not be open, and acquisitive outlaws try to avoid punishment. Nevertheless, these actions may be legitimate, when they are driven by needs that outweigh the harm entailed in violating the property rights of others.[29]

According to Katyal and Peñalver, the actions of acquisitive outlaws are also important sources of information that identify inadequacies or unfairness in the law. The actions of acquisitive outlaws are quite different from the communicative strategies employed by expressive outlaws and even farther from the practices of public reason, yet they still may be justified in terms of a democratic theory that emphasizes the epistemic features of democracy. The epistemic account of democracy holds that democratic institutions generate the best public policies because they are able to gather and process the information necessary for fair decision-making.[30]

Non-compliance is a way of communicating the intensity of a preference to change the rules and to reopen a debate about how to share public space under conditions of economic inequality.[31]

Does this mean that these very different approaches—"civil disobedience" and "savage democracy"—end up in the same place? Ultimately, the answer is no, but there are similarities. There is an element of falliblism in both. Habermas does not call democracy an empty place, but he gets at something similar when he describes the constitution as an "unfinished project."[32] He insists that the constitutional state is not a finished structure but a "fallible and revisable" enterprise.[33] The three theories of civil disobedience (Rawls, Habermas, Katyal/Peñalver) can be placed on a continuum. They all agree that the legitimacy of the law rests on the proper functioning of democratic institutions, and that some form of lawbreaking may be a justified response to democratic deficits. They differ on the relative importance of stability and the range of activities that can be considered communicative. In contrast to Lefort's approach, however they all treat conflicts as potentially resolvable and democratic deficits as exceptions to the rule.

Both "civil disobedience" and "savage democracy" recognize the importance of sustaining and legitimizing the extralegal, but they differ about the importance they assign to this dimension. For Abensour, the ideological function of the state is a primary concern. The main problem is not a lack of legitimacy but an excess of legitimacy. Too often people are satisfied with the following take on the Mission Park conflict: "Keep it simple, stupid. If there is a rule to book the facility, book it and then play. No exceptions." For Habermas, on the other hand, cases of failure are important, but the task of legitimizing the constitutional state is the primary one. This difference is reflected in the terminology that each thinker uses. Habermas describes civil disobedience as a dimension of civil society, and concludes that the law cannot adopt this oppositional perspective as its own.[34] This is mostly correct. The law cannot legitimize the extralegal or it ceases to be law.[35] This is why Lefort insists on the need for two terms: "politics" and "the political." "Politics" describes the world of policy, interest, power, and law. "The political" is a meta-account that can incorporate the stabilizing function of law and the destabilizing effect of "savage democracy"; while recognizing both, it privileges the latter.

In *Between Fact and Norms*, Habermas's modified account of deliberative democracy incorporates non-rationalist modes of persuasion that scholars felt were missing from his earlier account of discourse ethics. He notes that public opinion is a "wild complex"[36] of overlapping networks with different modes of communication. It is only when public opinion is institutionalized in law that "communicative power" must take a distinctive form.[37] In the process of lawmaking, deliberation must be free of coercion and based on the cognitive criteria of "rational acceptability."[38] To a large degree this is correct, both as an ideal and as a description of the type of arguments made in the political public sphere. In a democracy, when people advance their own interests, they have to do so in a language that appeals to the interests of others. When proposing a cut on capital gains taxes, the wealthy beneficiaries don't argue that they want to pay a lower share of the cost of government; they say that such cuts promote productive investment which creates jobs and grows the economy, thereby benefitting everyone. When employers fight minimum wage laws, they don't argue that they want to distribute profits as dividends rather than wages; they claim to worry that such laws increase unemployment, thereby harming their own workers, or that such laws increase prices, harming their customers.

The problem with the deliberative approach to democracy is that even when it narrows the scope of the rationalist-cognitivist sphere to lawmaking, it misses some important factors that may actually play important roles in bringing about fair agreement between citizens. First, the cognitive criterion of "rational acceptability" obscures the way that things come to seem rationally acceptable. This outcome comes about through habit, power, and ideology. If this is correct, then something may be false or partially false, but nevertheless promote truth simply by breaking the discursive lock of dominant ways of thinking and perceiving. The ideal of the populist public or what the Mission Park soccer players called the community may be this type of truth-promoting myth. By "myth" I mean that the idealized image of inclusive community may not exactly be true, but a truth-effect is produced by questioning or combatting the alternative.

Democratic society and the democratic state are like siblings: agonistic but also symbiotic. I use the term "democratic society" to describe the subset of civil society that engages in collective self-government or political activity. There is both tension and interdependence between democratic society and the state. The state is necessary for the reasons explained by republican theorists, as well as solidarists and social democrats. Groups such as criminal gangs, aristocratic families, guilds, religious orders, and corporations can wield considerable power, and a corresponding concentration of power is necessary to regulate, dismantle, and counterbalance these concentrated forces. The state, however, can also turn into a powerful agent of particular interests if it is not checked through some form of accountability or limited in some way. Democratic society plays this role.[39] This leads to the paradox that democratic society is both the problem and the solution. Self-governing associations can use their power to exclude outsiders and promote the interests of their members, but they can also protect the vulnerable and decentralize potentially despotic concentrations of power.[40] In order to distinguish between them, we need a theory of the public good.

DEMOCRACY AND SOLIDARISM

Gated communities and exclusive suburbs are two examples of associations that have used the ideal of democracy to justify exclusion.[41] These associations use the language of self-government, community, and freedom of contract to pursue of self-interest. They hire private security and build private recreational amenities, while opposing the taxes that would provide these things for everybody.[42] Wealthy neighborhoods also invoke "community" to justify limiting outsiders' access to public spaces. For example, in one of Toronto's wealthiest neighborhoods, a community tennis club that runs programs on public courts specifies that lessons are only open to children who live in the neighborhood or attend the neighborhood school. In contravention of city rules, the club's website makes it clear that the children living in modernist high-rises a kilometer away—most of whom are immigrants—are not welcome. This is also society against the state.[43]

In his book *Arguments and Fists*, Mika Lavaque-Manty examined two forms of political mobilization around local land use issues: NIMBYism and the environmental justice movement. From the standpoint of democratic theory, NIMBYism and the environmental justice movement look very much alike. In both types of organizations, residents mobilize in order to convince policymakers not to site a "locally unwanted land-use" (LULU) in their neighborhood. Lavaque-Manty suggests that the key difference is that NIMBYism is a politics of narrow self-interest, and the environmental justice movement seeks structural solutions based on general principles. NIMBYs want to pay less than others for a public good; they want cell phone reception but no cell phone tower in the neighborhood. They want homeless people off the street, but do not want a homeless shelter in their neighborhood. They focus on the way that a particular policy affects them, rather than the broader needs that a policy is designed to meet, and the fairest way to distribute the cost of meeting those needs.[44]

The environmental justice movement is similar in so far is it also mobilizes residents against LULUs, but it places these decisions in a broader context.[45] The environmental justice movement emerged in low-income and minority communities that had long borne a disproportionate share of the externalities of modern, urban life.[46] These include unwanted and dangerous facilities such as garbage dumps and toxic waste disposal sites.[47] Sometimes the geographic link between environmental hazards and poorer neighborhoods emerged indirectly. Before car ownership was widespread, workers had to live in close proximity to industrial employment, and therefore they ended up living near contaminated industrial sites. In other cases hazardous waste dumps were intentionally located in areas that policymakers felt were less likely to effectively mobilize opposition. The environmental justice movement linked local issues with broader concerns about the need for procedural equity (the right to participate),[48] geographical equity (the redress of a history of disparate impact), and social equity (targeted programs to deal with ongoing effects of past practices). While all political movements try to frame their interests in terms of general principles, NIMBYs tend to emphasize property rights, traditional character, or community control rather than equity or justice.

This contrast between the two different place-based political movements is instructive. Lavaque-Manty emphasizes that the two movements also draw on very different conceptions of liberalism. NIMBYs understand democracy as a system of regulated competition that enables individuals to pursue their interests. From this perspective, social relations are contractual relations that are based on interest and choice. The environmental justice movement, on the other hand, draws on a more egalitarian understanding of liberalism. This latter approach emphasizes that in addition to individual interests, there are also social interests that exist independent of the individual's direct interest.[49]

Lavaque-Manty argues that both positions are rationally defensible in a minimal sense, but he also concludes that the environmental justice movement is a better approach. He makes two arguments to justify this conclusion. The first is basically Kantian. He notes that the NIMBYs implicitly make a claim that cannot meet the test of public reason. The test of public reason is the question "Is this a position that all others could accept?"[50] The desire to benefit from collective goods without sharing the burden would not meet this test. Social cooperation creates benefits, but it also imposes burdens, and both should be shared fairly. The people living in the neighborhood that gets all of the loud traffic and hazardous waste dumps could hardly accept a system of allocation that allowed some neighborhoods to refuse their share.

The problem with this analysis is that it abstracts from the broader context of economic inequality and locational choice. By this I mean that affluent homeowners would probably respond that they purchased homes in quieter, safer, less toxic areas and paid for these amenities in the form of higher home prices. Indeed, homes located in the areas burdened by externalities of social cooperation cost less, and someone like Hayek might say that this reflects a rational choice based on the individual's assessment of the balance of benefits versus costs. Perhaps one family prefers to live in a three-bedroom home in a neighborhood with air pollution, as opposed to a studio apartment in a more pristine environment.

NIMBYs could make two responses to the argument that fairness should govern decisions about siting future LULUs. The first one is that the proposed "public goods" are not really public goods, and therefore not things that they need to subsidize. For example, the residents of suburban Richmond viewed regional public transit in this way. A second response is the efficiency argument, which emphasizes that the economic cost of placing LULUs in high-cost neighborhoods is higher than placing them in low-cost neighborhoods. According to the doctrine of regulatory takings, property owners should be compensated for policies that decrease the value of their properties, and these costs would be much higher in expensive neighborhoods.[51]

These objections remind us that the standard of public reason invoked above is abstract, and there are plausible arguments on both sides. If the claim is really that just social arrangements are ones that everyone could accept, then the basic structure of society itself is unjust and the problem isn't just who gets stuck living near a garbage dump, but why people don't have decent food, shelter, leisure time, adequate education, health care, technology, or even access to luxuries like restaurants, gym membership, vacations, tennis lessons, expensive wine, and cool gadgets. The claim that the only justified policies are ones that everyone affected would reasonably accept tells us very little.

Lavaque-Manty hints at a different way of responding to these "unreasonable" objections, but never fully works it out. He suggests that the NIMBYs may be wrong because they misrecognize or devalue social goods. In order to illustrate the difference between individual and social goods, Lavaque-Manty introduces Charles Taylor's discussion of friendship. According to Taylor, the benefits of friendship are not simply instrumental. There is something valuable about the social relationship that is not reducible to the aggregate of individual utility. Taylor suggests that other modes of commonality such as language, religion, and even patriotism have a similar, irreducibly social characteristic. This implies that there are collective values or goods that are not reducible to individual preferences or interests.

This phenomenological account of the social is convincing, but it remains unclear what role it can play in a normative defense of egalitarian liberalism. The implication seems to be that failing to recognize these social goods, and prioritizing private ones, is a cognitive and moral error. This is one way of explaining why the environmental justice approach is superior to the NIMBY or home-voter, who considers issues from the standpoint of private interest rather than public good. Lavaque-Manty, however, does not fully defend the "misrecognition of the social" argument, perhaps because it seems to rest on the "is-ought" fallacy. Just because there are social goods doesn't mean that we are obliged to value them over individual ones.

There are a couple of other responses to this argument that we should prioritize the public or social good. One is the standard liberal, Smithian argument that public goods are best achieved through individual, self-interested behavior. The butcher, baker, and candlestick-maker fulfill our needs by pursuing their interests. The second response is that the home-voter and the environmental justice activist both value social goods, but they are not the same social goods. The home-voter does value a certain kind of community and one can discern how much s/he values it by the price s/he is willing to pay. The content, however, can vary. For example, the security and familiarity of the gated suburban neighborhood and the hip, modern, youthful lifestyle of the downtown condo scene are two very different visions of community, but they are both ways that the individual can buy the experience of, or at least the fantasy of, a social good. Keally McBride made this point in "Consuming Community," her astute analysis of Celebration, Florida.[52] The appeal of Disney's town is precisely the promise of reconciling freedom and community. You can purchase a ready-made community. In the town of Celebration, prices are much higher than comparable homes nearby, and the reason is that you are buying a social good or at least a simulacra.

The solidarist theory of the common-wealth provides a way of responding to the home-voter.[53] It does so by defending a specific way of thinking about the public good. Late-19th-century solidarists made the empirical claim that the division of labor and the conditions of modern capitalist, industrial production generate a social product. This is still true today, but in a slightly different way; the post-industrial economy depends on a division of labor that is not only on the factory floor but also in social networks, supply chains, and technological infrastructure developed through collaboration.[54] The distribution of the social product is based on the power of capital and labor,[55] and the indirect contributions of collective investment in education, infrastructure, and technology are also undervalued or privatized. For the solidarists, this did not mean that private property was illegitimate, but rather that the allocation between state and private control and among individuals was not justifiable.[56] The public good is best understood as a program aimed at dismantling extreme inequality, filling basic needs, and achieving a fairer balance between private ownership and forms of social or state ownership that ensure access to the common-wealth. This approach to the public good emphasizes the redistributive component, but the public good is also an ethos, a way of describing and imagining the world as something which we all share and for which we are all responsible.[57] This is where public space and Taylor's phenomenological account of the social have a role to play. Public space— the parks, plazas, schools, and promenades—are sites of low-level conflict, but they are also places where we imagine ourselves as connected to one another.

The solidarist approach also provides some answers to the logic of NIMBYism. If we all benefit from the common-wealth—from the contributions of others and the inheritance of past generations, from our embeddedness in a common world—then we do have a responsibility to repair it, maintain it, and cultivate it. If we want to cultivate our own private garden we must protect the air quality and the ground water that we all share. If this is true of nature, it is even more applicable to the physical and social infrastructure of collective life: the roads that secure our freedom, the parks that enable us to play together, and the social practices that allow us to live together. The concepts of reciprocity and debt explain why we are *obliged* to cultivate the common world that we inherit rather than destroy it.

The second objection made by the NIMBYs is that the magic of the invisible hand guarantees that self-interest rather than misguided solidarity does a better job meeting everyone's needs. Again, solidarism explains why this is not true. It was not by accident that Adam Smith chose to use the butcher and baker rather than the pin factory worker as his illustration of the magic of the market. The pin factory workers, whom he introduces to illustrate the efficiency gained through the division of labor, do not exchange their products. The metal roller does not sell the flattened metal to the grinder. The labor process is controlled by authority, and the wages are set through a process of negotiation in which even Smith admits that the employer has much more power. The solidarists argued that we are a society of pin workers, and this socialized form of labor requires conscious collective control.

The home-voter might reply that while this is true of the workplace, it is not an accurate characterization of residential life. In the real estate market, individuals do make self-interested choices that rationally respond to price signals, achieving collective coordination without intentional organization. In fact, urban life is the most vivid illustration of the way that private choices affect and are affected by others in ways that do not fit the model of contract and consent. Economists use the term "neighborhood effects" to describe positive and negative externalities of other people's economic choices. Today it is no longer common for city dwellers to empty chamber pots into the streets, but noise, odor, and pollution are all ways that peoples' actions affect those who live nearby.[58] Government regulation of urban property has been nearly a permanent fixture of urban life. The first building code dates back at least to the time of Roman emperor Augustus, who limited the height of structures to 70 feet. In 5th-century Constantinople, houses larger than ten stories were prohibited.[59] This means that there are always at least four or five parties that are involved in a real estate transaction: the buyer, the seller, the government, and the neighbors. Non-residents are also indirectly affected. Home-voters use the franchise to promote their economic interests through regulation, which creates barriers to entry for others. Zoning regulations such as minimum lot sizes, setbacks, and restrictions on multi-family dwellings are notorious examples. It is deeply misleading to use the "invisible hand" of the market to justify self-interested behavior when this self-interested behavior takes the form of promoting restrictive government regulation.

· What about the objection that citizens who engage in what looks like anti-solidarist politics may reasonably disagree about what constitutes a public good? Like the suburbanites in Richmond, Virginia, 61.7 percent of voters in Vancouver, British Columbia, rejected a referendum proposal for a 0.5 percent increase to the provincial sales tax to raise the $8 billion needed to finance public transit infrastructure.[60] Opponents thought that transit is a service that users should pay for, not a public good that should be subsidized by everyone. I do not think that this is a position that we can dismiss as unreasonable or antidemocratic, but I do think it is wrong. Democracy is about persuasion, and this can be achieved through denaturalizing common sense or by linking things together in new ways. The theory of the urban commonwealth reworks common sense to provide an argument for supporting public transit and parks that are free for use by neighborhood kids. The city itself is common-wealth. Gentrification is increasing the cost of housing to the point where a share of this common-wealth is becoming inaccessible to the middle class, working class, and poor. Low-cost transit is the easiest way to ensure access not only to jobs but also to leisure, culture, and what the French call *centralité*. The rising economic inequality that is being felt across society is manifest in intensified spatial forms in the most prosperous cities, especially superstar cities like Vancouver and San Francisco. At the level of the polity, the solution is to increase collective control over private capital through something like citizen funds, but at the level of the city, a start is to improve public transit and to preserve the oases of public space.

CONCLUSION

The theories of democracy and the public good are attempts to think through the Mission Park Playground conflict. The conflict reminds us of the gap between legality and legitimacy, and the need for a political strategy that is mindful of this gap. To insist that democracy is an empty place, as Lefort does, is only a starting point. The real work of political theory involves trying to fill that gap by making arguments and telling stories that help us make sense of where we are and where we want to go.[61] To fill the gap, however, is not to abolish the gap, as totalitarianism tries to do. These arguments are revisable judgments about what should be done and why. The vision of the public good proposed above is one such project. It rests on a diagnosis of the contemporary condition as one in which the concentration of wealth and power in private hands has reached unjustifiable extremes. Against the logic of privatization, it celebrates the pleasures of public life and the equalizing effect of public things.

[9]

HETERO-RIGHTS TO THE CITY

There is an extensive literature in urban studies that has vividly described—and astutely analyzed—the way that rising inequality has transformed cities.[1] In political philosophy, scholars have used normative and critical theory to deepen our understanding of rights, justice, and equality. This book brings these two approaches together. It explains why displacement through gentrification, slum clearance, and destruction of public housing are wrong and why public space must be both a stage for political disagreement and a shared thing (res publica) that brings us together.

This book draws on contemporary political theory, but it also has a historical dimension. I reconstruct the intellectual history of solidarism because it is the forgotten foundation of social policies and ideas that are under attack today. In newspaper editorials, policy papers, and everyday life, the language of neo-liberalism is hegemonic: personal responsibility, choice, freedom, markets, efficiency, and desert. Moreover, even in places like San Francisco where this language does not predominate in public life, the practices of economic segregation and privatization still flourish.

There are alternative visions of the city: the inclusive city,[2] the creative city,[3] the smart city.[4] However, these also have limitations. The creative city and the smart city can function ideologically to legitimize economic inequalities and to prioritize the needs of educated, elite professionals.[5] Inclusivity sounds more promising, but it also implies that the city naturally belongs to certain people who include others on their own terms. The right to the city has a different rhetorical effect. It has a capillary structure that draws power from below rather than above. The term "right" implies a legitimate demand and depicts this demand as something obligatory rather than discretionary. The term "right" also has an agonistic quality. In Europe, rights emerged historically as limits on the power of the king. At first they were negotiated privileges that granted power or immunities to individuals or groups. These rights were extended and generalized through a long process of struggle.[6]

In this book I have occasionally used the phrase the "right to the city" to describe struggles for housing, transit, and public space. I have relied on approaches to rights from egalitarian and liberal philosophers, and also drawn on forgotten resources from the radical-republican tradition of solidarism. My intent was to illuminate the right to the city by looking at it from a different perspective before returning to Lefebvre's own account to see how these different approaches fit together. This chapter provides a close reading of Lefebvre's *Le Droit à la Ville* and then explains how the theory of the urban commonwealth helps resolve some of the problems in this text.

LE DROIT À LA VILLE

In the past decade Henri Lefebvre's notion of "the right to the city" has become extremely popular.[7] His influence extends beyond academia. The concept has been enthusiastically embraced by housing activists, artists, and even international organizations.[8] The technocratic, social democratic left has adopted the "right to the city" as the rationale for a more inclusive and just approach to urban policy, and radical and anarchist subcultures have used it as a way of imagining an alternative to the state.[9] Lefebvre has inspired an extremely rich and productive discussion about different dimensions of the right to the city, such as housing, transit, public space, urban social movements, foreclosure, and political participation,[10] but the vastness of the literature is one of the things that makes it difficult to understand his distinctive approach.[11] There are at least two other reasons why Lefebvre's "right to the city" is difficult to interpret. The first is practical. Lefebvre's own take on rights changed over the course of a long and extremely prolific career, and some of the key texts haven't been translated into English. The second reason is that the tension between Lefebvre's historical-materialist approach and his utopian vision of urban renewal is problematic and remains unresolved in his work.

In this chapter, I present an account of Lefebvre's early theory of the right to city, the Marxian critique of rights, and a theory of hetero-rights that helps us rethink the right to the city in light of this critique. *Heteros* is the Greek work for "other." Both Foucault and Lefebvre used the term "heterotopia" to describe other spaces[12]—places both inside and outside of the dominant order. A hetero-right highlights the otherness of rights that are both inside and outside the framework of liberal rights. At the end of his life Lefebvre endorsed the notion of a "contract of citizenship" not as a way of resolving conflicts over right but as a way of staging such conflicts. The struggle over the public and private shares of the commonwealth provides an even more effective stage.

In a recent article, Mark Purcell has argued that Lefebvre's account of the "right to the city" is a coherent alternative to the dominant liberal approach to rights.[13] According to Purcell, Lefebvre understands the right to the city as an element of a wider struggle for revolution, and not a reformist, humanist rationale for alleviating urban social problems. For Lefebvre, rights are not deduced from abstract theory; they are produced through political struggle. Citizens and workers assert collective claims, creating new rights, which can then be incorporated into norms and legal codes. This incorporation, however, is not automatic. There are structural constraints and organized opposition to rights claims, which can unleash political mobilization. Lefebvre called for "a right to the city" in order to inspire this struggle.

This account is largely convincing, but it creates the impression of coherence by minimizing some of the problems and tensions in Lefebvre's theory. Purcell is correct to point out that the embrace of the right to the city by planners who use it to promote inclusive development—things like congestion pricing for roads, mixed-income housing projects, light rail to link the *banlieue* to employment hubs—fundamentally misunderstand Lefebvre's approach. He did not think it would be possible to find technocratic fixes to urban problems, though he did end the book on an oddly optimistic note.[14] Lefebvre called for a form of urban renewal that unleashes and incorporates the playful, ludic dimensions of social life,[15] the collective appropriation of space and time,[16] art as a form of social practice rather than a mode of distinction, and a right to active, authentic participation.[17]

These ideals are very attractive, but they seem even more remote today than they did when Lefebvre was writing in 1967. Is Lefebvre's right to the city too utopian and unconnected to the social forces that could bring it about? Purcell responds that Lefebvre's right to the city is not utopian, in the negative sense of the term. He argues that Lefebvre's urban renewal builds on the irreducible urbanity that endures in cities and enables encounters between people as well as appropriation of place and participation in politics. It helps us imagine "a task that is quite practical, concrete, and achievable: seek and learn to recognize the urban that is all around us but hidden, and then nurture it in whatever way we can."[18]

This is indeed Lefebvre's conclusion, but it is also inconsistent with other parts of his project. In order to support this claim, I focus on *Le Droit à la Ville*, particularly the concepts of spectre, dialectic, ideology, and praxis, which help us see why it is problematic to use Lefebvre's dialectical theory to justify an evolutionary approach to urban reform. Lefebvre concludes, "The right to the city manifests itself as a superior form of rights . . . The right to the *œuvre*, to participation and *appropriation* (clearly distinct from the right to property), are implied in the right to the city."[19] Lefebvre doesn't clarify what the "right to appropriation" means, but I think that it is best understood as an argument for social property.

Le Droit à la Ville is an analysis of the city, but it is also an extended discussion of methodology. Lefebvre is extremely critical of both abstract normative theory and positivist science. He thinks that both of these are incomplete, and both give a distorted picture of social phenomena. They also function ideologically. Both, in different ways, deny social conflict and contradiction. The scientific approach treats urban issues as matters of instrumental rationality. The goal is efficiency in achieving a certain end, but the ends are naturalized rather than examined. Normative theory also functions ideologically. It transposes problems from the material level to the level of abstract thought, so that they can be resolved in theory while continuing unimpeded in practice.

The city provides a powerful illustration of the way this works. According to Lefebvre, the city we imagine when we use that term has two historical roots: the city of classical antiquity and the pre-industrial city.

The paradigmatic space of the classical city is the agora, the place where the citizens assemble in person to deliberate about collective life. Structural changes in the scale of territory and the social organization of labor have completely undermined the material basis of this city, yet the image of democracy, citizenship deliberation, and rationality remains potent.

The physical structure of contemporary European cities derives in part from the pre-industrial mercantile city. Lefebvre points out that the pre-industrial cities were controlled by bankers and merchants who created an urban form devoted to use value, pleasure, beauty, and spaces of encounter. He notes the monumentality of guild halls, churches, civic buildings, and squares that were created in this period. These were not polities that had high levels of equality; on the contrary, they were riven by class conflict. Yet, according to Lefebvre, this struggle itself reinforced a sense of belonging. It was a society that was oppressive but also very creative. The church extracted surplus value from the countryside and channeled it into the construction of magnificent cathedrals. Similarly, the guilds controlled the labor of apprentices and concentrated resources that funded elaborate guild halls. These spaces were neither public nor private, but functioned as a hierarchically organized urban commons. In the pre-industrial era, the concept of productive investment was less prominent and exchange value was not hegemonic; this meant that conspicuous collective consumption and use (buildings, banquets, the fête, the city itself) could flourish.

Industrialization radically changed the city. Some industries located in peripheral areas because power (coal, water) was more accessible there. Other industries did the same thing because they wanted to break or circumvent the power of urban guilds. Industrialization unleashed centrifugal tendencies that accelerated even more rapidly after the construction of highways. Industrial employment also drew people from the countryside to the city, increasing density and intensity and generating spatial and social tensions that changed the structure of the city. In many places this left an older part of town with the physical characteristic of "urbanity" or "centrality" surrounded by varied zones of industrial production, circulation, slum housing, and new suburban residential areas.

What exactly does Lefebvre mean by urbanity? The urban is a characteristic of the pre-industrial city: a center of social and political life; a site of intensified sensibility; a physical environment where one can accumulate knowledge and skill as well as wealth. In order to explain urbanity he draws a contrast between a work (*oeuvre*) and a product (*produit*). A work is oriented toward use value and a product is oriented toward exchange value.[20] The city itself is not something that can be exchanged, in part because it is shared among people rather than traded between them. According to Lefebvre, the primary use of the city was the festival, an unproductive expenditure of resources that brought nothing other than prestige and pleasure.

With industrialization, the cultural and structural forces that sustained the urban were destroyed, but the built environment of the city remained. The city endures as an aesthetically pleasing form, but one that is empty of content because the social praxis that underpinned it has been destroyed. This set the stage for the transformation from the urban as a form of social practice to the city as ideology. According to Lefebvre, the historical nucleus of the old city plays a new role, not as a site of encounter but as a site of consumption. It is a site of consumption in two ways: a privileged place for the buying and selling of specialized, luxury goods, and a place that is itself consumed.[21] A version of this argument became extremely influential in urban studies in the 1990s. A number of scholars drew attention to a new hybrid style of retail development that marketed private commercial space using the aesthetics of public space. This style took a variety of forms including historic waterfronts, festival marketplaces, new urbanist neighborhoods, and "ye old commons"-style shopping malls.[22] Lefebvre, however, goes a step farther. He emphasizes that the authentic, historical city—not merely the ersatz city—has the ideological function of disguising the disappearance of the urban itself. Historical preservationists try to protect the image of *centrality* while ignoring the structural forces that sustain or destroy centrality.[23]

The most important concept in *Le Droit à la Ville* is one that has received little attention. This is the concept of the *spectre*, and it is developed in the chapter immediately preceding "The Right to the City."[24] Lefebvre introduces the *spectre* in the context of a discussion about spatial segregation in cities. He notes an apparent paradox. At the level of abstract principle, opposition to segregation is almost complete. No one in government or academia or even in commerce directly defends residential segregation, because this would contradict the basic universalist tenets of liberal humanism.[25] At the same time, however, the practice of segregation is increasing rather than diminishing, and we know that it has accelerated more quickly in the 50 years since he wrote the book. Lefebvre notes that residential space is not the only space becoming segregated; this process is transforming leisure and social spaces too. He concludes that it reflects an either conscious or unconscious class strategy. As Friedrich Engels already pointed out in the mid-19th century, spatial segregation is one of the things that makes it possible for elites to ignore the contradictions of capitalism, because it literally hides them from view.[26] Lefebvre pushes this idea a step further, however, and points out that the city—precisely because it seems to be full of variety, encounter, and beauty—plays an important ideological role in mystifying this segregation. The conviviality of the historical core, with its nostalgic shops sustained by tourism, helps us ignore the reality of segregation.

Lefebvre uses the term *spectre*, but a better simile would be that the capitalist city is like a vampire rather than a ghost. It looks human, like the humanist city of the ancient agora or Renaissance city-state, but it is not what it seems. It sucks the life force from the countryside and the urban periphery, leaving lifeless remains. "Spectral analysis" is supposed to use the ghostly presence of the dead urban society to help us see *both* our desire for use value, festival, creativity, and encounter *and* the impossibility of fulfilling this desire in the world as it is currently structured. This is very similar to Walter Benjamin's dialectical image, which takes desires expressed in dreams (including historical ones) and juxtaposes them with the (im)possibilities of the present.[27] In his more optimistic moments, Benjamin hoped that this juxtaposition could be politicizing. Like *Ideologiekritik*, the dialectical image penetrates the dominant way of seeing, but does so through aesthetic rather than purely rationalist insight. Some critics, however, have questioned the effectiveness of this approach. The dialectical image may render contradictions visible, but perhaps this achieves little in a society where contradiction no longer produces cognitive dissonance, let alone political action.[28]

Contemporary urban theorists, even radical ones, have tried to turn Lefebvre's theory into something that can be employed for the project of urban reform. In order to do this, they have emphasized the passages where Lefebvre celebrates alternative ways of living in non-dominated spaces.[29] The main argument of *Le Droit à la Ville*, however, is the opposite. Up until the last chapter, Lefebvre does not look for hopeful signs of genuine urbanity in the capitalist city; instead, he uses spectral analysis to teach the reader to see through hopeful signs. We could use spectral analysis to think about "creative cities."[30] At first, the link between urbanism and creativity might seem consistent with Lefebvre's vision, given that the concept of *oeuvre* (work of art) is central to his analysis. In fact, creative cities are the ones with large numbers of elites (educated professionals) and they tend to be the cities with the highest levels of income inequality.[31] Moreover, the production and consumption of culture function to disguise or legitimize these inequalities. For Lefebvre, the idea of "creative cities" is problematic in much the same way that the humanist city is. He rejects classic humanism because it rests on an image of man and society that does not exist in capitalist society: man as an autonomous producer of his own life and society as composed of equals with similar interests.

Is it possible to contest the "class strategy" that creates a segregated and unequal city and to revitalize the urban at the same time? According to Lefebvre, planners and even well-meaning policymakers cannot do very much. History has proven Lefebvre correct. In spite of almost 50 years of investment in public housing, spatial segregation, homelessness, and dispossession have increased rather than decreased. In *Le Droit à la Ville*, Lefebvre identifies two different kinds of praxis, which point to very different understandings of politics. At several points he uses the term "praxis" in connection with the argument that the working class is the only social force capable of bringing about genuine urban renewal.[32] This is broadly consistent with the analysis of segregation. Workers and unemployed people are expelled to peripheral areas where they cannot share the use value of the city. The visible work of artists and the invisible labor of service workers make glamorous city living possible, but in enabling the city of consumption, they also contribute to their own exclusion through gentrification. This is a classic dialectical contradiction that could spark a political movement.[33]

The second form of praxis, however, is the one that contemporary urban theorists have emphasized: the already operative moments of play, creativity, and participation that flourish in the interstices of the existing city. If these alternative ways of inhabiting already exist, then all that needs to be done is to nurture, foster, and replicate them. This is basically an evolutionary approach and it informs much of progressive urban politics today. For example, in Toronto there is a nonprofit organization called Artscape that leverages public and private money to create low-cost space for artists and arts organizations. Artscape developed the Wychwood Barns, an award-winning project that transformed outdated urban infrastructure (industrial buildings that had once been used to store and repair streetcars) into an arts hub. The main barn now contains 26 live-work studios and 14 work-only studios for artists as well as a community gallery. Other buildings provide office and meeting space for nonprofit arts, educational, community, and environmental organizations. There is also a greenhouse, bake oven, educational garden, compost center, farmers market, and playground.

The project cost over $18 million, which came largely from the local and provincial governments, including funds designated for low-income housing.[34] The city of Toronto leases the site to Artscape, for one dollar per year, and also provides additional ongoing support in the form of tax abatements. The project is considered a success and in a certain sense it is.[35] A vibrant neighborhood public space was created through the leadership of a progressive city council member and the collaboration of local residents. The final design was the result of a long process of participatory planning, which engaged a large number of highly mobilized local residents. It was a contentious process in which citizens considered very different visions for the space.[36] The final result seems to incorporate many Lefebvrian themes—play, de-commodification of space, art, creativity, and ongoing self-management.

Yet examining the project from a materialist perspective helps us see some of the tensions that this project makes visible. First, in so far as the right to the city is introduced as a remedy for economic segregation, it is hard to see how this type of project helps. Economic segregation in Toronto takes the same form that it does in Paris: an increasingly wealthy historic inner city is surrounded by a ring of poor suburbs with low-quality high-rise apartments.[37] A community arts hub in the central city does nothing to dismantle this structure, and actually reinforces it by accelerating gentrification. Second, since much of the money for this project came from the very limited funds for "community benefits" and low-income housing, support for the arts reduced the resources available to help poor families. Finally, Wychwood Barns functions at least in part as an instance of the city-as-ideology that Lefebvre criticized in *Le Droit à la Ville*. The industrial chic arts space is a widely replicated model of urban renewal.[38] It blurs the line between use value and exchange value, which is the key to a certain kind of fantasy. By consuming "use value," city dwellers are able to both deny and enjoy capitalism. The creative children's activities run by the arts organization—like the organic products at the farmers' market—are purchased by the white, wealthy professionals who increasingly dominate the neighborhood.[39]

It is tempting to describe existing practices of participation, play, and creativity as the roots of a rhizomatic counter-colonization of the city. This interpretation seems preferable to cynical despair and more viable than revolution. Yet this approach (cultivating heterotopias, places of authentic dwelling) fails to identify the social forces that could resolve these contradictions in a way that advances social justice. Reading Lefebvre against Lefebvre's own conclusion, I argue we should try to think about the right to the city differently.

In *Le Droit à la Ville*, Lefebvre repeatedly states that the right to housing is not the same as the right to the city. In fact, he suggests that the focus on housing can be a distraction from the broader project of rethinking what it means to inhabit urban space.[40] I think he dismisses the right to housing far too quickly, but this probably reflects the context of the late 1960s, a period when the state had constructed high-rise public housing on a massive scale and observers were beginning to notice that housing when separated from community, aesthetics, and other social needs generated new problems.[41]

The key contribution of *Le Droit à la Ville* is twofold: a focus on the spatial dimension of urban inequality and the ideological role of the city in disguising this inequality. "Centralité ludique," as appealing as this is, is no solution. A more promising approach is a materialist and dialectical take on the right to the city. Near the end of his life, Lefebvre asked "Wasn't it a grave error of the Marxist tendency to underestimate and overlook both the rights of man and the global struggle to advance and deepen these rights?"[42] The next section of this chapter introduces an approach to rights that highlights the agonistic dimension. I call this approach "hetero-rights."

LEFEBVRE ON MARX ON RIGHTS

In *Du Contrat de Citoyenneté* Lefebvre explicitly criticizes Marxist theory for failing to recognize the role of rights in political struggle and rejects the Marxist view that rights are depoliticizing. In order to understand this shift, we must first examine the Marxist critique of rights. Lefebvre is a helpful guide in exploring this issue because he was both a proponent and critic of rights. In *Le manifeste différentialiste*, Lefebvre engages in an extended analysis of Marx's *On the Jewish Question*.[43] According to Lefebvre, Marx's critique of rights was based on an objection to the reductionist character of political emancipation. Political emancipation bifurcates the human being into economic and political man. The role of the citizen or moral person is abstracted from the underlying social conditions and therefore emancipating political man has no real effect. According to Marx, after acquiring political rights, the Jew may become a citizen, but the social order remains deeply Christian. Similarly, the worker may gain the right to vote but the capitalist economic order is presupposed and protected. The key to Lefebvre's reading of Marx is this issue of abstraction. He insists that written law is ineffective and real change is achieved at the level of "moeurs," in other words, social practice.[44]

Lefebvre's formulation, however, is a bit misleading. The problem with civil and political rights under liberalism is not excessive abstraction but rather an unacknowledged embeddedness. By this I mean that the liberal understanding of rights *fails* to abstract the rights-bearing individual from social relations. The link between citizen and property owner is actually reinforced, and the two identities are conflated rather than separated. The obligation of government and thus the responsibility of the citizen, as Marx explains, is to protect civil society as an arena for competition and the fulfillment of private interest. For Marx, the real problem with rights is not abstraction but mystification. The status of equal citizen with political rights serves to disguise the social inequality that is attached to it.

The liberal approach to rights involves a kind of sleight of hand. By "liberalism" I mean to describe an approach that encompasses an equal right to political participation and a set of individual rights (particularly property) that are naturalized as pre-political. The political rights are not abstracted; instead, they are understood as intrinsically linked to the other rights of bourgeois man, such as the right to private property. Lefebvre reaches this conclusion when he points out that real change is possible only if we reject the basic presupposition that the source of law (*droit*) is private property, and this would require a social revolution.

Lefebvre noted that the range of rights was continually expanding in his day. *Le manifeste différentialiste* was published in 1970, and this post-68 period saw the growth of rights claims emerging out of new social movements, including the rights of children and women.[45] Lefebvre treats these rights as part of a war of position that can achieve real improvements for excluded groups, but he also insists that they tie people to a system of domination. For Lefebvre, rights will always be contradictory as long as they are conceived in reformist terms. The reason is that these reforms serve to reinforce the prestige of the state.[46] The emancipatory side of rights also strengthens a mechanism of domination.

This discussion helps clarify the two main critiques of rights from the left. First, the rhetoric of rights mystifies power by deflecting attention from the production of inequalities to struggles over how to mitigate the worst effects. Second, it is a kind of governmentality in so far as it produces subjects who see the state as the source of salvation. In other words, a rights-based claim upon the state increases the power of sovereign authority and therefore is ambivalent at best.

With these critiques in mind, we can better understand the distinctiveness of Lefebvre's right to the city. The right to the city is best understood as an attempt to rework the meaning of rights in response to Marx's critique in *On the Jewish Question*. In asserting a right to the city, Lefebvre challenges the bifurcation of civil and political society. The right to the city does not build on the right to private property. Given the scale and diversity of the city, it is difficult to imagine it as another variant of the typical models of private property: the body, the home, the castle. From the perspective of private property, a right to the city is incomprehensible. No person can own a city as private property. This is a consequence of the definition of the city that Lefebvre provides in *The Urban Revolution*. After introducing the broader concept of the urban, he disaggregates the urban into component parts. According to Lefebvre, Level M (mixed, mediator, intermediary) is the level of the city.[47] It is what remains when you look at a map of the city and remove all of the privately owned buildings and all of the "global" institutions such as ministries, prefectures, and cathedrals. What remains are streets, squares, parish churches, community centers: an ensemble that links together the site and the structures that surround it. Although the legal titles to these mixed spaces of the city include a patchwork of forms of ownership—corporate, individual-private, and state-public—the spaces themselves are experienced phenomenologically as a commons.[48]

From this perspective, the right to the city could be described as a hetero-right. Just as Foucault and Lefebvre used the term "heterotopias" to describe other spaces—places both inside and outside of the dominant order—a hetero-right highlights the otherness of rights that are both inside and outside the framework of liberal rights. The right to the city is a logical impossibility in so far as no one can assert a conventional property right to the city. The right to public housing functions in a similar way. The right to public housing asserts something which is contradictory. It claims a property right to something which is not a possession. Asserting a right to public housing is a polemical claim that juxtaposes the property right of the public housing agency as a landlord, the political right of the public as a group of citizens, and the social rights of people in need of housing. It exposes the instability of the "public" as a subject, a bearer of rights, and a desired object. Jeremy Waldron's claim that freedom is only possible in a communist or solidarist society functions in a similar way.[49] It reminds us that the homeless person's right to *be* comes into conflict with the foundational right to private property. In his seminal essay "Homelessness and Freedom" he points out that the subject of rights is an embodied subject. In order to be free, the individual must be able to actualize freedom in the external world. This means that people need a place to carry out basic life functions such as sleeping, eating, and other physical functions. Hegel recognized this, and it is the reason that he identified the right to private property as the foundational right. In so far as homeless people have no place that they may legitimately carry out basic life functions, they effectively have no right to existence. Drawing on this analysis, Waldron argues in favor of collective property rights that ensure access to a place where basic needs can be met. He suggests that freedom is only possible in so far as society is communist, in the sense of protecting a commons where the homeless have a right to be. The dispossessed person's right to the commons is also a hetero-right. It is a rights claim that casts doubts on the dominant way of thinking about rights. It highlights the paradox that the right to property is also the basis of dispossession. It reminds us that the right to private property cannot be universalized, because there is always a limiting moment when there is no more commons to be appropriated, and one person must violate another's right or be left without "as much and as good" land as the first person who claimed a share.

When I say that hetero-rights exceed the conventional logic of rights, I do not intend to invoke the increasingly popular notion of "aspirational" rights. Hetero-rights are not "emergent" or "aspirational" rights.[50] Aspirational rights describe normative principles that are not justiciable within the current legal system but may be invoked to guide public policy. Hetero-rights are something more and also something less. They are more because they expose the limits of dominant ways of thinking about political problems, but they are less in the sense that they cannot be realized by gradually expanding existing rights. They are political tools, because they make claims about injustice that cannot be resolved without political change.

Do the rights to the city, to housing, and to public space have the same features as the civil and political rights that Marx subjected to critique? The main objection to Jewish emancipation was that such emancipation could be granted without fundamentally changing the Christian underpinnings of the state. This is not true of the rights to the city, to housing, and to public space. To recognize the people's right to occupy public space would be tantamount to reconfiguring the notion of state sovereignty. The right to housing challenges the right to private property. Invoking these rights does not mystify the real distribution of power; it exposes it.

The second Marxian objection to rights is the sovereigntist objection. In *Dispossession*, Judith Butler makes a version of this argument. She writes, "Even when we have our rights, we are dependent on a mode of governance and a legal regime that confers and sustains those rights. And so we are already outside of ourselves before any possibility of being dispossessed of our rights, land, and modes of belonging."[51] One response is that the rights claims described above are not addressed to the legal regime, and therefore do not simply strengthen the prestige of the state and reinforce the dependence of the citizen. This response, however, is only partially true. The anarchist component of the Occupy protest movements did try to imagine, create, and sustain alternative modes of organization outside of the state, but my sense is that a larger group of participants and supporters did not aspire to an anarchist utopia; they sought a deeper democracy and a more just city. Asserting popular sovereignty outside the institutional structures of a formally democratic state is not the same as imagining a stateless polity. It is reformist in that it challenges the bureaucratic and technocratic state in the name of the people. It also reminds us of the distinction between the government, the people, and the majority, but it does so in order to better realize the democratic ideal of equalizing power.

In *Le manifeste différentialiste*, Lefebvre was ambivalent about rights because he was ambivalent about reformism. He argued that as long as the right to private property is treated as the source of law (*droit*), other rights claims will secure only marginal improvements. Writing in the late 1960s, Lefebvre sided with Rosa Luxemburg against Eduard Bernstein, and Jules Guesde against Léon Bourgeois; he worried that reformism weakened the unity and resolution of the forces that could bring about a social revolution.

In *Le Droit à la Ville* Lefebvre explicitly rejects the theory of the urban commonwealth proposed in this book. He insists that the only way to overcome the contradictions of urban society is to abolish exchange value. He argues the evolutionary, statist solutions to urban problems generate further contradictions, such as segregation-through-gentrification.[52] He is particularly critical of something that sounds very similar to solidarism: *la socialisation de la société*. According to Lefebvre, proponents of this theory think that the socialization of production and expansion of communication have created the conditions that make rational planning and regulation viable. Lefebvre thinks this rests on the problematic fantasy that you can have the public good without conflict, and capitalism without exploitation.

Does the idea of the urban commonwealth reinforce the ideological belief in universal interests and weaken the ability to recognize conflicting interests? The concept of the common could function in this way. For example, common interest developments (essentially gated communities with shared amenities) employ the rhetoric and semiotics of the common to disguise the fact that this form of collective private property is exclusive and intended as an alternative to public goods that must be shared with diverse others. But the urban commonwealth, as employed in this book, functions in the opposite way. It is a challenge to the hegemonic assumption that the city naturally belongs to those who can pay the high cost of admission, which in most places takes the form of high rent or expensive real estate. The notion of common-wealth is mobilized against the hegemonic view that private property and the commodity form are the only natural, legitimate, and efficient ways of relating people to places. In this sense, it is closer to the strategy of antagonism than consensus, but it draws on elements of both. Like all political claims it has two sides; it challenges the distribution of things and the sensibilities that enable us to perceive these distributions as either legitimate or natural. At the same time, the political asserts a new universal; it claims that the new approach is not just the particular interest of some, but rather that it should be the shared project of all.

THE RIGHT TO THE URBAN COMMONWEALTH

Hetero-rights are rights understood politically, not metaphysically, and as sources of productive tension rather than gradual evolution. In 1990, one year before he died, Lefebvre published a collection of essays with the "Groupe de Navarrenx." Entitled *Du Contrat de Citoyenneté*, it is a final account of his theory of rights. In his contribution, Lefebvre still calls for new rights of citizenship, including the rights to identity and difference, to culture, to *autogestion*, and the right to the city.[53] He also provides a new rationale for a politics of rights. He notes that his own reconsideration of the issue of rights was inspired by an obscure Spanish court decision in July 1986. The plaintiff brought a suit against the governing socialist party (Partido Socialista Obrero Español [PSOE]) on the grounds that it had violated the promises it made during the election. The judge agreed that the PSOE had violated an implied contract with the electorate. At first this might seem like a

THE DEATH AND LIFE OF THE URBAN COMMONWEALTH

case that illustrates the problem with liberal rights, since it privileges contract and decontextualizes rights, but Lefebvre reaches the opposite conclusion. He emphasizes that it is a legal recognition of the idea that the state is subordinate and the citizens are sovereign. It gives substance and reality to the abstract principle of accountability. The key is not the form of right but rather its effect, which in this case is to deepen democracy through the mechanism of a contract of citizenship. Understood in this way, right does not resolve social conflict, but it does provide a new terrain of struggle.

We should understand the argument presented in this book—the right to a share of the urban commonwealth—in a similar way. I also want to suggest that this argument is consistent with the political strategy that Lefebvre endorsed at the end of his life in *Du Contrat de Citoyenneté*. The idea of social property and debt could provide a new terrain for struggle over how to share the common-wealth. The right to a share of social property is a hetero-right; it highlights the tension between the right to private property and the social infrastructure that supports it. Like Obama's claim "You didn't build that," it is both obviously true and disconcerting. It is both reflected in the existing practice of regulation, public insurance, and taxation and also potentially revolutionary at the same time. The space between the status quo and the potentially radical implications of the idea is the terrain of struggle.

[10]

CONCLUSION

The struggle over the right to the city can take place in the courts, in the policy arena, on the street, and in the workplace. The theory of the urban commonwealth is a way of thinking about our connection with the people who share the space of the city and it has practical consequences. It is a rationale for policies such as inclusionary zoning, rent control, value capture, taxation of capital gains from the sale of real estate, and community benefits agreements.[1] It provides an alternative to the legal doctrine of regulatory takings, a concept that was developed to convince the courts that the government should compensate the private property owner for the costs associated with regulation.[2] The doctrine of regulatory takings is basically the inverse of the theory of solidarism: it insists that the benefits of cooperation should be privatized and costs should be socialized. This doctrine has been gaining influence in the courts, where it was recently used to challenge the constitutionality of inclusionary zoning.[3]

In 2010, San Jose, a city near Silicon Valley with some of the highest real estate prices in the nation, passed a law requiring that new residential developments of at least 20 homes include affordable units for low-income buyers.[4] In the rationale for the ordinance, the city council explained how real estate development affects both the supply and demand of affordable housing. First, market-rate residential development decreases the already limited amount of land available for affordable housing. Second, real estate development draws construction and service workers to the city, which puts further pressure on the limited supply of affordable housing.[5] The California Building Industry filed suit, claiming that such policies go beyond normal local police powers and violate the constitutional prohibition on taking private property without compensation. The Superior

Court agreed, but the city of San Jose appealed to the California Supreme Court, which affirmed that municipalities could use all reasonable means to meet the challenge of providing affordable housing.[6] The case is important because of the way that it articulates two very different approaches to local land use. One is the theory of the urban commonwealth, which treats the city as common property and, given the conditions of scarcity, places modest limits on the market exchange of land in order to meet the need for affordable housing. It situates real estate development in the context of the social and physical infrastructure of the city, and considers what is minimally necessary to sustain that infrastructure. The alternative abstracts from this context, and focuses on the benefits accrued to the contracting parties without considering how this affects everyone else. This book has tried to explain why the urban commonwealth is a better approach.

In *Social Justice and the City*, David Harvey drew attention to what he called "the hidden mechanisms" of redistribution that are the object of urban political struggles. He argued that the distribution of real income via these hidden mechanisms benefits the rich and disadvantages the poor.[7] We see this when a wealthy neighborhood gets a new playground and a poor neighborhood gets a new garbage incinerator. These outcomes are not surprising since they are the result of a bargaining process in which the wealthy have more financial resources and social capital. When wealthy people are concentrated in physical space, these benefits are magnified, which provides a further incentive to exclude others. This book builds on and radicalizes this point. It tries to show that displacement and exclusion from cities is also a hidden mechanism of distribution that gives some people a larger share of the common-wealth and prevents others from enjoying the public and social infrastructure that belongs to everyone.

There are two main objections to the approach that I have taken in this book. Both of these objections point to the limits of normative theory, but from slightly different directions. The first critique faults liberal theory for failing to fully consider the impact of structural forces, and the second one questions normative theory from a political-tactical perspective. In this conclusion, I would like to briefly respond to these objections.

The remedies most frequently mentioned in this book are place-based: investment in public transit and affordable housing, protection against displacement, and provision of democratic public spaces. Are these remedies appropriate and effective tools for repairing the thick injustice[8] that is visible in urban areas? The critical urban theorist David Imbroscio has pointed out some of the problems with a liberal, place-based approach to urban problems. According to Imbroscio, the problem with the liberal approach is that it doesn't understand the source of the inequalities that are manifest in cities. It treats space as a cause of the problem rather than an effect. For example, liberal urban theory emphasizes the mismatch between inner-city workers and suburban jobs, or wealthy suburban tax bases and inner-city needs. According to Imbroscio, however, this account seriously misdiagnoses the source of urban injustice; the empirical story itself is inaccurate and the solutions it implies—such as greater administrative centralization and the relocation of people to more suitable places—are counterproductive.[9]

Critical urban theory promotes a different set of solutions. In order to address the systematic structural roots of urban injustice, structural remedies are required. The key is to foster locally embedded forms of economic activity such as worker cooperatives, small entrepreneurs, local markets, community development banks, and social and public enterprises.[10] Critical urban theory argues that the best way to diminish inequality is by diffusing ownership rather than by collecting taxes and distributing welfare benefits. Rather than increasing bureaucratic coordination across large territories, this approach is more oriented toward decentralization and localism. Instead of moving people to new places to achieve a better social mix, it aspires to help people flourish in their communities by building the capacity to fulfill their own needs.

In many ways, critical urban theory reassembles the proposals of the solidarists in belle epoque France. The solidarists were concerned about rising inequality and urban social problems, and they promoted worker cooperatives and local development banks as remedies. Today, new technology has opened up additional possibilities such as peer-to-peer exchange, collaboration based on open-source platforms, re-localized production, and crowd-sourcing.[11] Like the solidarists a century earlier, Hardt and Negri and their followers see these as positive developments because they can bring together freedom and sociability.[12] I agree that alternative forms of production and exchange (social enterprise, open-source collaboration, worker cooperatives, cooperative housing, etc.) should be fostered, both for their direct contribution to economic sustainability and for their indirect contribution to an ethos of solidarity. These are practices that help us understand ourselves as citizens working together to solve shared problems—or as individuals building on the innovations of others to create and share something new—rather than as consumers or clients.

Unlike Hardt and Negri, however, I am not optimistic that "biopolitical" production is poised to replace capitalist enterprise. Hardt and Negri don't offer any evidence in favor of this claim and there is considerable reason to doubt it. It rests on the assumption that capital is no longer a source of economic and political power, and therefore they mistakenly conclude that it is possible to surpass capitalism without actually dispersing the ownership of capital.

Similarly, the local economic development promoted by critical urban theory is a good idea but only a partial solution. In areas that are suffering from extreme dis-investment, it may be the best option available, and in more prosperous areas, such initiatives still are important since they diversify the economic base, strengthen the local economy, stabilize employment cycles, and foster a political culture of solidarity. While the goal is to transform the structure of capital, in practice this involves encouraging alternative economies to fill the gaps created by the dominant modes of production and exchange, and this leaves much of the power of capital intact. Self-help and local economic development can mitigate some of the effects of structural inequality, but their real power is their ability to diffuse a more solidaristic ethos and create a political constituency that mobilizes in favor of solidarist policies.

The updated solidarism promoted in this book incorporates both state-directed and more capillary forms of solidarity. The state is the institution that can compel the repayment of social debt through the partial reallocation of social property. This could be achieved through wage earner funds, de-commodification of public goods, or a minimum income. These are all mechanisms that give everyone a share in the resources derived from capital. This would also enhance freedom by increasing choice about how to allocate one's labor. Some people would choose full-time work in highly productive corporations and others would spend more time on care work, research, creative pursuits, sports, leisure, social enterprise, or craft production.

In *Social Justice and the City*, David Harvey criticized reformist approaches to urban inequality, noting that liberal anti-poverty programs had no effect on the distribution of income. Recent research, however, has challenged the view that public policies have little effect on poverty and inequality. Thomas Piketty showed that pretax income inequality is increasing in all developed countries but that the level of inequality after taxes and transfers varies dramatically.[13] This reflects the use of social and tax policy to reshape the distribution of income. Public policies can also have an impact on pre–"tax-and-transfer" distribution of income by facilitating or preventing the ability of labor unions to bargain with capital.[14]

This brings me to the second criticism, which asks whether normative theorizing is an effective political tool in the struggle for a just city. In his paper on the failed attempt to expand public transit in Richmond, Virginia, Williamson admits that Machiavellian tactics may be the only way to challenge powerful interests. He concludes that local politics is not an ideal speech situation, but a street fight in which victory goes to the powerful, cunning, or audacious. A stronger version of this argument is that Kantian concepts are detrimental to the struggle for local justice, because they rely on and reinforce a misleading understanding of politics. Normative theory depicts opponents as people who have made errors of moral reasoning rather than as adversaries pursuing incompatible goals. Normative theory may actually be counterproductive if it means that activists are unable or unwilling to use all of the tools necessary to win a street fight.

Following Hans Sluga, I have treated normative theory as a component of practical political judgment.[15] This book has drawn on normative theory as a diagnostic tool. Sluga describes the diagnostic approach as one that attends to concrete situations and develops specific inferences for action from the resulting insights.[16] The arguments about the right to the city and the wrong of dispossession are always connected to an analysis of the forms for struggle that have advanced local justice. These struggles have been fought through public reason and rhetoric but also through action, in plazas and parks, and even on the marshy riverbanks where people have literally materialized their claim to the city using concrete, sand, and stone.[17] This book examines the meaning of local justice as well as the forms of deliberation, dissent, and disobedience necessary to defend it.

Local justice is the inverse of global justice; instead of asking what we owe to distant others,[18] local justice forces us to consider what we owe to those closest to us. Spatial analysis is powerful tool of critical theory because it brings the abstract and concrete together. An abstract right to housing is actually quite easy to endorse, at least when it means that homeless people will be given shelter somewhere else. A homeless shelter in one's neighborhood is something very different because the "others" are no longer distant. In contemporary political theory, justice in nation-states[19] and then global justice[20] have been the dominant scales of inquiry. The concept of global justice expands the extent of political and moral obligation and highlights global inequalities, but it does so in a way that rests on and reinforces the distance between the moral agent and object of concern.[21] It is relatively easy to affirm an obligation to distant others when this obligation entails something like support for a tax on global resource extraction.[22] It is very different when it requires living in proximity to a public housing project or a busy bus station. In these latter cases, there is a strong experiential and subjective dimension and it is precisely this visceral dimension that abstraction cannot take into account. This blindness is both the strength and weakness of abstract theory. It is a strength when it functions as a tool that we can use to subject our intuitions to critique and examination. It is a problem when theoretical conviction comes to function as a substitute for praxis. This happens when the affective attachment to ideals seems so real—and so significant to our identity—that it makes practice seem less relevant.

It is beyond the scope of this book—and perhaps any book—to prove that arguments about justice have an effect on political outcomes, yet I think they do matter. A strong sense of right is a part of political mobilization. Any individual who is simply pursuing his or her self-interest is unlikely to become involved in political struggle; the risk of failure is usually large, and the costs of participation are high compared to the personal benefits that are secured. There must be some extra nugget of enjoyment to motivate participation, either the pleasure of principle or enjoyment of the struggle itself. Affect and principle are linked: a sense of justice is a way of securing attachment to the political project.

Examining justice in particular places and contexts is important because it enables what Slavoj Žižek calls a "parallax view." The parallax was a principle that astronomers used to measure distances from objects in space. By comparing the distance from two different points, they were able to estimate the position of the object. The method employed here is somewhat similar. It is not the obvious point that social phenomena appear different from different perspectives. Instead, by noting the distance between justice when examined up close, in cities and neighborhoods, and what it looks like from far away, we may gain a better understanding of the concept. What the parallax view of justice shows us is a divided self, which means that in a certain way Plato, the first theorist of both justice and the city, was right. We are appetitive and proud and capable of reason and these human characteristics are legible in the city, which is a place of conspicuous consumption and competition as well as a place of deliberation, solidarity, and creativity.[23] Segregated cities and regions are a way of ensuring that the divided self does not become a schizophrenic one. Exposure to difference is limited and controlled. This, of course, was the solution in *The Republic*: assign everyone to one task; separate groups and fix them in their appropriate place.[24] Yet this was never a plausible solution. If each person is divided, then spatial segregation will never be able to put people in their proper place. This analysis also means that there is no such thing as the just city, at least if this term is meant to describe a fully harmonious city, a place where there is no part that is excluded or uncounted.[25]

Even though there is no such thing as a just city, the pursuit of local justice is still important. While I have not defended a comprehensive theory of justice, I have explained how the solidarist approach and the concepts of rent, debt, and social property are diagnostic tools that help us see new solutions to struggles over urban space. Of course, these concepts could also be applied on the national and even global scale, but it is beyond the scope of the book to explore the insights—and challenges—that might result from expanding the scope of the theory. Limiting the scope in this way is consistent with the diagnostic, problem-driven approach of this book. In this book I chose to focus on displacement and dispossession in cities. I did so because access to housing and urban infrastructure is enormously important and because I felt that approaching these issues from the standpoint of justice and right could help. In everyday discourse, dispossession and exclusion are treated as unavoidable, indeed as natural features of urban life. When people have learned to see themselves as home-voters, it seems irrational to use urban infrastructure to dismantle rather than reinforce inequality. As a social imaginary, solidarism presents a way to see ourselves differently, as joint beneficiaries of a shared inheritance and trustees with fiduciary responsibility to others. The city is only part of this inheritance, but it is a part that helps us think about the whole.

I don't want to romanticize the city as a more diverse, pluralistic version of the communitarian idyll. It is not unusual for there to be struggles over how to share a bequest. In the city we are also compelled to struggle with both the pleasure and challenge of physical proximity. Solidarism was both an acknowledgment of the fact of interdependence and a judgment about its normative significance, notably the claim that a share of social value should secure the common good. Precisely what this means in practice cannot be determined through an algorithm, because it requires balancing, context-specific knowledge, and practical judgment. The theory of solidarism, however, is intended to provide some guidance. By denaturalizing private property, we see that untapped financial resources are available, which in turn makes new solutions to urban problems imaginable. The city, however, is not just a problem to be solved. It is also a place where solidarity and plurality are lived and materialized.

NOTES

Chapter 1

1. "Toronto home prices surge as sales far outpace new listings," *Globe and Mail*, March 3, 2016. http://www.theglobeandmail.com/report-on-business/economy/housing/toronto-home-prices-surge-as-sales-far-outpace-new-listings/article29007589/, accessed April 9, 2016.

2. Alex Alsup, "Detroit Foreclosure Auction: All the Basics You Need to Know Before You Bid on Property," *Huffington Post* (2013). http://www.huffingtonpost.com/2013/08/09/detroit-foreclosure-auction-wayne-county-properties_n_3726834.html.

3. See Michael J. Sandel, *What Money Can't Buy: The Moral Limits of Markets* (New York: Farrar, Straus and Giroux, 2013).

4. Following Edward Soja, I treat urban life as something "nested within many geographical contexts above and below the administrative space of the city itself." Edward W. Soja, *Seeking Spatial Justice* (Minneapolis: University of Minnesota Press, 2010).

5. Susan S. Fainstein, *The Just City* (Ithaca, NY: Cornell University Press, 2011); Soja, *Seeking Spatial Justice*.

6. John R. Logan and Harvey L. Molotch, *Urban Fortunes: The Political Economy of Place* (Berkeley: University of California Press, 2007).

7. Peter Dreier, John Mollenkopf, and Todd Swanstrom, *Place Matters: Metropolitics for the Twenty-First Century*, 3rd ed. (Lawrence: University Press of Kansas, 2014).

8. Don Mitchell, *The Right to the City: Social Justice and the Fight for Public Space* (New York: Guilford Press, 2003).

9. My approach builds on the influential work of Nicholas K. Blomley in *Unsettling the City: Urban Land and the Politics of Property* (New York: Routledge, 2004) and justifies "entitlements not easily captured by ownership" (37). It also seeks to provide a more detailed account of what Peter Marcuse called "commons planning." See Peter Marcuse, "From Justice Planning to Commons Planning," in *Searching for the Just City: Debates in Urban Theory and Practice*, ed. Peter Marcuse et al. (London: Routledge, 2009), 91–102.

10. There is also an emerging literature in Italian on "la città come bene comune": the city as common good. Edoardo Salzano defines the city as the home of the community. See Edoardo Salzano, "La città come bene comune: Costruire il futuro partendo dalla storia," *Historia Magistra*, 2012; Chiara Belingardi, "Città bene comune e diritto alla città," paper presented at the conference Abitare di Nuovo, Naples, 2012. http://www.researchgate.net/profile/Chiara_ Belingardi/publication/273137347_Citt_Bene_Comune_e_Diritto_alla_ Citt/links/54f980170cf2ccffe9e152ce.pdf.

11. For a particularly nuanced and comprehensive discussion of the relationship between democracy and the urban, see Mark Purcell, *Recapturing Democracy: Neoliberalization and the Struggle for Alternative Urban Futures* (New York: Routledge, 2008).

12. Neil Smith, *The New Urban Frontier: Gentrification and the Revanchist City* (London: Routledge, 1996); David Harvey, *Social Justice and the City*, rev. ed. (Athens: University of Georgia Press, 2009).

13. See Harvey, *Social Justice and the City*, 153–194.

14. Sam Roberts, "More Apartments Are Empty yet Rented or Owned, Census Finds," *New York Times* (July 6, 2011, sec. N.Y./Region). http://www.nytimes. com/2011/07/07/nyregion/more-apartments-are-empty-yet-rented-or- owned-census-finds.html.

15. This does not mean that investment and profit play no role in individual decisions. Canada does not allow homeowners to deduct mortgage interest payments from taxes, but it does exempt the profit on the sale of a primary residence from capital gains taxes. This is basically a way of subsidizing homeowners, who have higher incomes than renters, and it is an incentive to purchase a large house that is a home/investment package. See David Hulchanski, "A Tale of Two Canadas: Homeowners Getting Richer, Renters Getting Poorer," *Centre for Urban and Community Studies Research Bulletin* (2001). http:// www.urbancentre.utoronto.ca/pdfs/researchbulletins/02.pdf. Even though "exchange value" does play an important secondary role, I argue it is misleading to approach the issue exclusively from this perspective because it oversimplifies a complex issue.

16. Joseph Gyourko, Christopher Mayer, and Todd Sinai, "Superstar Cities," National Bureau of Economic Research (2006). http://www.nber.org/papers/ w12355.

17. See also Thad Williamson, David Imbroscio, and Gar Alperovitz, *Making a Place for Community: Local Democracy in a Global Era* (New York: Routledge, 2003); Martin O'Neill and Thad Williamson, *Property-Owning Democracy: Rawls and Beyond* (Malden, MA: Wiley-Blackwell, 2012).
18. Charles Taylor, "Modern Social Imaginaries," *Public Culture* 14, no. 1 (2002): 91–124.
19. Margaret Kohn, *Brave New Neighborhoods: The Privatization of Public Space* (London: Routledge, 2004).
20. Blomley, *Unsettling the City*; Nicholas K. Blomley, "Enclosure, Common Right and the Property of the Poor," *Social & Legal Studies* 17, no. 3 (2008): 311–331.
21. Shishir Mathur, *Innovation in Public Transport Finance: Property Value Capture* (Burlington, VT: Ashgate Publishing, 2014); Martim O. Smolka, *Implementing Value Capture in Latin America* (Cambridge, MA: Lincoln Institute of Land Policy, 2013).
22. Richard Delgado, "On Telling Stories in School: A Reply to Farber and Sherry," *Vanderbilt Law Review* 46 (1993): 665–676; Patricia J. Williams, "Alchemical Notes: Reconstructing Ideals from Deconstructed Rights," *Harvard Civil Rights–Civil Liberties Law Review* 22 (1987): 401–434.
23. Cécile Fabre, *Social Rights under the Constitution: Government and the Decent Life* (Oxford: Oxford University Press, 2000); Thomas Humphrey Marshall, *Citizenship and Social Class* (London: Pluto Press, 1992).
24. *Olga Tellis v. Bombay Municipal Corporation*, AIR 1986 SC 180.
25. Thad Williamson, "Mobility and Its Opponents: Richmond, Virginia's Refusal to Embrace Mass Transit," paper presented at the Urban Affairs Association meeting, April 2013.
26. Hannah Arendt and Jonathan Schell, *On Revolution* (New York: Penguin, 2006).
27. Jane Mansbridge, "Using Power/Fighting Power," *Constellations* 1, no. 1 (1994): 53–73.
28. On the symbolic dimension of gated communities, see Setha Low, *Behind the Gates: Life, Security, and the Pursuit of Happiness in Fortress America* (London: Routledge, 2004).
29. Stuart Hodkinson, "The New Urban Enclosures," *City* 16, no. 5 (2012): 500–518.
30. Thomas Piketty, *Capital in the Twenty-First Century* (Cambridge, MA: Harvard University Press, 2014).

Chapter 2

1. For a thorough and compelling account of the theory that underpins this claim, see Gar Alperovitz and Lew Daly, *Unjust Deserts: How the Rich Are Taking Our Common Inheritance* (New York: New Press, 2008).

2. Wendy Brown, "American Nightmare: Neoliberalism, Neoconservatism, and De-Democratization," *Political Theory* 34, no. 6 (2006): 690–714; George Lakoff, *Moral Politics: How Liberals and Conservatives Think* (Chicago: University of Chicago Press, 2002); Corey Robin, *The Reactionary Mind: Conservatism from Edmund Burke to Sarah Palin* (New York: Oxford University Press, 2011).

3. Jonas Pontusson, "Once Again a Model," in *What's Left of the Left*, ed. James E. Cronin, George W. Ross, and James Shoch (Durham, NC: Duke University Press, 2011), 89–115; Peter J. Katzenstein, *Small States in World Markets: Industrial Policy in Europe* (Ithaca, NY: Cornell University Press, 1985); Gøsta Esping-Andersen, *The Three Worlds of Welfare Capitalism* (Princeton, NJ: Princeton University Press, 1990).

4. Joseph M. Schwartz, *The Future of Democratic Equality: Rebuilding Social Solidarity in a Fragmented America* (London: Routledge, 2008); Thomas Piketty, *Capital in the Twenty-First Century* (Cambridge, MA: Harvard University Press, 2014); G. A. Cohen, *Rescuing Justice and Equality* (Cambridge, MA: Harvard University Press, 2009).

5. Tom Malleson, "Rawls, Property-Owning Democracy, and Democratic Socialism," *Journal of Social Philosophy* 45, no. 2 (2014): 228–251; Martin O'Neill and Thad Williamson, eds., *Property-Owning Democracy: Rawls and Beyond* (Malden, MA: Wiley-Blackwell, 2012).

6. Thomas Humphrey Marshall, *Citizenship and Social Class* (London: Pluto Press, 1992).

7. Marie-Claude Blais, *La solidarité: Histoire d'une idée* (Paris: Gallimard, 2007).

8. A similar set of arguments circulated in England and the United States in the 19th century. Drawing on Ricardo's theory of rent, John Stuart Mill argued that land should not be private property and Henry George advanced the claim that unearned increases of value should be allocated to the public rather than distributed as private property. See Alperovitz and Daly, *Unjust Deserts*, 109–125.

9. Thomas Paine and Nancy J. Altman, *Agrarian Justice: With a New Foreword, "Social Security, Thomas Paine, and the Spirit of America"* (CreateSpace Independent Publishing Platform, 2015).

10. Edwin Morley-Fletcher, "Vouchers and Personal Welfare Accounts," paper presented at 9th B.I.E.N International Congress (2002), 48.

11. For an overview, see Walter Van Trier, "Who Framed Social Dividend?," USBIG discussion paper no. 26 (March 2002).

12. Philippe Van Parijs, "Basic Income: A Simple and Powerful Idea for the Twenty-First Century," *Politics & Society* 32, no. 1 (2004): 7–39; Philippe Van Parijs, "Competing Justifications of Basic Income," in *Arguing for Basic Income: Ethical Foundations for a Radical Reform* (London: Verso: 1992), 1–43; Philippe Van Parijs, "Why Surfers Should Be Fed: The Liberal Case for an Unconditional Basic Income," *Philosophy & Public Affairs* 20, no. 2 (1991): 101–131; Philippe Van Parijs, "The Second Marriage of Justice and Efficiency," *Journal of Social Policy* 19, no. 1 (1990): 1–25.

NOTES

13. Van Parijs, "Why Surfers Should Be Fed."
14. Van Parijs, "Why Surfers Should Be Fed," 113.
15. Richard G. Lipsey and Kelvin Lancaster, "The General Theory of Second Best," *Review of Economic Studies* 24, no. 1 (1956): 11–32.
16. Michael Walzer, *Spheres of Justice: A Defense of Pluralism and Equality* (New York: Basic Books, 1984).
17. John R. Logan and Harvey L. Molotch, *Urban Fortunes: The Political Economy of Place* (Berkeley: University of California Press, 2007).
18. On republicanism in political theory, see Maurizio Viroli, *Republicanism*, trans. Antony Shugaar (New York: Hill and Wang, 2001); Philip Pettit, *Republicanism: A Theory of Freedom and Government* (Oxford: Oxford University Press, 1999); Cécile Laborde and John Maynor, *Republicanism and Political Theory* (Toronto: Wiley, 2009).
19. The last major article on solidarism in English was published in 1961 (Jack Ernest S. Hayward, "The Official Social Philosophy of the French Third Republic: Léon Bourgeois and Solidarism," *International Review of Social History* 6, no. 1 (1961): 19–48.) In his influential book *Solidarity* (Cambridge, MA: MIT Press, 2005), Hauke Brunkhorst does not mention Léon Bourgeois or solidarism. There are a few exceptions. There are brief discussions of solidarism in Michael Freeden, *Ideologies and Political Theory: A Conceptual Approach* (New York: Oxford University Press, 1998), and Terence Ball and Richard Bellamy, eds., *The Cambridge History of Twentieth-Century Political Thought* (Cambridge: Cambridge University Press, 2006).
20. Cited in Andreas Wildt, "Solidarität," *Historisches Worterbuch der Philosophie*, band 9 (Basel: Schwabe, 1995), 1005.
21. Hayward, "The Official Social Philosophy of the French Third Republic," 26.
22. Alfred Fouillée, *La propriété sociale et la Démocratie* (Paris: Hachette, 1884).
23. Fouillée, *La propriété sociale*, 14.
24. Fouillée, *La propriété sociale*, 16.
25. Fouillée, *La propriété sociale*, 17.
26. John Locke, *Locke: Two Treatises of Government*, ed. Peter Laslett, 3rd ed. (New York: Cambridge University Press, 1988); C. B. Macpherson, *The Political Theory of Possessive Individualism: Hobbes to Locke* (Don Mills, ON: Oxford University Press, 2011).
27. Barbara Arneil, *John Locke and America: The Defence of English Colonialism* (Oxford: Oxford University Press, 1996).
28. Fouillée, *La propriété sociale*, 18.
29. Samuel Fleischacker, *A Short History of Distributive Justice* (Cambridge, MA: Harvard University Press, 2005).
30. Herbert Spencer, *Spencer: Political Writings*, ed. John Offer (New York: Cambridge University Press, 1993); Richard Hofstadter, *Social Darwinism in American Thought*, reprint ed. (Boston: Beacon Press, 1992).

31. Jeremy Waldron, *God, Locke, and Equality: Christian Foundations in Locke's Political Thought* (New York: Cambridge University Press, 2002).
32. Fouillée, *La propriété sociale.*
33. David Harvey, *The New Imperialism* (Oxford: Oxford University Press, 2005).
34. Jeremy Waldron, "Two Worries about Mixing One's Labour," *Philosophical Quarterly* 33, no. 103 (1983): 37–44; Robert Nozick, *Anarchy, State, and Utopia* (New York: Basic Books, 1975).
35. Hofstadter, *Social Darwinism in American Thought.*
36. For a fuller discussion see Blais, *La solidarité.*
37. Hayward, "The Official Social Philosophy of the French Third Republic."
38. Émile Durkheim, *De la division du travail social: Étude sur l'organisation des sociétés supérieures* (Paris: Presses Universitaires de France, 1893).
39. For a more contemporary version of this argument, see Robert E. Goodin, "Vulnerabilities and Responsibilities: An Ethical Defense of the Welfare State," *American Political Science Review* 79, no. 3 (1985): 775–787.
40. Léon Bourgeois, *Solidarité* (Paris: Hachette Livre BnF, 2013).
41. Bourgeois, *Solidarité.*
42. Charles Gide and Charles Rist, *A History of Economic Doctrines from the Time of the Physiocrats to the Present Day,* trans. R. Richards (London: George Harrap, 1915), 552.
43. Gide and Rist, *Economic Doctrines,* 553.
44. Fouillée makes a similar argument in *La propriété sociale,* 20–22. He notes the higher value of agricultural land located in proximity to public infrastructure such as railroads and argues that this reflects the value of the social component.
45. Gide and Rist, *Economic Doctrines,* 569.
46. On the concept of desert in contemporary moral philosophy, see Richard J. Arneson, "Desert and Equality," in *Egalitarianism: New Essays on the Nature and Value of Equality,* ed. Nils Holtug and Kasper Lippert-Rasmussen (Oxford: Oxford University Press, 2007), 262–293; Robert Young, "Egalitarianism and Personal Desert," *Ethics* 102 (1992): 319–341.
47. The city is just one dimension of the common-wealth. Culture, technology, knowledge, and language are a shared inheritance too. Copyright principles such as fair use and limited duration reflect the idea that intellectual products too have both a private and a social dimension. The degree and kind of regulation will depend on which dimension is more vulnerable under existing circumstances. Since it is impossible to determine one's individual contribution to the cultural common-wealth, it makes sense to think of the needs of producers, the public, and the cultural domain as a whole. For example, in a society with a generous minimum income basic needs are provided for; therefore it is less important to ensure that independent cultural producers can effectively commodify their products. I also think that there is a strong case that intellectual products that are already subsidized by the government (e.g., research and technology

developed in public universities or supported by government grants) should be freely accessible and open source, since the producer has already been compensated through a salary.

48. On luck egalitarianism, see G. A. Cohen, *Rescuing Justice and Equality* (Cambridge, MA: Harvard University Press, 2009).

49. Bourgeois, *Solidarité*.

50. John Rawls, *A Theory of Justice* (Cambridge, MA: Harvard University Press, 2009).

51. David Robichaud and Patrick Turmel, *La juste part: Repenser les inégalités, la richesse et la fabrication des grille-pains* (Montreal: Atelier 10, 2012).

52. Jason Hackworth, *The Neoliberal City: Governance, Ideology, and Development in American Urbanism* (Ithaca, NY: Cornell University Press, 2006).

53. In 2013, the budget for HUD was just over $40 billion. The cost of the mortgage interest deduction is estimated to be around $70 billion. See Will Fischer and Chye-Ching Huang, "Mortgage Interest Deduction Is Ripe for Reform," Centre on Budget and Policy Priorities Report, Rev. June 25, 2013.

54. Shishir Mathur, *Innovation in Public Transport Finance: Property Value Capture* (Burlington, VT: Ashgate, 2014); Martim O. Smolka, *Implementing Value Capture in Latin America: Policies and Tools for Urban Development* (Cambridge, MA: Lincoln Institute of Land Policy, 2013).

55. Gide and Rist, *Economic Doctrines*, 567.

56. For some exceptions to the generalization, see Alperovitz and Daly, *Unjust Deserts*.

57. Giorgio Agamben, *Homo Sacer: Sovereign Power and Bare Life* (Stanford, CA: Stanford University Press, 1998).

58. This phrase comes from Mitt Romney's famous speech identifying the 47 percent of Americans who don't pay federal income tax as "takers." The majority of those people (61 percent) work and pay payroll taxes and a large minority (22 percent) are elderly and living on a low fixed income and savings. Romney fails to consider that the wealthy are paying the majority of federal income taxes because they themselves are the "takers," the ones who have taken a disproportionate share of the wealth produced collectively through the division of labor. See Ezra Klein, "Romney's Theory of the 'Taker Class,' and Why It Matters," *Washington Post*, September 17, 2012, http://www.washingtonpost.com/blogs/wonkblog/wp/2012/09/17/romneys-theory-of-the-taker-class-and-why-it-matters/.

59. Richard A. Epstein, *Takings* (Cambridge, MA: Harvard University Press, 1985).

Chapter 3

1. For an overview of the scale of slums, see Mike Davis, "Planet of Slums," *New Left Review* 28 (2003): 5–34; Mike Davis, *Planet of Slums* (London: Verso, 2007); M. Rahman, "India's Slumdog Census Reveals Poor Conditions for

One in Six Urban Dwellers," *Guardian,* March 22, 2013. http://www.theguard
ian.com/world/2013/mar/22/india-slumdog-census-poor-conditions.

2. *Olga Tellis v. Bombay Municipal Corporation,* AIR 1986 SC 180. For an example
   of this way of characterizing the decision, see Samuel D. Permutt, "Manual
   Scavenging Problem: A Case for the Supreme Court of India," *Cardozo Journal
   of International and Comparative Law* 20 (2011): 277.

3. For example, see below for a discussion of *Pitampura Sudhar Samiti
   v. Government of National Capital Territory of Delhi,* CWP 4215/1995;
   Balakrishnan Rajagopal, "Pro–Human Rights but Anti-Poor? A Critical
   Evaluation of the Indian Supreme Court from a Social Movement Perspective,"
   Human Rights Review 8, no. 3 (2007): 157–186.

4. Gautam Bhan, "'This Is No Longer the City I Once Knew': Evictions, the
   Urban Poor and the Right to the City in Millennial Delhi," *Environment
   and Urbanization* 21, no. 1 (2009): 127–142; *Pitampura Sudhar Samiti
   v. Government of National Capital Territory of Delhi,* CWP 4215/1995.

5. *Olga Tellis v. Bombay Municipal Corporation,* AIR 1986 SC 180.

6. UN-Habitat, "The Right to Adequate Housing." http://www.ohchr.org/
   Documents/Publications/FS21_rev_1_Housing_en.pdf; accessed February
   2015.

7. Arjun Appadurai, "Spectral Housing and Urban Cleansing: Notes on Millennial
   Mumbai," *Public Culture* 12, no. 3 (2000): 627–651.

8. Prashant Bhushan, "Misplaced Priorities and Class Bias of the Judiciary," *Economic
   and Political Weekly* 44, no. 14 (2009): 32–37; Oliver Mendelsohn, "The Supreme
   Court as the Most Trusted Public Institution in India," *South Asia: Journal of South
   Asian Studies* 23, supp. 1 (2000): 103–119. According to Mendelsohn, ". . . no case
   illustrates the extraordinary change in the stance of the Supreme Court during the
   early period of Public Interest Litigation than *Olga Tellis.* Acceptance by the Court
   of the proposition that there was a fundamental Constitutional right to squat on
   the pavements of Bombay was nothing less than stunning," 111.

9. According to Balakrishnan Rajagopal, the constitutional amendment that
   removed the right to private property's status as a fundamental right actually
   undermined the ability of petitioners to claim a right to housing. See Rajagopal,
   "Pro–Human Rights but Anti-Poor?"

10. Courtney Jung and Evan Rosevear, *Economic and Social Rights across Time,
    Regions, and Legal Traditions: A Preliminary Analysis of the TIESR Dataset,*
    SSRN Scholarly Paper (Rochester, NY: Social Science Research Network,
    March 4, 2013).

11. Isaiah Berlin, "Two Concepts of Liberty," in *Four Essays on Liberty,* by Isaiah
    Berlin (New York: Oxford University Press, 1969), 118–172; Ran Hirschl,
    "'Negative' Rights vs. 'Positive' Entitlements: A Comparative Study of Judicial
    Interpretations of Rights in an Emerging Neo-liberal Economic Order," *Human
    Rights Quarterly* 22, no. 4 (2000): 1060–1098; Charles Taylor, "What's Wrong

with Negative Liberty," in *The Idea of Liberty*, ed. Alan Ryan (Oxford: Oxford University Press, 1979), 175–194.

12. Ronald Dworkin, *Taking Rights Seriously* (Cambridge, MA: Harvard University Press, 1978).

13. *Olga Tellis v. Bombay Municipal Corporation*, AIR 1986 SC 180.

14. *Olga Tellis v. Bombay Municipal Corporation*, AIR 1986 SC 180.

15. This case came at the end of a period in which the ISC began to play a new role in addressing social issues. They did so by allowing public interest litigation or what Upendra Baxi has described as social action litigation. By expanding standing to allow new petitioners, including journalists and activists, and expanding jurisdiction to consider new issues, the Court created a new venue for considering and publicizing the concerns of subaltern citizens. Upendra Baxi, "Taking Suffering Seriously: Social Action Litigation in the Supreme Court of India," *Third World Legal Studies* 4 (1985): 107–132. See also Jamie Cassels, "Judicial Activism and Public Interest Litigation in India: Attempting the Impossible?," *American Journal of Comparative Law* 37 (1989): 495–519.

16. Government of India, Ministry of Law and Justice, *The Constitution of India*, 2011. http://lawmin.nic.in/olwing/coi/coi-english/Const.Pock%202Pg.Rom8 Fsss%287%29.pdf, accessed February 2015.

17. Namita Wahi, "State, Private Property and the Supreme Court," *Frontline Magazine* 29, no. 19 (2012); Namita Wahi, "The Tension between Property Rights and Social and Economic Rights: A Case Study of India," in *Social and Economic Rights in Theory and Practice*, ed. Helena Alviar et al. (London: Routledge, 2014): 138–157.

18. John Locke, *Second Treatise of Government*, ed. C. B. Macpherson (Indianapolis: Hackett, 1980).

19. Locke, *Second Treatise of Government*, par. 28–31.

20. Locke, *Second Treatise of Government*, par. 33.

21. Locke, *Second Treatise of Government*, par. 41.

22. James Harrington, *Harrington: The Commonwealth of Oceana and A System of Politics*, ed. J. G. A. Pocock (Cambridge: Cambridge University Press, 1992); Geoff Kennedy, *Diggers, Levellers, and Agrarian Capitalism: Radical Political Thought in 17th Century England* (Lanham, MD: Lexington Books, 2008); Gerrard Winstanley, *"The True Levellers' Standard Advanced," "The Law of Freedom" and Other Writings*, ed. Will Jonson (CreateSpace Independent Publishing Platform, 2014).

23. Locke, *Second Treatise of Government*, par 38.

24. Locke, *Second Treatise of Government*, par 35.

25. Locke, *Second Treatise of Government*, par. 87.

26. Richard Ashcraft, *Revolutionary Politics and Locke's* Two Treatises of Government (Princeton, NJ: Princeton University Press, 1986).

27. James Tully, *A Discourse on Property: John Locke and His Adversaries* (Cambridge: Cambridge University Press, 1983), 113.
28. Giorgio Agamben, *Homo Sacer: Sovereign Power and Bare Life* (Stanford, CA: Stanford University Press, 1998).
29. Rajagopal, "Pro-Human Rights but Anti-Poor?"
30. *Pitam Pura Sudhar Samiti v. Union of India* (2002), I.L.R. 2 (Del.) 393, ¶ 1 (Delhi H.C.).
31. *Almitra H. Patel and Anr. v. Union of India* (2000), 3 SCC 575 b. According to Justice Kirpal, "the department of slum clearance does not seem to have cleared any slum despite it's being in existence for decades. In fact more and more slums are coming into existence. Instead of 'Slum Clearance' there is 'Slum Creation' in Delhi. This in turn gives rise to domestic waste being strewn on open land in and around the slums. This can best be controlled at least, in the first instance, by preventing the growth of slums."
32. *Pitam Pura Sudhar Samiti v. Union of India* (2002), I.L.R. 2 (Del.) 393, ¶ 1 (Delhi H.C.).
33. *Pitam Pura Sudhar Samiti v. Union of India* (2002), I.L.R. 2 (Del.) 393, ¶ 1 (Delhi H.C.).
34. Charles Taylor, "Modern Social Imaginaries," *Public Culture* 14, no. 1 (2002): 91–124.
35. Srijit Mishra, "Risks, Farmers' Suicides and Agrarian Crisis in India: Is There a Way Out?," *Indian Journal of Agricultural Economics* 63, no. 1 (2008): 38–54; Ashok Vikhe Patil, K. V. Somasundaram, and R. C. Goyal, "Current Health Scenario in Rural India," *Australian Journal of Rural Health* 10, no. 2 (2002): 129–135.
36. Bhan, "This Is No Longer the City I Once Knew."
37. Bhan, "This Is No Longer the City I Once Knew."
38. James Holston, *The Modernist City: An Anthropological Critique of Brasilia* (Chicago: University of Chicago Press, 1989).
39. *Olga Tellis v. Bombay Municipal Corporation*, AIR 1986 SC 180.
40. *Olga Tellis v. Bombay Municipal Corporation*, AIR 1986 SC 180.
41. David Miller, *Principles of Social Justice* (Cambridge, MA: Harvard University Press, 1999).
42. Liam Murphy and Thomas Nagel, *The Myth of Ownership: Taxes and Justice* (Oxford: Oxford University Press, 2002).
43. Lloyd I. Rudolph and Suzanne H. Rudolph, *In Pursuit of Lakshmi: The Political Economy of the Indian State* (Chicago: University of Chicago Press, 1987); Atul Kohli, *Democracy and Discontent: India's Growing Crisis of Governability* (Cambridge: Cambridge University Press, 1990).
44. Rudolph and Rudolph, *In Pursuit of Lakshmi*, 33.
45. Jeffrey Evans Stake, "The Uneasy Case for Adverse Possession," *Georgetown Law Journal* 89, no. 8 (2000): 2419–2474.

46. Eduardo M. Peñalver and Sonia Katyal, *Property Outlaws: How Squatters, Pirates, and Protesters Improve the Law of Ownership* (New Haven, CT: Yale University Press, 2010).

47. On the debate about self-ownership, see Michael Otsuka, *Libertarianism without Inequality* (Oxford: Oxford University Press, 2003); Michael Otsuka, "Self-Ownership and Equality: A Lockean Reconciliation," *Philosophy & Public Affairs* 27, no. 1 (1998): 65–92; G. A. Cohen, *Self-Ownership, Freedom, and Equality* (Cambridge: Cambridge University Press, 1995).

48. See also Greogry S. Alexander et al., "A Statement of Progressive Property," *Cornell Law Review* 94, no. 4 (2008): 743–744; Robin Paul Malloy and Michael Diamond, *The Public Nature of Private Property* (Burlington, VT: Ashgate, 2011).

49. Peñalver and Katyal, *Property Outlaws*.

50. Jacob S. Hacker and Paul Pierson, *Winner-Take-All Politics: How Washington Made the Rich Richer—and Turned Its Back on the Middle Class* (New York: Simon and Schuster, 2011); Benjamin I. Page, Larry M. Bartels, and Jason Seawright, "Democracy and the Policy Preferences of Wealthy Americans," *Perspectives on Politics* 11, no. 1 (2013): 51–73; Mark E. Warren, "Citizen Participation and Democratic Deficits: Considerations from the Perspective of Democratic Theory," in *Activating the Citizen: Dilemmas of Participation in Europe and Canada*, ed. Joan DeBardeleban and Jon Pammet (London: Palgrave Macmillan, 2009), 17–40.

51. David Harvey, *Social Justice and the City* (Athens: University of Georgia Press, 2010), 79.

52. William E. Scheuerman, "Whistleblowing as Civil Disobedience: The Case of Edward Snowden," *Philosophy & Social Criticism* 40, no. 7 (2014): 609–628.

53. Sidney Verba and Norman H. Nie, *Participation in America: Political Democracy and Social Equality* (Chicago: University of Chicago Press, 1987).

54. Abhijit Banerjee and Rohini Somanathan, "The Political Economy of Public Goods: Some Evidence from India," *Journal of Development Economics* 82, no. 2 (2007): 287–314.

55. Ashok Swain, *Struggle against the State: Social Network and Protest Mobilization in India* (Farnham, UK: Ashgate, 2013).

56. Peñalver and Katyal, *Property Outlaws*.

57. This doesn't address the problem of criminal gangs who extort rent from pavement and shack dwellers. Here the fault seems to fall on the state for failing to enforce the law. That criminal gangs illegally extort rent does not invalidate the residents' right to housing.

58. *Modderklip Boerdery (Pty) Ltd v. Modder East Squatters and another*, 2001 (4) SA 385. See also *President of the Republic of South Africa and Anor. v. Modderklip Boerdery*, (Pty) Ltd 40 2005 (5) SA 3 (CC).

59. Peter Dreier, John Mollenkopf, and Todd Swanstrom, *Place Matters: Metropolitics for the Twenty-First Century* (Lawrence: University Press of Kansas, 2014).

Chapter 4

1. Alexis de Tocqueville, *Democracy in America and Two Essays on America*, ed. Isaac Kramnick and trans. Gerald Bevan (London: Penguin, 2003), 380.
2. Tocqueville, *Democracy in America*, 379.
3. Burke A. Hendrix, *Ownership, Authority, and Self-Determination* (University Park: Penn State University Press, 2008); James Tully, "The Struggles of Indigenous Peoples for and of Freedom," in *Political Theory and the Rights of Indigenous Peoples*, ed. Duncan Ivison and Paul Patton (Cambridge: Cambridge University Press, 2000), 36–59; Robert A. Williams Jr., *The American Indian in Western Legal Thought: The Discourses of Conquest* (Oxford: Oxford University Press, 1990); Carole Pateman and Charles Mills, *The Contract and Domination* (Cambridge: Polity Press, 2007); Dale Antony Turner, *This Is Not a Peace Pipe: Towards a Critical Indigenous Philosophy* (Toronto: University of Toronto Press, 2006). Glen Coulthard, *Red Skin, White Masks: Rejecting the Colonial Politics of Recognition* (Minneapolis: Univ of Minnesota Press, 2014).
4. There are important exceptions to this claim, especially in the literature in urban studies. See for example Mindy Fullilove, *Root Shock: How Tearing Up City Neighborhoods Hurts America, and What We Can Do about It* (New York: Random House, 2009).
5. Anna Stilz, "Occupancy Rights and the Wrong of Removal," *Philosophy & Public Affairs* 41, no. 4 (2013): 324–356; Margaret Moore, *A Political Theory of Territory* (Oxford: Oxford University Press, 2015).
6. Stilz, "Occupancy Rights and the Wrong of Removal."
7. Margaret Moore, "Which People and What Land? Territorial Right-Holders and Attachment to Territory," *International Theory* 6, no. 1 (2014): 121–140.
8. Stilz, "Occupancy Rights and the Wrong of Removal," 337.
9. Stilz, "Occupancy Rights and the Wrong of Removal," 338.
10. Moore, "Which People and What Land?"
11. Margaret Moore, "Place-Related Attachments and Global Distributive Justice," *Journal of Global Ethics* 9, no. 2 (2013): 215–226.
12. It is beyond the scope of this book to develop a theory of territorial rights. Territorial rights involve the relationship between a state, a people, and land, which adds an additional dimension of complexity. The right of occupancy is a theory developed to address the issue of internal colonialism and minority rights within a larger unit of government (state, federation, empire, etc.) On territorial rights see David Miller, "Territorial Rights: Concept and Justification," *Political Studies* 60, no. 2 (2012): 252–268; Anna Stilz, "Nations, States, and Territory," *Ethics* 121, no. 3 (2011): 572–601; Moore, *A Political Theory of Territory*.
13. Moore, "Which People and What Land?"
14. For an overview of different approaches inspired by Lefebvre's right to the city, see Stefan Kipfer, Parastou Saberi, and Thorben Wieditz, "Henri

Lefebvre: Debates and Controversies," *Progress in Human Geography* 37, no. 1 (2013): 115–130. My approach is most similar to the one Kipfer et al. describe as "social democratic" but, as will become clear in latter chapters, it also draws on dimensions of the "poetic and anarchist" side.

15. Arnold R. Hirsch, *Making the Second Ghetto: Race and Housing in Chicago 1940–1960* (Chicago: University of Chicago Press, 1998).

16. Brittany Scott, "Is Urban Policy Making Way for the Wealthy: How a Human Rights Approach Challenges the Purging of Poor Communities from US Cities," *Columbia Human Rights Law Review* 45 (2013): 863.

17. Ben Austen, "The Last Tower: The Decline and Fall of Public Housing," *Harper's*, May 2012. http://harpers.org/archive/2012/05/the-last-tower/.

18. Deirdre Oakley and Keri Burchfield, "Out of the Projects, Still in the Hood: The Spatial Constraints on Public-Housing Residents' Relocation in Chicago," *Journal of Urban Affairs* 31, no. 5 (2009): 589–614.

19. Lawrence J. Vale and Erin Graves, "The Chicago Housing Authority's Plan for Transformation: What Does the Research Show So Far?" Massachusetts Institute of Technology, Department of Urban Studies and Planning (2010), 10–11. http://www.macarthurfoundation.net/media/article_pdfs/valegraves_cha_pft_final-report.pdf. According to the CHA, as of 2010, 71.25 percent of the planned 25,000 units had been completed (Chicago Housing Authority, 2010). About half of the families with a "right of return" had either died, become incapacitated, lost eligibility, or lost contact with CHA.

20. Larry Bennett, *The Third City: Chicago and American Urbanism* (Chicago: University of Chicago Press, 2012), 175.

21. Danya E. Keene, Mark B. Padilla, and Arline T. Geronimus, "Leaving Chicago for Iowa's 'Fields of Opportunity': Community Dispossession, Rootlessness, and the Quest for Somewhere to 'Be OK,'" *Human Organization* 69, no. 3 (2010): 278.

22. Edward G. Goetz, "The Audacity of HOPE VI: Discourse and the Dismantling of Public Housing," *Cities* 35 (2012): 342–348; Edward G. Goetz, *New Deal Ruins: Race, Economic Justice, and Public Housing Policy* (Ithaca, NY: Cornell University Press, 2013).

23. This is from a scene in the documentary film *Cabrini Green: Mixing It Up*, by Ronit Bezalel.

24. On the relationship between identity, race, and place, see Clarissa Rile Hayward, *How Americans Make Race: Stories, Institutions, Spaces* (New York: Cambridge University Press, 2013).

25. This is based on interviews with residents featured in the documentary film *Voices of Cabrini*, by Ronit Bezalel.

26. Bonnie Honig, "The Politics of Public Things: Neoliberalism and the Routine of Privatization," *No Foundations: An Interdisciplinary Journal of Law and Justice* 10 (2013): 59.

27. Honig, "The Politics of Public Things."
28. In "Occupancy Rights and the Wrong of Removal," Stilz writes, "I don't deny that the Navajo removal was wrong in part because it featured compulsion. But I do deny that the wrong of compulsion captures all that is problematic about it." I point out the flaws of the "autonomy/coercion" argument because it is a prominent liberal trope and typical of the way people intuitively approach the issue.
29. Iris Marion Young, *Responsibility for Justice* (New York: Oxford University Press, 2013).
30. Alan Wertheimer, *Coercion* (Princeton, NJ: Princeton University Press, 1990).
31. Wertheimer, *Coercion*.
32. Karl Marx, *Capital*: vol. 1: *A Critique of Political Economy* (London; New York: Penguin, 1992).
33. Allen W. Wood, "The Marxian Critique of Justice," *Philosophy & Public Affairs* 1, no. 3 (1972): 244–282.
34. Liam Murphy and Thomas Nagel, *The Myth of Ownership: Taxes and Justice* (Oxford: Oxford University Press, 2002).
35. Stilz, "Occupancy Rights and the Wrong of Removal," 324–356.
36. Jason Hackworth, *The Neoliberal City: Governance, Ideology, and Development in American Urbanism* (Ithaca, NY: Cornell University Press, 2006).
37. Philip Pettit, *Republicanism: A Theory of Freedom and Government* (Oxford: Oxford University Press, 1999).
38. Oliver Wendell Holmes, Letter to Jeremy Bentham, April 1, 1907, cited in Jeffrey Evans Stake, "The Uneasy Case for Adverse Possession," *Georgetown Law Journal* 89, no. 8 (2000): 2419–2474.
39. Philip Pettit, *Just Freedom: A Moral Compass for a Complex World* (New York: Norton, 2014), 46.
40. Georg Wilhelm Friedrich Hegel, *Hegel: Elements of the Philosophy of Right*, ed. Allen W. Wood, trans. H. B. Nisbet (Cambridge: Cambridge University Press, 1991).
41. Jeremy Waldron, "Homelessness and the Issue of Freedom," *UCLA Law Review* 39, no. 1 (1991): 295–324.
42. Richard Teichgraeber, "Hegel on Property and Poverty," *Journal of the History of Ideas* 38, no. 1 (1977): 47–64.
43. Hegel, *Elements of the Philosophy of Right*.
44. Margaret Jane Radin, "Property and Personhood," *Stanford Law Review* 34 (1982): 957–1015; Margaret Jane Radin, *Reinterpreting Property* (Chicago: University of Chicago Press, 1993).
45. William P. Wilen, "The Horner Model: Successfully Redeveloping Public Housing," *Northwestern Journal of Law & Social Policy* 1 (2006): 62–303.
46. *Gautreaux v. Chi. Hous. Auth.*, 296 F. Supp. 907, 908 (N.D. Ill. 1969).
47. Peter H. Schuck, "Judging Remedies: Judicial Approaches to Housing Segregation," *Harvard Civil Rights–Civil Liberties Law Review* 37, no. 2 (2002): 289–368.

48. The plaintiffs claimed that by failing to maintain the Horner developments, the CHA's actions were a form of demolition that violated of 42 U.S.C. § 1437p of the United States Housing Act, the Annual Contributions Contract between the CHA and HUD, and the tenants' leases. See *Henry Horner Mothers Guild v. Chi. Hous. Auth.*, 824 F. Supp. 808, 810 (N.D. Ill. 1993).
49. *Henry Horner Mothers Guild v. Chi. Hous. Auth.*
50. *Henry Horner Mothers Guild v. Chi. Hous. Auth.*
51. Federal budget data. http://www.whitehouse.gov/sites/default/files/omb/budget/fy2014/assets/hist.pdf, accessed February 2015.
52. Scott, "Is Urban Policy Making Way for the Wealthy?"
53. Wilen, "The Horner Model."
54. Albert O. Hirschman, *Exit, Voice, and Loyalty: Responses to Decline in Firms, Organizations, and States* (Cambridge, MA: Harvard University Press, 1970).
55. Rolf Pendall, "Why Voucher and Certificate Users Live in Distressed Neighborhoods," *Housing Policy Debate* 11, no. 4 (2000): 881–910; Victoria Basolo and Mai Thi Nguyen, "Does Mobility Matter? The Neighborhood Conditions of Housing Voucher Holders by Race and Ethnicity," *Housing Policy Debate* 16, nos. 3–4 (2005): 297–324.
56. See *Cabrini-Green Local Advisory Council v. CHA* (1998).
57. According to William P. Wilen, most of the LACs in Chicago Public Housing projects were closely tied to the CHA and the building management companies. They were not effective at addressing the problems in the projects or at holding building management accountable for violations of rules. Only the Cabrini-Green LAC ever filed a lawsuit against the CHA. See Wilen, "The Horner Model."
58. Wilen, "The Horner Model."
59. "Fact Sheet–Urban Aboriginal Population in Canada," Urban and Aboriginal Affairs, https://www.aadnc-aandc.gc.ca/eng/1100100014298/1100100014302, accessed April 27, 2016.
60. This information is drawn from the court decision *Abbotsford (City) v. Shantz*, 2015 BCSC 1909, 14. "6.97% of urban Aboriginal people in Canada are considered to be homeless compared with 0.78% of the mainstream population. More than one in fifteen urban Aboriginal people are homeless, compared to one out of 128 non-Aboriginal Canadians."

Chapter 5

1. In my research on solidarism I have not come across this specific proposal, but I believe it is consistent with the principle of social property.
2. Jacques Derrida, *Dissemination* (London: A&C Black, 2004).

3. For an interesting discussion of the ethics of gentrification, see Nicholas K. Blomley, *Unsettling the City: Urban Land and the Politics of Property* (New York: Routledge, 2003), 78–81.

4. Neil Smith, *The New Urban Frontier: Gentrification and the Revanchist City* (London: Routledge, 1996), 30.

5. Jon Caulfield, *City Form and Everyday Life* (Toronto: University of Toronto Press, 1994); David Ley, "Artists, Aestheticisation and the Field of Gentrification," *Urban Studies* 40, no. 2 (2003): 2527–2544; David Ley, *The New Middle Class and the Remaking of the Central City* (Oxford: Oxford University Press, 1996); Tim Butler, *Gentrification and the Middle Classes* (Brookfield, VT: Ashgate, 1997); Ruth Glass, *London: Aspects of Change* (London: MacGibbon & Kee, 1964).

6. Glass, *London: Aspects of Change.*

7. Jason Hackworth, "Postrecession Gentrification in New York," *Urban Affairs Review* 37, no. 6 (2002): 815–843.

8. Tom Slater, "The Eviction of Critical Perspectives from Gentrification Research," *International Journal of Urban and Regional Research* 30, no. 4 (2006): 737–757; Loretta Lees, "Gentrification and Social Mixing: Towards an Inclusive Urban Renaissance?," *Urban Studies* 45, no. 12 (2008): 2449–2470.

9. Tom Slater, "Municipally Managed Gentrification in South Parkdale, Toronto," *Canadian Geographer* 48, no. 3 (2004): 303–325.

10. Joey Cosco, "A 30-Year-Old Law Is Creating a Crisis in San Francisco," *Business Insider*, July 22, 2014, accessed July 23, 2014. http://www.businessinsider.com/ ellis-act-ruining-san-francisco-2014-7#ixzz38UcY7TrI.

11. Robert Murdie and Carlos Teixeira, "The Impact of Gentrification on Ethnic Neighbourhoods in Toronto: A Case Study of Little Portugal," *Urban Studies* 48, no. 1 (2011): 71.

12. Jacob Vigdor, Douglas S. Massey, and Alice M. Rivlin, "Does Gentrification Harm the Poor?," *Brookings-Wharton Papers on Urban Affairs* (2002): 133–173.

13. Lance Freeman, "Displacement or Succession? Residential Mobility in Gentrifying Neighborhoods," *Urban Affairs Review* 40, no. 4 (2005): 463–491.

14. Rowland Atkinson, "Measuring Gentrification and Displacement in Greater London," *Urban Studies* 37, no. 1 (2000): 149–165.

15. Lees, "Gentrification and Social Mixing."

16. Garry Robson and Tim Butler, "Coming to Terms with London: Middle-Class Communities in a Global City," *Journal of Urban and Regional Research* 25, no. 1 (2001): 78.

17. F. A. Hayek, *The Constitution of Liberty* (Chicago: University of Chicago Press, 1960), 340–357.

18. Hayek, *The Constitution of Liberty.*

19. Charles Tiebout, "A Pure Theory of Local Expenditures," *Journal of Political Economy* 64, no. 5 (1956): 416–424.

20. Edward Glaeser, *Triumph of the City: How Our Greatest Invention Makes Us Richer, Smarter, Greener, Healthier, and Happier* (New York: Penguin Books, 2012).
21. Elizabeth Anderson, "What Is the Point of Equality?," *Ethics* 109, no. 2 (1999): 287–337.
22. Ronald Dworkin, *Sovereign Virtue: The Theory and Practice of Equality* (Cambridge, MA: Harvard University Press, 2000), 12.
23. Amartya Sen, "Equality of What?," in *Liberty, Equality, and Law: Selected Tanner Lectures on Moral Philosophy*, ed. Sterling M. McMurrin (Cambridge: Cambridge University Press, 1987).
24. G. A. Cohen, "On the Currency of Egalitarian Justice," *Ethics* 99 (1989): 906–944.
25. Cohen, "On the Currency of Egalitarian Justice," 923.
26. Dworkin, *Sovereign Virtue*, 288.
27. G. A. Cohen, "Expensive Tastes Rides Again," in *Dworkin and His Critics*, ed. Justine Burley (Malden, MA: Blackwell, 2004): 1–29.
28. Ronald Dworkin, "Ronald Dworkin Replies," in *Dworkin and His Critics*, ed. Justine Burley (Malden, MA: Blackwell, 2004), 337–396.
29. Richard Florida, *The Rise of the Creative Class* (New York: Basic Books, 2002).
30. Loren King, "Democratic Hopes in the Polycentric City," *Journal of Politics* 66 (2004): 203–223.
31. Yi-Fu Tuan, *Topophilia: A Study of Environmental Perceptions, Attitudes, and Values* (New York: Columbia University Press, 1974), 4, 247.
32. Richard Sennett, *The Uses of Disorder: Personal Identity and City Life* (New Haven, CT: Yale University Press, 2008).
33. Dworkin, "Ronald Dworkin Replies," 347.
34. Dworkin, *Sovereign Virtue*, 298.
35. Michael Hardt and Antonio Negri, *Commonwealth* (Cambridge, MA: Harvard University Press, 2011).
36. Michael Walzer, *Spheres of Justice: A Defense of Pluralism and Equality* (New York: Basic Books, 1983).
37. See Blomley, *Unsettling the City*.
38. Kerry Gold, "Grandview Park Redevelopment Incites Class War," *Globe and Mail*, July 28, 2010. http://www.theglobeandmail.com/news/british-columbia/grandview-park-redevelopment-incites-class-war/article1212680/. For a broader analysis of the cultural transformations associated with gentrification, see Rebecca Solnit and Susan Schwartzenberg, *Hollow City: The Siege of San Francisco and the Crisis of American Urbanism* (London: Verso, 2002).
39. Brianna Goldberg, "All We Need Is a Starbucks; Residents of Oakwood and Vaughan Desperately Seek Gentrification," *National Post*, June 18, 2008, s3.
40. Avery Kolers, *Land, Conflict, and Justice: A Political Theory of Territory* (Cambridge: Cambridge University Press, 2009), 3.

41. Kolers, *Land, Conflict, and Justice*, 52.
42. Dworkin, *Sovereign Virtue*, 65.
43. Kolers, *Land, Conflict, and Justice*, 53.
44. Dworkin, *Sovereign Virtue*, 67.
45. Kolers, *Land, Conflict, and Justice*, 67.
46. Murdie and Teixeira, "The Impact of Gentrification on Ethnic Neighbourhoods in Toronto."
47. Marshall Berman, *On the Town: One Hundred Years of Spectacle in Times Square* (London: Verso, 2009).
48. See Nancy Love, "'You Are Standing on the Indian': The Settler Contract, Terra Nullis, and White Supremacy," paper presented at the American Political Science Association meeting, Washington, DC, August 2014.
49. Michel Foucault and Jay Miskowiec, "Of Other Spaces," *Diacritics* 16, no. 1 (1986): 22–27.
50. Berman, *On the Town*.
51. Alan Walks and Richard Maaranen, "Gentrification, Social Mix, and Social Polarization: Testing the Linkages in Large Canadian Cities," *Urban Geography* 29, no. 4 (2008): 293–326.
52. Walks and Maaranen, "Gentrification, Social Mix, and Social Polarization," 293–326.
53. Glass, *London: Aspects of Change*.
54. Susan Bickford, "Constructing Inequality: City Spaces and the Architecture of Citizenship," *Political Theory* 28, no. 3 (2000): 355–376; Iris Marion Young, "Residential Segregation and Differentiated Citizenship," *Citizenship Studies* 3, no. 2 (1999): 237–252.
55. Gary Bridge, Tim Butler, and Loretta Lees, *Mixed Communities: Gentrification by Stealth?* (Chicago: Policy Press, 2013).
56. Robert David Sack, *Human Territoriality: Its Theory and History* (New York: Cambridge University Press, 1986).
57. Young, "Residential Segregation and Differentiated Citizenship."
58. For a similar argument, see Edward Soja's distinction between enclaves, which can have positive functions, and discriminatory or disadvantaged ghettoes: Edward Soja, *Seeking Spatial Justice* (Minneapolis: University of Minnesota Press, 2010), 55.
59. Jason Hackworth, *The Neoliberal City: Governance, Ideology, and Development in American Urbanism* (Ithaca, NY: Cornell University Press, 2006).
60. Susan S. Fainstein, *The Just City* (Ithaca, NY: Cornell University Press, 2010); Aline Kan Wong and Stephen Hua Kuo Yeh, eds., *Housing a Nation: 25 Years of Public Housing in Singapore* (Singapore: Maruzen Asia, 1985).
61. David Imbroscio, "From Redistribution to Ownership: Toward an Alternative Urban Policy for America's Cities," *Urban Affairs Review* 49, no. 6 (2013): 787–820.

Chapter 6

1. Sarah McBride, "Google Bus Blocked in San Francisco Gentrification Protest," Reuters, December 10, 2013. http://www.reuters.com/article/2013/12/10/us-google-protest-idUSBRE9B818J20131210.
2. Avigail Ferdman, "The Human Flourishing Justification for the Distribution of Non-universal Public Goods," paper presented at the workshop "Approaches to Public Goods," University of Toronto, May 2016.
3. U.S. Department of Transportation, "Summary of Travel Trends," p. 19. http://nhts.ornl.gov/2009/pub/stt.pdf.
4. Mark Garrett and Brian Taylor, "Reconsidering Social Equity in Public Transit," *Berkeley Planning Journal* 13, no. 1 (1999), http://escholarship.org/uc/item/1mc9t108.pdf.
5. John Pucher, "Discrimination in Mass Transit," *Journal of the American Planning Association* 48, no. 3 (1982): 315–326; John Pucher, "Who Benefits from Transit Subsidies? Recent Evidence from Six Metropolitan Areas," *Transportation Research* Part A: 17, no. 1 (1983): 39–50.
6. Edward W. Soja, *Seeking Spatial Justice* (Minneapolis: University of Minnesota Press, 2010).
7. Thad Williamson, "Mobility and Its Opponents: Richmond, Virginia's Refusal to Embrace Mass Transit," paper presented at the Urban Affairs Association meeting (April 2013).
8. Arthur Ripstein, *Force and Freedom: Kant's Legal and Political Philosophy* (Cambridge, MA: Harvard University Press, 2009).
9. Tim Cresswell, "The Right to Mobility: The Production of Mobility in the Courtroom," *Antipode* 38, no. 4 (2006): 735.
10. Susan Fainstein also concludes that one way to promote equity in cities is to subsidize public transit and to promote planning solutions that do not disproportionately benefit the already well-off. See Susan S. Fainstein, *The Just City* (Ithaca, NY: Cornell University Press, 2010), 173. See also Karel Martens, "Justice in Transport as Justice in Accessibility: Applying Walzer's 'Spheres of Justice' to the Transport Sector," *Transportation* 39, no. 6 (2012): 1035–1053; Karel Martens, *Transport Justice: Designing Fair Transportation Systems* (New York: Routledge, 2016).
11. Ripstein, *Force and Freedom*, 232–266.
12. Ripstein, *Force and Freedom*, 237.
13. Immanuel Kant, *Kant: Political Writings*, ed. H. S. Reiss (New York: Cambridge University Press, 1991).
14. Kant, *Kant: Political Writings*, 147.
15. Kant, *Kant: Political Writings*, 149.
16. Kant, *Kant: Political Writings*, 149.
17. Ripstein, *Force and Freedom*.

18. Ripstein, *Force and Freedom,* 244.
19. For a discussion of pedestrianism and the regulation of public roads in England and the United States, see Nicholas K. Blomley, *Rights of Passage: Sidewalks and the Regulation of Public Flow* (New York: Routledge, 2011).
20. Thad Williamson, "Mobility and Its Opponents: Richmond, Virginia's Refusal to Embrace Mass Transit," paper presented at the Urban Affairs Association meeting (April 2013), 2.
21. The spatial mismatch is a concept originally introduced by John F. Kain. See "Housing Segregation, Negro Employment, and Metropolitan Decentralization," *Quarterly Journal of Economics* 82, no. 2 (1968): 175–197. Also see a comprehensive review of 28 newer empirical studies: Keith R. Ihlanfeldt and David L. Sjoquist, "The Spatial Mismatch Hypothesis: A Review of Recent Studies and Their Implications for Welfare Reform," *Housing Policy Debate* 9, no. 4 (1998): 849–892. One interesting study examined different reasons for the variation in the percentage of black workers at suburban fast-food restaurants and found that the presence of a public transit stop within walking distance had the strongest correlation. See Keith R. Ihlanfeldt and Madelyn V. Young, "The Spatial Distribution of Black Employment between the Central City and the Suburbs," *Economic Inquiry* 34, no. 4 (1996): 693–707.
22. Williamson, "Mobility and Its Opponents," 2.
23. Williamson, "Mobility and Its Opponents," 4.
24. Clarissa Rile Hayward, *How Americans Make Race: Stories, Institutions, Spaces* (New York: Cambridge University Press, 2013), 45.
25. Clarissa Rile Hayward and Todd Swanstrom, eds., *Justice and the American Metropolis* (Minneapolis: University of Minnesota Press, 2011).
26. This account draws on Williamson, "Mobility and Its Opponents."
27. According to 2006 census data, Scarborough is 33 percent white and the city of Toronto is 53 percent white. http://www.citiescentre.utoronto.ca/Assets/Cities+Centre+2013+Digital+Assets/Cities+Centre/Cities+Centre+Digital+Assets/pdfs/publications/Cowen+Torontos+Inner+Suburbs+2011.pdf.
28. "Transit Deserts and Hulchanski's Three Cities," Martin Prosperity Insights, http://martinprosperity.org/images/stories/jmc/cache/mpi-transit-deserts-hulchanskis-three-cities.pdf. The method is described as follows: the score is based on data from the Toronto Transit Commission and looks at the number and frequency of stops within 500 meters of the centroid of a census block. It is weighted for mode of transportation (subway, bus, streetcar).
29. The data for the city of Toronto comes from the University of Toronto Data Management Group's report "Transportation Tomorrow Survey" (2011), http://www.dmg.utoronto.ca/pdf/tts/2011/travel_summaries_for_the_gtha/Toronto/City_of_Toronto.pdf. The data for the inner suburbs is drawn from Paul Hess and Jane Farrow, *Walkability in Toronto's High-Rise Neighbourhoods—Final Report* (Toronto: Cities Centre, University of Toronto, 2010).

The report includes eight neighborhoods, one of which is in the center city. I averaged the car ownership rates in the seven suburban neighborhoods.

30. A recent study provides evidence that seems to refute the suggestion that there is a spatial mismatch in Toronto and finds that less advantaged census tracts are better served by public transit. This study, however, includes both the city of Toronto and the Greater Toronto Metropolitan Area, which includes affluent, car-dependent suburbs that are not on the public bus system (TTC). A better comparison would be transit equity within the city of Toronto itself. See Nicole Foth, Kevin Manaugh, and Ahmed M. El-Geneidy, "Towards Equitable Transit: Examining Transit Accessibility and Social Need in Toronto, Canada, 1996–2006," *Journal of Transport Geography* 29 (2013): 1–10.

31. Annelise Grube-Cavers and Zachary Patterson, "Urban Rapid Rail Transit and Gentrification in Canadian Urban Centres: A Survival Analysis Approach," *Urban Studies* 52, no. 1 (2015): 178–194; Vladimir Bajic, "The Effects of a New Subway Line on Housing Prices in Metropolitan Toronto," *Urban Studies* 20, no. 2 (1983): 147–158.

32. Fainstein, *The Just City.*

33. Noel Cass, Elizabeth Shove, and John Urry, "Social Exclusion, Mobility and Access," *Sociological Review* 53, no. 3 (2005): 539–555.

34. Royson James, "New Subway's Coming, but a Subdued Mood Is Here," *Toronto Star*, October 10, 2013.

35. C. W. Mills, "'Ideal Theory' as Ideology," *Hypatia* 20, no. 3 (2005): 165–183.

36. Hayward and Swanstrom, *Justice and the American Metropolis.*

37. Joseph Heath, *The Efficient Society: Why Canada Is as Close to Utopia as It Gets* (Toronto: Penguin Canada, 2002).

38. Jason Henderson, *Street Fight: The Politics of Mobility in San Francisco* (Amherst: University of Massachusetts Press, 2013), 146.

39. Ixhchel Delaporte, "La gratuité comme antidote à l'austérité," *L'Humanité* (December 30, 2013). The city financed the initiative by raising the transport tax on large businesses from 0.6 to 1.8 percent.

40. Ixhchel Delaporte, "À Aubagne, la petite révolution des bus gratuits," *L'Humanité*, December 20, 2013.

41. The right to mobility is not the same as the right to be left alone in public space. For an interesting discussion of this issue, see Nicholas Blomley, "The Right to Pass Freely: Circulation, Begging, and the Bounded Self," *Social & Legal Studies* 19, no. 3 (2010): 331–350.

Chapter 7

1. Jason Hackworth, *The Neoliberal City: Governance, Ideology, and Development in American Urbanism* (Ithaca, NY: Cornell University Press, 2007); Neil Brenner, Peter Marcuse, and Margit Mayer, eds., *Cities for People, Not for Profit: Critical*

Urban Theory and the Right to the City (London: Routledge, 2012); Timothy Paul Ryan Weaver, "Neoliberalism in the Trenches: Urban Policy and Politics in the United States and the United Kingdom," 2012. http://repository.upenn. edu/dissertations/AAI3542903/.

2. This is based on average individual income from the Canadian census. A census tract is "middle income" if the average income is between 20 percent above and 20 percent below the average for the census metropolitan area (CMA). It is low income if it is more than 20 percent below the CMA. David Hulchanski, *The Three Cities within Toronto: Income Polarization among Toronto's Neighborhoods, 1970–2005* (Toronto: Cities Centre, University of Toronto, 2001).

3. Grace-Edward Galabuzi, *Canada's Economic Apartheid: The Social Exclusion of Racialized Groups in the New Century* (Toronto: Canadian Scholars' Press, 2006).

4. Simone Chambers, "Justice or Legitimacy, Barricades or Public Reason," in *Property-Owning Democracy: Rawls and Beyond*, ed. Martin O'Neill and Thad Williamson (Malden, MA: Wiley-Blackwell, 2012), 17–32.

5. Gregory Smithsimon and Sharon Zukin, "The City's Commons: Privatization vs. Human Rights," in *The Future of Human Rights in an Urban World*, ed. Thijs van Lindert and Doutje Lettinga (Netherlands: Amnesty International, 2014), 41–44.

6. Judith Butler, *Notes Toward a Performative Theory of Assembly* (Cambridge, MA: Harvard University Press, 2015), 137.

7. Fergus Millar, *The Crowd in Rome in the Late Republic* (Ann Arbor: University of Michigan Press, 2002).

8. Butler, *Notes toward a Performative Theory of Assembly*, 129.

9. This was the view endorsed in the court decisions to uphold the evictions of occupiers in New York City and Toronto. The courts also relied on depositions from individuals who advanced this view.

10. William Connolly, *The Terms of Political Discourse*, 3rd ed. (Princeton, NJ: Princeton University Press, 1993).

11. Jean Bethke Elshtain, *Public Man, Private Woman: Women in Social and Political Thought* (Princeton, NJ: Princeton University Press, 1993).

12. Jeff Weintraub and Krishan Kumar, *Public and Private in Thought and Practice* (Chicago: University of Chicago Press, 1997).

13. *Batty v. City of Toronto*, 2011 ONSC 6862, 1.

14. See *Waller v. City of New York*, Index No. 112957/2011.

15. *Batty v. Toronto*, 2011, 3.

16. *Batty v. Toronto*, 2011, 3.

17. Jodi Dean, "Claiming Division, Naming a Wrong," *Theory & Event* 14, no. 4 (2011). https://muse.jhu.edu/article/459208.

18. The international movement predates OWS, which was itself inspired by Tahrir Square and the Spanish *Real Democracy Now!* encampments. In late October 2011, 1,000 cities across the globe had active occupations.

See Jeffrey S. Juris, "Reflections on #Occupy Everywhere: Social Media, Public Space, and Emerging Logics of Aggregation," *American Ethnologist* 39, no. 2 (2012): 259–279.

19. From the standpoint of legal analysis, there are some important differences between American and Canadian constitutional law. The legal precedents governing symbolic expression and "time, place, manner restrictions" on free speech are not identical. Moreover, the Canadian Charter of Rights and Freedoms contains a provision specifically stating that the scope of rights is subject to "reasonable limits prescribed by law as can be demonstrably justified in a free and democratic society." The US Supreme Court relies on balancing too, but the standards that have emerged through case law and are not encoded in an explicit constitutional provision. These differences, however, are not important for the purposes of this chapter, because I treat the arguments advanced in the court decisions as expressions of public reason rather than narrow legal analysis.

20. *Batty v. Toronto*, 2011.

21. Timothy Zick, *Speech Out of Doors* (Cambridge: Cambridge University Press, 2008).

22. *Hague v. CIO*, 307 U.S. 496 (1939).

23. Francis Dupuis-Déri, "Qui a peur du peuple? Le débat entre l'agoraphobie politique et l'agoraphilie politique," *Variations: Revue internationale de théorie critique* 15 (2011): 49–74.

24. Thomas Hobbes, *Leviathan* (New York: Penguin Books, 1985).

25. Hobbes, *Leviathan*, 275.

26. Quentin Skinner, *Visions of Politics,* vol. 2, *Renaissance Virtues* (Cambridge: Cambridge University Press, 2002), 14.

27. Jürgen Habermas, "Right and Violence: A German Trauma," *Cultural Critique* 1 (1985): 125–139.

28. Peter E. Quint, *Civil Disobedience and the German Courts* (New York: Routledge, 2008).

29. Habermas, "Right and Violence," 136; see also Hannah Arendt, *Crises of the Republic* (New York: Harcourt, 1972); Stephen White and Evan Farr, "'No-Saying' in Habermas," *Political Theory* 40, no. 1 (2011): 32–57.

30. Weintraub and Kumar, *Public and Private*, 11.

31. John P. McCormick, "Machiavelli against Republicanism," *Political Theory* 31, no. 5 (2003): 615–653; John P. McCormick, *Machiavellian Democracy* (Cambridge: Cambridge University Press, 2011). By invoking Machiavelli, my goal is not to provide a reading of Machiavelli but rather to use his work to help identify the features of the populist theory of the public. This more modest goal reflects the considerable challenges involved in interpreting inconsistent passages both within the *Discourses* and between the *Discourses* and other writings.

32. Benedetto Fontana, "Sallust and the Politics of Machiavelli," *History of Political Thought* 24, no. 1 (2003): 86–108; Philip Pettit, *Republicanism: A Theory of Freedom and Government* (Oxford: Oxford University Press, 1997);

Quentin Skinner, "The Republican Idea of Political Liberty," in *Machiavelli and Republicanism*, ed. Gisela Bock, Quentin Skinner, and Maurizio Viroli (Cambridge: Cambridge University Press, 1990), 293–309; Skinner, *Visions of Politics*.

33. McCormick, "Machiavelli against Republicanism"; McCormick, *Machiavellian Democracy*; Miguel Vatter, "The Quarrel between Populism and Republicanism: Machiavelli and the Antinomies of Plebeian Politics," *Contemporary Political Theory* 11, no. 3 (2012): 242–263.

34. Niccolo Machiavelli, *Selected Political Writings*, trans. David Wooton (Indianapolis: Hackett, 1994), I.4.

35. Machiavelli, *Selected Political Writings*.

36. Machiavelli, *Selected Political Writings*, I.17.

37. Machiavelli, *Selected Political Writings*, I.58.

38. Frances Fox Piven and Richard Cloward, *Poor People's Movements: Why They Succeed, How They Fail* (New York: Vintage, 1978); Charles Tilly and Sidney Tarrow, *Contentious Politics* (Boulder, CO: Paradigm, 2006).

39. Contemporary theorists have also identified strands of this approach in the work of Hannah Arendt [Jeffrey C. Isaac, *Democracy in Dark Times* (Ithaca, NY: Cornell University Press, 1998)], including her reworking of the political to foreground the Greek concept of isonomy, which she translated as "no-rule"; see Hannah Arendt, *On Revolution* (New York: Penguin Books, 1965), 30; Patchen Markell, "The Rule of the People: Arendt, Archê, and Democracy," *American Political Science Review* 100, no. 1 (2006): 1–14; Vatter, "The Quarrel between Populism and Republicanism." Machiavelli himself does not suggest that "no-rule" is a viable political option, and instead emphasizes the importance of law, given the tendency of elites to exercise domination and, to a lesser degree, the people's susceptibility to corruption.

40. Note that Zuccotti Park is a privately owned public space. Justice Stallman decided not to address the issue of whether or not this type of privately owned public space constituted a traditional public forum. He felt that this was not necessary because the eviction met the higher level of constitutional scrutiny required to enforce anti-camping bylaws in a public space.

41. *Waller v. City of New York.*

42. Jerold Kayden, *Privately Owned Public Space: The New York City Experience* (Toronto: Wiley, 2000).

43. *Clark v. Community for Creative Non-violence* 468 U.S. 288 (1984).

44. Zick, *Speech Out of Doors*, 203.

45. Michael J. Shapiro, "Street Politics," *Journal of Critical Globalisation Studies* 5 (2012): 127–128.

46. Jürgen Habermas, *The Theory of Communicative Action: Lifeworld and System: A Critique of Functionalist Reason*, vol. 2 (Boston: Beacon Press, 1985).

47. *Batty v. Toronto*, 35.

48. *Batty v. Toronto*, 39.

49. 1982, section 1.
50. *Batty v. Toronto*, 2011, 44.
51. My own experience visiting the park was very different from the one that Justice Brown described. Despite my bourgeois attire, I painted a sign, was offered a hug, and talked about anarchism with people in the library yurt. For similar first-hand accounts of OWS, see Carla Blumenkranz et al., eds., *Occupy!: Scenes from Occupied America* (London: Verso, 2011).
52. Ernesto Laclau, *On Populist Reason* (London: Verso, 2005).
53. Jason Frank, *Constituent Moments: Enacting the People in Postrevolutionary America* (Durham, NC: Duke University Press, 2010), 3; see also Bonnie Honig, *Emergency Politics: Paradox, Law, Democracy* (Princeton, NJ: Princeton University Press, 2009).
54. Butler, *Notes toward a Performative Theory of Assembly*, 170.
55. Blumenkranz et al., *Occupy!*
56. Gayatri Chakravorty Spivak, "Can the Subaltern Speak?," in *Marxism and the Interpretation of Culture* (Urbana: University of Illinois Press, 1988), 271–313.
57. Hanna Fenichel Pitkin, *The Concept of Representation* (Berkeley: University of California Press, 1967).
58. Giorgio Agamben, *Means without End: Notes on Politics* (Minneapolis: University of Minnesota Press, 2000); cited in Frank, *Constituent Moments*.
59. Jacques Rancière, *Disagreement: Politics and Philosophy*, trans. Julie Rose (Minneapolis: University of Minnesota Press, 1999), 41; Jacques Rancière, "Democracy, Republic, Representation," *Constellations* 13, no. 3 (2006): 302.
60. Rancière, *Disagreement*, 28.
61. Rancière, *Disagreement*, 29–30.
62. Rancière, *Disagreement*, 32.
63. Rancière, *Disagreement*, 40.
64. Maple Razsa and Andrej Kurnik, "The Occupy Movement in Žižek's Hometown: Direct Democracy and a Politics of Becoming," *American Ethnologist* 39, no. 2 (2012): 239.
65. Michael Stothard, "Corporation of London Draws Protesters' Ire," *Financial Times*, November 19, 2011, p. 2.
66. Sidney G. Tarrow, *Power in Movement: Social Movements and Contentious Politics*, 3rd ed. (Cambridge: Cambridge University Press, 2011), 101.
67. Stuart Schrader and David Wachsmuth, "Reflections on Occupy Wall Street, the State and Space," *City* 16, no. 2 (2012): 243–248.
68. I would like to thank Timothy Weaver for drawing my attention to this case.
69. Margaret Kohn, *Brave New Neighborhoods: The Privatization of Public Space* (London: Routledge, 2004).
70. Jeffrey Green, *The Eyes of the People: Democracy in the Age of Spectatorship* (Oxford: Oxford University Press, 2011).

71. John Parkinson, *Democracy and Public Space: The Physical Sites of Democratic Performance* (Oxford: Oxford University Press, 2012).
72. Arendt, *Crises of the Republic.*

Chapter 8

1. San Francisco's Latino population grew by 11 percent between 2000 and 2010, but the percentage of Latinos in the Mission District decreased by 22 percent. See http://missionlocal.org/2011/06/latinos-make-gains-everywhere-except-in-the-mission/.
2. Julia Carrie Wong, "The Fight over San Francisco's Public Spaces," *New Yorker*, October 23, 2014. http://www.newyorker.com/tech/elements/dropbox-airbnb-fight-san-franciscos-public-spaces.
3. Edward W. Soja, *Seeking Spatial Justice* (Minneapolis: University of Minnesota Press, 2010), 45.
4. MissionCreekVideo, "Mission Playground Is Not for Sale," YouTube. https://www.youtube.com/watch?v=awPVY1DcupE, accessed November 28, 2014.
5. These comments were posted on "Mission Playground Is Not for Sale." https://www.youtube.com/watch?v=awPVY1DcupE. "These entitled douchebags couldn't care less about the community and the people they're kicking out."
6. Kim-Mai Cutler, "Hundreds Protest at San Francisco City Hall after Soccer Conflict with Dropbox, Airbnb Employees," *TechCrunch*, October 16, 2014. http://techcrunch.com/2014/10/16/soccer-dropbox-airbnb/.
7. Cutler, "Hundreds Protest at San Francisco City Hall."
8. M. P. Saffon and N. Urbinati, "Procedural Democracy, the Bulwark of Equal Liberty," *Political Theory* 41, no. 3 (June 1, 2013): 441–481, doi:10.1177/0090591713476872.
9. Chantal Mouffe, "Deliberative Democracy or Agonistic Pluralism?," *Social Research* 66, no. 3 (1999): 745–758.
10. Jane Mansbridge, "Using Power/Fighting Power," *Constellations* 1, no. 1 (1994): 53–73.
11. James D. Ingram, "The Politics of Claude Lefort's Political: Between Liberalism and Radical Democracy," *Thesis Eleven* 87, no. 1 (2006): 33–50.
12. Claude Lefort, *The Political Forms of Modern Society: Bureaucracy, Democracy, Totalitarianism*, ed. David Thompson (Cambridge, MA: MIT Press, 1986), 285.
13. Lefort, *The Political Forms of Modern Society*, 279.
14. Miguel Abensour, *Democracy against the State: Marx and the Machiavellian Movement* (Cambridge: Polity, 2011), 105.
15. Abensour, *Democracy against the State.*
16. Abensour, *Democracy against the State*, 104.

17. Richard J. F. Day, *Gramsci Is Dead: Anarchist Currents in the Newest Social Movements* (Toronto: Pluto Press, 2005).
18. Claude Lefort, *Democracy and Political Theory*, trans. David Macey (Cambridge: Polity, 1991), 17.
19. Jürgen Habermas, *Between Facts and Norms: Contributions to a Discourse Theory of Law and Democracy*, ed. William Rehg (Cambridge, MA: MIT Press, 1998).
20. Habermas, *Between Facts and Norms*, 382.
21. Habermas, *Between Facts and Norms*, 381.
22. William Smith, "Civil Disobedience and the Public Sphere," *Journal of Political Philosophy* 19, no. 2 (2011): 145–166.
23. John Rawls, *A Theory of Justice* (Cambridge, MA: Harvard University Press, 2009).
24. John Rawls, "The Justification of Civil Disobedience," *Collected Papers* (Cambridge, MA: Harvard University Press, 1999), 176–189.
25. Nine out of the ten most expensive real estate markets in America are located in the San Francisco Bay Area. Julie Zeveloff, "The 20 Most Expensive Housing Markets in America," *Business Insider* (November 12, 2014). http://www.businessinsider.com/most-expensive-housing-markets-2014-11?op=1.
26. Eduardo M. Peñalver and Sonia Katyal, *Property Outlaws: How Squatters, Pirates, and Protesters Improve the Law of Ownership* (New Haven, CT: Yale University Press, 2010).
27. See also Kimberley Brownlee, *Conscience and Conviction: The Case for Civil Disobedience* (Oxford: Oxford University Press, 2012).
28. Peñalver and Sonia Katyal, *Property Outlaws*.
29. They also argue that a second situation that justifies the actions of acquisitive outlaws is when "consensual transfers are somehow blocked."
30. Hélène Landemore, *Democratic Reason: Politics, Collective Intelligence, and the Rule of the Many* (Princeton, NJ: Princeton University Press, 2013).
31. Brownlee, *Conscience and Conviction*.
32. Habermas, *Between Facts and Norms*, 384.
33. Habermas, *Between Facts and Norms*, 384.
34. Habermas, *Between Facts and Norms*, 384.
35. See William E. Scheuerman, "Whistleblowing as Civil Disobedience: The Case of Edward Snowden," *Philosophy & Social Criticism* 40, no. 7 (2014): 609–628.
36. Habermas, *Between Facts and Norms*, 307.
37. William Smith, "Civil Disobedience and Social Power: Reflections on Habermas," *Contemporary Political Theory* 7, no. 1 (2008): 72–89.
38. Habermas, *Between Facts and Norms*, 151.
39. See Robert Putnam, *Making Democracy Work: Civic Traditions in Modern Italy* (Princeton, NJ: Princeton University Press, 1994). Putnam argued that the key to the relationship between successful democracy and civil society is trust.

NOTES

I have argued that the mechanism is actually distrust—a mobilized citizenry that holds officials accountable. Margaret Kohn, "Civic Republicanism versus Social Struggle: A Gramscian Approach to Associationalism in Italy," *Political Power and Social Theory* 13 (1999): 201–238.

40. Nancy L. Rosenblum, *Membership and Morals: The Personal Uses of Pluralism in America* (Princeton, NJ: Princeton University Press, 2000); Mark E. Warren, *Democracy and Association* (Princeton, NJ: Princeton University Press, 2000).

41. Evan McKenzie, *Privatopia: Homeowner Associations and the Rise of Residential Private Government* (New Haven, CT: Yale University Press, 1996); Evan McKenzie, *Beyond Privatopia: Rethinking Residential Private Government* (Washington, DC: Urban Institute Press, 2011).

42. Margaret Kohn, *Brave New Neighborhoods: The Privatization of Public Space* (London: Routledge, 2004).

43. In Abensour's work, the term "democratic society" may be intended to signal that all forms of opposition to state policies are not the same. Some are driven by elites and others by the subaltern. For many political theorists, the adjective democratic evokes the classical/ancient Greek idea of rule by the many, the poor, or the common people. From this perspective, democracy is understood not as a set of procedures but as a form of rule that uses political equality to mitigate the effects of economic inequality. While I agree that democracy is more than pure proceduralism, I think it is confusing to expand the concept of democracy until it becomes a synonym for equality or justice. If we don't simply equate social justice or equality with democracy, then how do we understand the relationship between them? Invoking the people does not solve this problem. Once we give up Rousseau's metaphysical understanding of the General Will, the people loses its foundational status as a guarantor of truth and justice.

44. Mika LaVaque-Manty, *Arguments and Fists: Political Agency and Justification in Liberal Theory* (East Sussex, UK: Psychology Press, 2002).

45. Denis J. Brion, "An Essay on Lulu, Nimby, and the Problem of Distributive Justice," *BC Environmental Affairs Law Review* 15, no. 3 (1987): 437–504.

46. Isabelle Anguelovski, *Neighborhood as Refuge: Community Reconstruction, Place Remaking, and Environmental Justice in the City* (Cambridge, MA: MIT Press, 2014). Susan L. Cutter, "Race, Class and Environmental Justice," *Progress in Human Geography* 19, no. 1 (1995): 111–122; Robert D. Bullard, ed. *Environmental Justice and Communities of Color* (San Francisco: Sierra Club Books, 1996).

47. Eileen Maura McGurty, "From NIMBY to Civil Rights: The Origins of the Environmental Justice Movement," *Environmental History* 2 (1997): 301–323.

48. Christian Hunold and Iris Marion Young, "Justice, Democracy, and Hazardous Siting," *Political Studies* 46, no. 1 (1998): 82–95.

49. LaVaque-Manty, *Arguments and Fists*, 113.

50. LaVaque-Manty, *Arguments and Fists*, 118.

51. Richard A. Epstein, *Takings* (Cambridge, MA: Harvard University Press, 1985).

52. Keally D. McBride, *Collective Dreams: Political Imagination & Community* (Cambridge: Cambridge University Press, 2005).

53. William A. Fischel, *The Homevoter Hypothesis: How Home Values Influence Local Government Taxation, School Finance, and Land-Use Policies* (Cambridge, MA: Harvard University Press, 2009).

54. Michael Hardt and Antonio Negri, *Commonwealth* (Cambridge, MA: Harvard University Press, 2011).

55. Thomas Piketty, *Capital in the Twenty-First Century* (Cambridge, MA: Harvard University Press, 2014).

56. Of course, the solidarists were describing belle epoque France, but, according to Piketty, our economic structure is now coming to resemble this earlier period.

57. Ella Myers, *Worldly Ethics: Democratic Politics and Care for the World* (Durham, NC: Duke University Press, 2013).

58. The first modern zoning law was introduced in Germany in 1845. It created three zones in order to restrict the location of enterprises that emitted unhealthy or unpleasant odors: F. B. Williams, *The Law of City Planning and Zoning* (New York: Macmillan, 1922).

59. Derek Keene, "Tall Buildings in Medieval London: Precipitation, Aspiration and Thrills," *London Journal* 33, no. 3 (2008): 201–215.

60. Lisa Johnson and Tamara Baluja, "Transit Referendum: Voters Say No to New Metro Vancouver Tax, Transit Improvements," *CBC News*, July 2, 2015. http:// www.cbc.ca/news/canada/british-columbia/transit-referendum-voters-say-no-to-new-metro-vancouver-tax-transit-improvements-1.3134857.

61. Ernesto Laclau, *Emancipation(s)* (London: Verso, 2007).

Chapter 9

1. Theresa Erin Enright, "Mass Transportation in the Neoliberal City: The Mobilizing Myths of the Grand Paris Express," *Environment and Planning A* 45, no. 4 (2013): 797–813; Jason Hackworth, *The Neoliberal City: Governance, Ideology, and Development in American Urbanism* (Ithaca, NY: Cornell University Press, 2006); Gillad Rosen and Eran Razin, "The Rise of Gated Communities in Israel: Reflections on Changing Urban Governance in a Neo-liberal Era," *Urban Studies* 46, no. 8 (2009): 1702–1722; Neil Brenner and Nik Theodore, "Cities and the Geographies of 'Actually Existing Neoliberalism,'" *Antipode* 34, no. 3 (2002): 349–379; David Harvey, *A Brief History of Neoliberalism* (Oxford: Oxford University Press, 2005); Timothy Paul Ryan Weaver, "Neoliberalism in the Trenches: Urban Policy and Politics in the United States

and the United Kingdom" (2012). http://repository.upenn.edu/dissertations/
AAI3542903/.

2. Julia Gerometta, Hartmut Haussermann, and Giulia Longo, "Social Innovation
and Civil Society in Urban Governance: Strategies for an Inclusive City," *Urban
Studies* 42, no. 11 (2005): 2007–2021.

3. Allen J. Scott, "Creative Cities: Conceptual Issues and Policy Questions,"
Journal of Urban Affairs 28, no. 1 (2006): 1–17; Graeme Evans, "Creative Cities,
Creative Spaces and Urban Policy," *Urban Studies* 46, nos. 5–6 (2009): 1003–1040;
Jamie Peck, "Struggling with the Creative Class," *International Journal of Urban
and Regional Research* 29, no. 4 (2005): 740–770.

4. Robert G. Hollands, "Will the Real Smart City Please Stand up? Intelligent,
Progressive or Entrepreneurial?," *City* 12, no. 3 (2008): 303–320.

5. Eugene J. McCann, "Inequality and Politics in the Creative City-
Region: Questions of Livability and State Strategy," *International Journal of
Urban and Regional Research* 31, no. 1 (2007): 188–196.

6. Thomas Humphrey Marshall, *Citizenship and Social Class* (London: Pluto
Press, 1992).

7. David Harvey, *Rebel Cities: From the Right to the City to the Urban Revolution*
(London: Verso, 2012); Edésio Fernandes, "Constructing the 'Right to the
City' in Brazil," *Social & Legal Studies* 16, no. 2 (2007): 201–219; Mark Purcell,
"Excavating Lefebvre: The Right to the City and Its Urban Politics of the
Inhabitant," *GeoJournal* 58, nos. 2–3 (2002): 99–108; Neil Brenner, Peter
Marcuse, and Margit Mayer, eds., *Cities for People, Not for Profit: Critical Urban
Theory and the Right to the City* (London: Routledge, 2012); Margit Mayer,
"The 'Right to the City' in the Context of Shifting Mottos of Urban Social
Movements," *City* 13, nos. 2–3 (2009): 362–374; Mehmet Barış Kuymulu,
"The Vortex of Rights: 'Right to the City' at a Crossroads," *International Journal
of Urban and Regional Research* 37, no. 3 (2013): 923–940; Peter Marcuse,
"From Critical Urban Theory to the Right to the City," *City* 13, nos. 2–3
(2009): 185–197; Lila Leontidou, "Urban Social Movements in 'Weak' Civil
Societies: The Right to the City and Cosmopolitan Activism in Southern
Europe," *Urban Studies* 47, no. 6 (2010): 1179–1203.

8. Right to the City Alliance, "We Call These Projects Home: Solving the Housing
Crisis from the Ground Up," 2010. http://cdp.urbanjustice.org/sites/default/
files/We_Call_These_Projects_Home_Summary.pdf. Also see Alison Brown
and Annali Kristiansen, "Urban Policies and the Right to the City: Rights,
Responsibilities and Citizenship" (UNESCO/UN-Habitat, 2009). http://
unesdoc.unesco.org/images/0017/001780/178090e.pdf.

9. Stefan Kipfer, Parastou Saberi, and Thorben Wieditz, "Henri Lefebvre
Debates and Controversies," *Progress in Human Geography* 37, no. 1 (2013):
115–134.

10. Kanishka Goonewardena et al., *Space, Difference, Everyday Life: Reading Henri
Lefebvre* (London: Routledge, 2008); Stuart Elden, "Politics, Philosophy,

Geography: Henri Lefebvre in Recent Anglo-American Scholarship," *Antipode* 33, no. 5 (2001): 809–825.

11. Mark Purcell, "Possible Worlds: Henri Lefebvre and the Right to the City," *Journal of Urban Affairs* 36, no. 1 (2014): 141–154.

12. Michel Foucault and Jay Miskowiec, "Of Other Spaces," *Diacritics* 16, no. 1 (1986): 22–27; Henri Lefebvre, *Le manifeste différentialiste* (Paris: Gallimard, 1970); Henri Lefebvre, *Writings on Cities*, trans. Eleonore Kofman and Elizabeth Lebas (Malden, MA: Blackwell, 1996). Both Foucault and Lefebvre used the term in work written in 1967.

13. Purcell, "Possible Worlds," 142.

14. In the preface to the third French edition, Remi Hess, a former assistant of Lefebvre, suggests that the book was completed in the latter part of 1967 when "May 68" mobilization was already starting in Nanterre (p. vi). See also Laurence Costes, *Henri Lefebvre: Le droit à la ville: Vers la sociologie de l'urbain* (Paris: Lire-Elipses, 2009).

15. Lefebvre, *Writings on Cities*, 171.

16. Lefebvre, *Writings on Cities*, 173.

17. Lefebvre, *Writings on Cities*, 174.

18. Purcell, "Possible Worlds."

19. Lefebvre, *Writings on Cities*, 173–174.

20. Lefebvre, *Writings on Cities*, 66.

21. Lefebvre, *Writings on Cities*, 73.

22. Michael Sorkin, *Variations on a Theme Park: Scenes from the New American City and the End of Public Space* (New York: Hill and Wang, 1992). Kohn, *Brave New Neighborhoods*; Andrew Ross, *The Celebration Chronicles: Life, Liberty, and the Pursuit of Property Value in Disney's New Town* (New York: Ballantine Books, 2011); Sharon Zukin, *Loft Living: Culture and Capital in Urban Change* (New Brunswick, NJ: Rutgers University Press, 2014).

23. Lefebvre, *Writings on Cities*, 106–107.

24. Lefebvre, *Writings on Cities*, 142.

25. Lefebvre, *Writings on Cities*, 140.

26. Friedrich Engels, *The Condition of the Working Class in England*, ed. David McLellan (Oxford: Oxford University Press, 2009).

27. Susan Buck-Morss, *The Dialectics of Seeing: Walter Benjamin and the Arcades Project*, reprint ed. (Cambridge, MA: MIT Press, 1991); Walter Benjamin, *The Arcades Project*, ed. Rolf Tiedemann, trans. Howard Eiland and Kevin McLaughlin (Cambridge, MA: Harvard University Press, 2002).

28. Stephen Bronner, *Of Critical Theory and Its Theorists* (Oxford: Wiley-Blackwell, 1994).

29. Purcell, "Possible Worlds"; Purcell, "Excavating Lefebvre"; Kipfer, Saberi, and Wieditz, "Henri Lefebvre Debates and Controversies."

30. Richard Florida, *The Rise of the Creative Class—Revisited: Revised and Expanded* (New York: Basic Books, 2014); Peter Hall, "Creative Cities and Economic

Development," *Urban Studies* 37, no. 4 (2000): 639–649; Allen J. Scott, "Creative Cities: Conceptual Issues and Policy Questions," *Journal of Urban Affairs* 28, no. 1 (2006): 1–17; Evans, "Creative Cities, Creative Spaces and Urban Policy."

31. Peck, "Struggling with the Creative Class"; McCann, "Inequality and Politics in the Creative City-Region."

32. See Lefebvre, *Writings on Cities*, 143, 150, 157.

33. Harvey, *Rebel Cities*.

34. Creative Placemaking Case Studies, "Artscape Wychwood Barns." http://www.artscapediy.org/Case-Studies/Artscape-Wychwood-Barns.aspx.

35. See for example, Christopher Hume, "Urban Revival Balances Past and Present: Rejuvenation of Wychwood Barns Maintains Link to the Past While Successfully Creating Perfect Mix of Beauty and Utility," *Toronto Star*, November 20, 2008, p. A10.

36. Carl Grodach and Daniel Silver, *The Politics of Urban Cultural Policy: Global Perspectives* (London: Routledge, 2012).

37. David Hulchanski, *The Three Cities within Toronto: Income Polarization among Toronto's Neighbourhoods, 1970–2005* (Toronto: Cities Centre, University of Toronto, 2010).

38. Zukin, *Loft Living*; Margaret Kohn, "Dreamworlds of Deindustrialization," *Theory & Event* 12, no. 4 (2009).

39. Rachelle Marie Campigotto, "Farmers' Markets and Their Practices Concerning Income, Privilege, and Race: A Case Study of Wychwood Artscape Barns in Toronto" (MA thesis, University of Toronto, 2010). https://tspace.library.utoronto.ca/handle/1807/24545.

40. Lefebvre, *Writings on Cities*, 126.

41. Jane Jacobs, *The Death and Life of Great American Cities* (New York: Vintage, 1992).

42. Henri Lefebvre, *Du contrat de citoyenneté* (Paris: Éditions Syllepse, 2007), 29: "Une grave erreur de la tendance marxiste, ne serait-ce pas d'avoir sous-estimé et meme négligé à la fois les droits de l'homme et la lute mondiale autour de ces droits, pour leur extension et leur approfondissement."

43. Lefebvre, *Le manifeste différentialiste*.

44. Lefebvre, *Le manifeste différentialiste*, 45.

45. Lefebvre, *Le manifeste différentialiste*.

46. Lefebvre, *Le manifeste différentialiste*, 47.

47. Henri Lefebvre, *The Urban Revolution*, trans. Robert Bononno (Minneapolis: University of Minnesota Press, 2003), 80.

48. Lefebvre, *The Urban Revolution*, 101–103.

49. Jeremy Waldron, "Homelessness and the Issue of Freedom," *UCLA Law Review* 39, no. 1 (1991): 295–324.

50. Ellen Wiles, "Aspirational Principles or Enforceable Rights: The Future for Socio-economic Rights in National Law," *American University International Law Review* 22 (2006): 35.
51. Judith Butler and Athena Athanasiou, *Dispossession: The Performative in the Political* (Malden, MA: Polity, 2013).
52. Lefebvre, *Writings on Cities*, 124.
53. Lefebvre, *Du contrat de citoyenneté*, 36.

Chapter 10

1. Aaron A. Moore, "Trading Density for Benefits: Section 37 Agreements in Toronto," *IMFG Perspectives* 2 (2013): 1–7.
2. Richard Allen Epstein, *Takings* (Cambridge, MA: Harvard University Press, 1985).
3. *California Building Industry Assn. v. City of San Jose*, 216 Cal. App. 4th 1373, 157 Cal. Rptr. 3d 813 (Ct. App. 2013).
4. The law required that 15 percent of the homes be "affordable" or, alternately, the developer could select to pay a $122,000 contribution to help build affordable housing offsite.
5. Kevin D. Siegel and Matthew D. Visick, "Inclusionary Zoning for Affordable Housing under Attack" (2014). http://www.bwslaw.com/tasks/sites/bwslaw/assets/Image/Siegel%20Visick%20PLJ%20Article%20Summer%202014.pdf.
6. *California Building Industry Assn. v. City of San Jose*.
7. David Harvey, *Social Justice and the City*, revised ed. (Athens: University of Georgia Press, 2009).
8. Clarissa Rile Hayward and Todd Swanstrom, eds., *Justice and the American Metropolis* (Minneapolis: University of Minnesota Press, 2011).
9. David Imbroscio, "American Cities and American Political Science: A Look at Thick Injustice," *Perspectives on Politics* 10, no. 3 (2012): 736–738.
10. David Imbroscio, *Urban America Reconsidered: Alternatives for Governance and Policy* (Ithaca, NY: Cornell University Press, 2011); David L. Imbroscio, *Reconstructing City Politics: Alternative Economic Development and Urban Regimes* (London: Sage, 1997); Thad Williamson, David Imbroscio, and Gar Alperovitz, *Making a Place for Community: Local Democracy in a Global Era* (New York: Routledge, 2003).
11. Michel Bauwens, *Sauver le monde: Vers une économie post-capitaliste avec le peer-to-peer* (Paris: Les Liens qui libèrent, 2015).
12. Michael Hardt and Antonio Negri, *Commonwealth* (Cambridge, MA: Harvard University Press, 2011).
13. Thomas Piketty, *Capital in the Twenty-First Century* (Cambridge, MA: Harvard University Press, 2014).

14. Thomas W. Volscho and Nathan J. Kelly, "The Rise of the Super-rich: Power Resources, Taxes, Financial Markets, and the Dynamics of the Top 1 Percent, 1949 to 2008," *American Sociological Review* 77, no. 5 (2012): 679–699; Ünal Töngür and Adem Yavuz Elveren, "Deunionization and Pay Inequality in OECD Countries: A Panel Granger Causality Approach," *Economic Modelling* 38 (2014): 417–425; Bruce Western and Jake Rosenfeld, "Unions, Norms, and the Rise in U.S. Wage Inequality," *American Sociological Review* 76, no. 4 (2011): 513–537.

15. Hans Sluga, *Politics and the Search for the Common Good* (Cambridge: Cambridge University Press, 2014).

16. Sluga, *Politics and the Search for the Common Good*, 25.

17. Judith Butler, *Notes toward a Performative Theory of Assembly* (Cambridge, MA: Harvard University Press, 2015).

18. Leif Wenar, "What We Owe to Distant Others," *Politics, Philosophy & Economics* 2, no. 3 (2003): 283–304.

19. John Rawls, *The Law of Peoples: With "The Idea of Public Reason Revisited"* (Cambridge, MA: Harvard University Press, 2001).

20. Thomas W. Pogge, *World Poverty and Human Rights*, 2nd ed. (Cambridge: Polity, 2008); Lea Ypi, *Global Justice and Avant-Garde Political Agency* (Oxford: Oxford University Press, 2012).

21. Makau W. Mutua, "Savages, Victims, and Saviors: The Metaphor of Human Rights," *Harvard International Law Journal* 42, no. 1 (2001): 201–245.

22. Pogge, *World Poverty and Human Rights*.

23. Ash Amin and Nigel Thrift, *Cities: Reimagining the Urban* (Cambridge: Polity Press, 2002).

24. Jacques Rancière, *The Philosopher and His Poor* (Durham, NC: Duke University Press, 2004).

25. Jacques Rancière, *Disagreement: Politics and Philosophy* (Minneapolis: University of Minnesota Press, 2004).

BIBLIOGRAPHY

Abensour, Miguel. *Democracy against the State: Marx and the Machiavellian Movement.* Cambridge: Polity Press, 2011.

Agamben, Giorgio. *Homo Sacer: Sovereign Power and Bare Life.* Stanford, CA: Stanford University Press, 1998.

Agamben, Giorgio. *Means without End: Notes on Politics.* Minneapolis: University of Minnesota Press, 2000.

Alexander, Greogry S., Eduardo M. Peñalver, Joseph William Singer, and Laura S. Underkuffler. "A Statement of Progressive Property." *Cornell Law Review* 94, no. 4 (2008): 743–744.

Alperovitz, Gar, and Lew Daly. *Unjust Deserts: How the Rich Are Taking Our Common Inheritance.* New York: New Press, 2008.

Alsup, Alex. "Detroit Foreclosure Auction: All the Basics You Need to Know before You Bid on Property." *Huffington Post,* 2013. http://www.huffingtonpost.com/2013/08/09/detroit-foreclosure-auction-wayne-county-properties_n_3726834.html.

Amin, Ash, and Nigel Thrift. *Cities: Reimagining the Urban.* Cambridge: Polity Press, 2002.

Anderson, Elizabeth. "What Is the Point of Equality?" *Ethics* 109, no. 2 (1999): 287–337.

Anguelovski, Isabelle. *Neighborhood as Refuge: Community Reconstruction, Place Remaking, and Environmental Justice in the City.* Cambridge, MA: MIT Press, 2014.

Appadurai, Arjun. "Spectral Housing and Urban Cleansing: Notes on Millennial Mumbai." *Public Culture* 12, no. 3 (2000): 627–651.

Arendt, Hannah. *Crises of the Republic.* New York: Harcourt, 1972.

BIBLIOGRAPHY

Arendt, Hannah. *On Revolution*. New York: Penguin, 2006.

Arneil, Barbara. *John Locke and America: The Defence of English Colonialism*. Oxford: Oxford University Press, 1996.

Arneson, Richard J. "Desert and Equality." In *Egalitarianism: New Essays on the Nature and Value of Equality*. Edited by Nils Holtug and Kasper Lippert-Rasmussen. Oxford: Oxford University Press, 2006: 262–293.

Ashcraft, Richard. *Revolutionary Politics and Locke's Two Treatises of Government*. Princeton, NJ: Princeton University Press, 1986.

Austen, Ben. "The Last Tower: The Decline and Fall of Public Housing." *Harper's* (May 2012). http://harpers.org/archive/2012/05/the-last-tower/.

Bajic, Vladimir. "The Effects of a New Subway Line on Housing Prices in Metropolitan Toronto." *Urban Studies* 20, no. 2 (1983): 147–158.

Ball, Terence, and Richard Bellamy, eds. *The Cambridge History of Twentieth-Century Political Thought*. Cambridge: Cambridge University Press, 2006.

Banerjee, Abhijit, and Rohini Somanathan. "The Political Economy of Public Goods: Some Evidence from India." *Journal of Development Economics* 82, no. 2 (2007): 287–314.

Basolo, Victoria, and Mai Thi Nguyen. "Does Mobility Matter? The Neighborhood Conditions of Housing Voucher Holders by Race and Ethnicity." *Housing Policy Debate* 16, nos. 3–4 (2005): 297–324.

Bauwens, Michel (with Jean Lievens). *Sauver le monde: Vers une économie post-capitaliste avec le peer-to-peer*. Paris: Éditions Les Liens qui libèrent, 2015.

Baxi, Upendra. "Taking Suffering Seriously: Social Action Litigation in the Supreme Court of India." *Third World Legal Studies* 4 (1985): 107–132.

Belingardi, Chiara. "Città bene comune e diritto alla città." Paper presented at the conference Abitare di Nuovo, Naples, 2012. http://www.researchgate.net/profile/Chiara_Belingardi/publication/273137347_Citt_Bene_Comune_e_Diritto_alla_Citt/links/54f980170cf2ccffe9e152ce.pdf.

Benjamin, Walter. *The Arcades Project*. Edited by Rolf Tiedemann. Translated by Howard Eiland and Kevin McLaughlin. Cambridge, MA: Harvard University Press, 2002.

Bennett, Jane. *Vibrant Matter: A Political Ecology of Things*. Durham, NC: Duke University Press, 2010.

Bennett, Larry. *The Third City: Chicago and American Urbanism*. Chicago: University of Chicago Press, 2012.

Berlin, Isaiah. "Two Concepts of Liberty." In *Four Essays on Liberty*. Edited by Isaiah Berlin. New York: Oxford University Press, 1970: 118–172.

Berman, Marshall. *On the Town: One Hundred Years of Spectacle in Times Square*. London: Verso, 2009.

Bhan, Gautam. "'This Is No Longer the City I Once Knew': Evictions, the Urban Poor and the Right to the City in Millennial Delhi." *Environment and Urbanization* 21, no. 1 (2009): 127–142.

Bhushan, Prashant. "Misplaced Priorities and Class Bias of the Judiciary." *Economic and Political Weekly* 44, no. 14 (2009): 32–37.

Bickford, Susan. "Constructing Inequality: City Spaces and the Architecture of Citizenship." *Political Theory* 28, no. 3 (2000): 355–376.

Blais, Marie-Claude. *La solidarité: Histoire d'une idée*. Paris: Gallimard, 2007.

Blomley, Nicholas K. "Enclosure, Common Right and the Property of the Poor." *Social & Legal Studies* 17, no. 3 (2008): 311–331.

Blomley, Nicholas K. "The Right to Pass Freely: Circulation, Begging, and the Bounded Self." *Social & Legal Studies* 19, no. 3 (2010): 331–350.

Blomley, Nicholas K. *Rights of Passage: Sidewalks and the Regulation of Public Flow*. New York: Routledge, 2011.

Blomley, Nicholas K. *Unsettling the City: Urban Land and the Politics of Property*. New York: Routledge, 2004.

Blumenkranz, Carla, Keith Gessen, Mark Greif, Sarah Leonard, Sarah Resnick, Nikil Saval, Eli Schmitt, and Astra Taylor, eds. *Occupy!: Scenes from Occupied America*. London: Verso, 2011.

Bourdieu, Pierre. *The State Nobility: Elite Schools in the Field of Power*. Stanford, CA: Stanford University Press, 1998.

Bourgeois, Léon. *Solidarité*. Paris: Hachette Livre BnF, 2013.

Brenner, Neil, Peter Marcuse, and Margit Mayer. *Cities for People, Not for Profit: Critical Urban Theory and the Right to the City*. London: Routledge, 2012.

Brenner, Neil, and Nik Theodore. "Cities and the Geographies of 'Actually Existing Neoliberalism.'" *Antipode* 34, no. 3 (2002): 349–379.

Bridge, Gary, Tim Butler, and Loretta Lees. *Mixed Communities: Gentrification by Stealth?* Bristol, UK: Chicago: Policy Press, 2013.

Brion, Denis J. "An Essay on Lulu, Nimby, and the Problem of Distributive Justice." *BC Environmental Affairs Law Review* 15, no. 3 (1987): 437–504.

Bronner, Stephen. *Of Critical Theory and Its Theorists*. Oxford: Wiley-Blackwell, 1994.

Brown, Alison and Annali Kristiansen. "Urban Policies and the Right to the City: Rights, Responsibilities and Citizenship." UNESCO/UN-Habitat, 2009. http://unesdoc.unesco.org/images/0017/001780/178090e.pdf.

Brown, Wendy. "American Nightmare Neoliberalism, Neoconservatism, and De-democratization." *Political Theory* 34, no. 6 (2006): 690–714.

Brownlee, Kimberley. *Conscience and Conviction: The Case for Civil Disobedience*. Oxford: Oxford University Press, 2012.

Brunkhorst, Hauke. *Solidarity: From Civic Friendship to a Global Legal Community*. Translated by Jeffrey Flynn. Cambridge, MA: MIT Press, 2005.

Buck-Morss, Susan. *The Dialectics of Seeing: Walter Benjamin and the Arcades Project*. Reprint ed. Cambridge, MA: MIT Press, 1991.

Bullard, Robert D., ed. *Environmental Justice and Communities of Color*. San Francisco: Sierra Club Books, 1996.

Butler, Judith. *Notes toward a Performative Theory of Assembly*. Cambridge, MA: Harvard University Press, 2015.

Butler, Judith, and Athena Athanasiou. *Dispossession: The Performative in the Political*. Malden, MA: Polity Press, 2013.

Butler, Tim. *Gentrification and the Middle Classes*. Burlington, VT: Ashgate, 1997.

Campigotto, Rachelle Marie. "Farmers' Markets and Their Practices Concerning Income, Privilege, and Race: A Case Study of Wychwood Artscape Barns in Toronto." MA thesis, University of Toronto, 2010. https://tspace.library.utoronto.ca/handle/1807/24545.

Cass, Noel, Elizabeth Shove, and John Urry. "Social Exclusion, Mobility and Access." *Sociological Review* 53, no. 3 (2005): 539–555.

Cassels, Jamie. "Judicial Activism and Public Interest Litigation in India: Attempting the Impossible?" *American Journal of Comparative Law* 37 (1989): 495–519.

Caulfield, Jon. *City Form and Everyday Life: Toronto's Gentrification and Critical Social Practice*. Toronto: University of Toronto Press, 1994.

Chambers, Simone. "Justice of Legitimacy, Barricades or Public Reason." In *Property Owning Democracy: Rawls and Beyond*. Edited by Martin O'Neil and Thad Williamson. Malden, MA: Wiley-Blackwell, 2012: 17–32.

Cohen, Gerald Allan. "Expensive Taste Rides Again." In *Dworkin and His Critics*. Edited by Justine Burley. Hoboken, NJ: Wiley, 2004: 1–29.

Cohen, Gerald Allan. "On the Currency of Egalitarian Justice." *Ethics* 99 (1989): 906–944.

Cohen, Gerald Allan. *Rescuing Justice and Equality*. Cambridge, MA: Harvard University Press, 2009.

Cohen, Gerald Allan. *Self-Ownership, Freedom, and Equality*. Cambridge: Cambridge University Press, 1995.

Connolly, William. *The Terms of Political Discourse*. 3rd ed. Princeton, NJ: Princeton University Press, 1993.

Cosco, Joey. "A 30-Year-Old Law Is Creating a Crisis in San Francisco." *Business Insider*, July 22, 2014. http://www.businessinsider.com/ellis-act-ruining- san-francisco-2014-7#ixzz38UcY7TrI.

Costes, Laurence. *Henri Lefebvre: Le droit à la ville: Vers la sociologie de l'urbain*. Paris: Lire-Elipses, 2009.

Coulthard, Glen Sean. *Red Skin, White Masks: Rejecting the Colonial Politics of Recognition*. Minneapolis: Univ of Minnesota Press, 2014.

Cresswell, Tim. "The Right to Mobility: The Production of Mobility in the Courtroom." *Antipode* 38, no. 4 (2006): 735–754.

Cutler, Kim-Mai. "Hundreds Protest at San Francisco City Hall after Soccer Conflict with Dropbox, Airbnb Employees." *TechCrunch* (2014). http://techcrunch.com/2014/10/16/soccer-dropbox-airbnb/.

Cutter, Susan L. "Race, Class and Environmental Justice." *Progress in Human Geography* 19, no. 1 (1995): 111–122.

Davis, Mike. "Planet of Slums." *New Left Review* 28 (2003): 5–34.

Davis, Mike. *Planet of Slums*. London: Verso, 2007.

Day, Richard J. F. *Gramsci Is Dead: Anarchist Currents in the Newest Social Movements.* Toronto: Pluto Press, 2005.

Dean, Jodi. "Claiming Division, Naming a Wrong." *Theory & Event* 14, no. 4 (2011). https://muse.jhu.edu/article/459208.

Delaporte, Ixhchel. "À Aubagne, la petite révolution des bus gratuits." *L'Humanité,* December 20, 2013.

Delaporte, Ixhchel. "La gratuité comme antidote à l'austérité." *L'Humanité,* December 30, 2013.

Delgado, Richard. "On Telling Stories in School: A Reply to Farber and Sherry." *Vanderbilt Law Review* 46, no. 3 (1993): 665–676.

Derrida, Jacques. *Dissemination.* London: A&C Black, 2004.

Donzelot, Jacques. "The Promotion of the Social." *Economy and Society* 17, no. 3 (1988): 395–427.

Dreier, Peter, John Mollenkopf, and Todd Swanstrom. *Place Matters: Metropolitics for the Twenty-First Century.* 3rd ed. Lawrence: University Press of Kansas, 2014.

Dupuis-Déri, Francis. "Qui a peur du peuple? Le débat entre l'agoraphobie politique et l'agoraphilie politique." *Variations: Revue internationale de théorie critique* 15 (2011): 49–74.

Durkheim, Émile. *De la division du travail social: Étude sur l'organisation des sociétés supérieures.* Paris: Presses Universitaires de France, 1893.

Dworkin, Ronald. "Ronald Dworkin Replies." In *Dworkin and His Critics.* Edited by Justine Burley. Malden, MA: Blackwell, 2004: 337–396.

Dworkin, Ronald. *Sovereign Virtue: The Theory and Practice of Equality.* Cambridge, MA: Harvard University Press, 2000.

Dworkin, Ronald. *Taking Rights Seriously.* Cambridge, MA: Harvard University Press, 1978.

Elden, Stuart. "Politics, Philosophy, Geography: Henri Lefebvre in Recent Anglo-American Scholarship." *Antipode* 33, no. 5 (2001): 809–825.

Elshtain, Jean Bethke. *Public Man, Private Woman: Women in Social and Political Thought.* Princeton, NJ: Princeton University Press, 1993.

Engels, Friedrich. *The Condition of the Working Class in England.* Edited by David McLellan. Reissue ed. Oxford: Oxford University Press, 2009.

Enright, Theresa Erin. "Mass Transportation in the Neoliberal City: The Mobilizing Myths of the Grand Paris Express." *Environment and Planning A* 45, no. 4 (2013): 797–813.

Epstein, Richard A. *Takings.* Cambridge, MA: Harvard University Press, 1985.

Esping-Andersen, Gøsta. *The Three Worlds of Welfare Capitalism.* Princeton, NJ: Princeton University Press, 1990.

Evans, Graeme. "Creative Cities, Creative Spaces and Urban Policy." *Urban Studies* 46, nos. 5–6 (2009): 1003–1040.

Fabre, Cécile. *Social Rights under the Constitution: Government and the Decent Life.* Oxford: Oxford University Press, 2000.

Fainstein, Susan S. *The Just City*. Ithaca, NY: Cornell University Press, 2011.

Ferdman, Avigail. "The Human Flourishing Justification for the Distribution of Non-universal Public Goods." Paper presented at the workshop "Approaches to Public Goods," University of Toronto, May 2016.

Fernandes, Edésio. "Constructing the 'Right to the City' in Brazil." *Social & Legal Studies* 16, no. 2 (2007): 201–219.

Fischel, William A. *The Homevoter Hypothesis: How Home Values Influence Local Government Taxation, School Finance, and Land-Use Policies*. Cambridge, MA: Harvard University Press, 2009.

Fischer, Will, and Chye-Ching Huang. "Mortgage Interest Deduction Is Ripe for Reform." Centre on Budget and Policy Priorities Report, Rev. June 25, 2013.

Fleischacker, Samuel. *A Short History of Distributive Justice*. Cambridge, MA: Harvard University Press, 2009.

Florida, Richard. *The Rise of the Creative Class—Revisited: Revised and Expanded*. New York: Basic Books, 2014.

Fontana, Benedetto. "Sallust and the Politics of Machiavelli." *History of Political Thought* 24, no. 1 (2003): 86–108.

Foth, Nicole, Kevin Manaugh, and Ahmed M. El-Geneidy. "Towards Equitable Transit: Examining Transit Accessibility and Social Need in Toronto, Canada, 1996–2006." *Journal of Transport Geography* 29 (2013): 1–10.

Foucault, Michel, and Jay Miskowiec. "Of Other Spaces." *Diacritics* 16, no. 1 (1986): 22–27.

Fouillée, Alfred. *La propriété sociale et la Démocratie*. Paris: Hachette, 1884.

Freeden, Michael. *Ideologies and Political Theory: A Conceptual Approach*. Oxford: Oxford University Press, 1998.

Freeman, Lance. "Displacement or Succession? Residential Mobility in Gentrifying Neighborhoods." *Urban Affairs Review* 40, no. 4 (2005): 463–491.

Fullilove, Mindy. *Root Shock: How Tearing Up City Neighborhoods Hurts America, and What We Can Do about It*. New York: Random House, 2009.

Galabuzi, Grace-Edward. *Canada's Economic Apartheid: The Social Exclusion of Racialized Groups in the New Century*. Toronto: Canadian Scholars' Press, 2006.

Garrett, Mark, and Brian Taylor. "Reconsidering Social Equity in Public Transit." *Berkeley Planning Journal* 13, no. 1 (1999).

Gerometta, Julia, Hartmut Haussermann, and Giulia Longo. "Social Innovation and Civil Society in Urban Governance: Strategies for an Inclusive City." *Urban Studies* 42, no. 11 (2005): 2007–2021.

Gide, Charles, and Charles Rist. *A History of Economic Doctrines from the Time of the Physiocrats to the Present Day*. Translated by R. Richards. London: George Harrap, 1915.

Glaeser, Edward. *Triumph of the City: How Our Greatest Invention Makes Us Richer, Smarter, Greener, Healthier, and Happier*. Reprint ed. New York: Penguin Books, 2012.

Glass, Ruth. *London: Aspects of Change*. London: MacGibbon & Kee, 1964.

Goetz, Edward G. "The Audacity of HOPE VI: Discourse and the Dismantling of Public Housing." *Cities* 35 (2012): 342–348.

Goetz, Edward G. *New Deal Ruins: Race, Economic Justice, and Public Housing Policy*. Ithaca, NY: Cornell University Press, 2013.

Gold, Kerry. "Grandview Park Redevelopment Incites Class War." *Globe and Mail*, July 28, 2010. http://www.theglobeandmail.com/news/british-columbia/grandview-park-redevelopment-incites-class-war/article1212680/.

Goldberg, Brianna. "All We Need Is a Starbucks; Residents of Oakwood and Vaughan Desperately Seek Gentrification." *National Post*, June 18, 2008, s3.

Goldman, Alexandra. "The Google Shuttle Effect: Gentrification and San Francisco's Dot Com Boom 2.0." Report submitted for MA in City Planning at UC Berkeley, 2013. http://svenworld.com/wp-content/uploads/2014/01/Goldman_PRFinal.pdf.

Goodin, Robert E. "Vulnerabilities and Responsibilities: An Ethical Defense of the Welfare State." *American Political Science Review* 79, no. 3 (1985): 775–787.

Goonewardena, Kanishka, Stefan Kipfer, Richard Milgrom, and Christian Schmid. *Space, Difference, Everyday Life: Reading Henri Lefebvre*. London: Routledge, 2008.

Graham, Mary. "Some Thoughts about the Philosophical Underpinnings of Aboriginal Worldviews." *Worldviews: Global Religions, Culture, and Ecology* 3, no. 2 (1999): 105–118.

Green, Jeffrey. *The Eyes of the People: Democracy in the Age of Spectatorship*. Oxford: Oxford University Press, 2011.

Grengs, Joe. "The Abandoned Social Goals of Public Transit in the Neoliberal City of the USA." *City* 9, no. 1 (2005): 51–66.

Grodach, Carl, and Daniel Silver. *The Politics of Urban Cultural Policy: Global Perspectives*. London: Routledge, 2012.

Grube-Cavers, Annelise, and Zachary Patterson. "Urban Rapid Rail Transit and Gentrification in Canadian Urban Centres: A Survival Analysis Approach." *Urban Studies* 52, no. 1 (2015): 178–194.

Gyourko, Joseph, Christopher Mayer, and Todd Sinai. "Superstar Cities." National Bureau of Economic Research, 2006. http://www.nber.org/papers/w12355.

Habermas, Jürgen. *Between Facts and Norms: Contributions to a Discourse Theory of Law and Democracy*. Edited by William Rehg. Cambridge, MA: MIT Press, 1998.

Habermas, Jürgen. *The Theory of Communicative Action: Lifeworld and System: A Critique of Functionalist Reason*. Vol. 2. Boston, MA: Beacon Press, 1985.

Habermas, Jürgen. "Right and Violence: A German Trauma." trans. Martha Calhoun. *Cultural Critique* 1 (1985): 125–139.

Hacker, Jacob S., and Paul Pierson. *Winner-Take-All Politics: How Washington Made the Rich Richer—and Turned Its Back on the Middle Class.* New York: Simon and Schuster, 2011.

Hackworth, Jason. *The Neoliberal City: Governance, Ideology, and Development in American Urbanism.* Ithaca, NY: Cornell University Press, 2006.

Hackworth, Jason. "Postrecession Gentrification in New York." *Urban Affairs Review* 37, no. 6 (2002): 815–843.

Hall, Peter. "Creative Cities and Economic Development." *Urban Studies* 37, no. 4 (2000): 639–649.

Hardt, Michael, and Antonio Negri. *Commonwealth.* Cambridge, MA: Harvard University Press, 2011.

Harrington, James. *Harrington: The Commonwealth of Oceana and A System of Politics.* Edited by J. G. A. Pocock. Cambridge: Cambridge University Press, 1992.

Harvey, David. *A Brief History of Neoliberalism.* Oxford: Oxford University Press, 2005.

Harvey, David. *The New Imperialism.* Oxford: Oxford University Press, 2005.

Harvey, David. *Rebel Cities: From the Right to the City to the Urban Revolution.* London: Verso, 2012.

Harvey, David. *Social Justice and the City.* Revised ed. Athens: University of Georgia Press, 2009.

Hayek, F. A. *The Constitution of Liberty.* Chicago: University of Chicago Press, 1960.

Hayward, Clarissa Rile. *How Americans Make Race: Stories, Institutions, Spaces.* New York: Cambridge University Press, 2013.

Hayward, Clarissa Rile, and Todd Swanstrom, eds. *Justice and the American Metropolis.* Minneapolis: University of Minnesota Press, 2011.

Hayward, Jack Ernest S. "The Official Social Philosophy of the French Third Republic: Léon Bourgeois and Solidarism." *International Review of Social History* 6, no. 1 (1961): 19–48.

Heath, Joseph. *The Efficient Society: Why Canada Is as Close to Utopia as It Gets.* Toronto: Penguin Canada, 2002.

Hegel, Georg Wilhelm Friedrich. *Hegel: Elements of the Philosophy of Right.* Edited by Allen W. Wood. Translated by H. B. Nisbet. Cambridge: Cambridge University Press, 1991.

Henderson, Jason. *Street Fight: The Politics of Mobility in San Francisco.* Amherst: University of Massachusetts Press, 2013.

Hendrix, Burke A. *Ownership, Authority, and Self-Determination.* University Park: Penn State University Press, 2008.

Hess, Paul, and Jane Farrow. *Walkability in Toronto's High-Rise Neighbourhoods—Final Report.* Toronto: Cities Centre, University of Toronto, 2011.

Hirsch, Arnold R. *Making the Second Ghetto: Race and Housing in Chicago 1940–1960.* Chicago: University of Chicago Press, 1998.

Hirschl, Ran. "'Negative' Rights vs. 'Positive' Entitlements: A Comparative Study of Judicial Interpretations of Rights in an Emerging Neo-liberal Economic Order." *Human Rights Quarterly* 22, no. 4 (2000): 1060–1098.

Hirschman, Albert O. *Exit, Voice, and Loyalty: Responses to Decline in Firms, Organizations, and States.* New ed. Cambridge, MA: Harvard University Press, 1970.

Hobbes, Thomas. *Leviathan.* New York: Penguin Books, 1985.

Hodkinson, Stuart. "The New Urban Enclosures." *City* 16, no. 5 (2012): 500–518.

Hofstadter, Richard. *Social Darwinism in American Thought.* Reprint ed. Boston: Beacon Press, 1992.

Hollands, Robert G. "Will the Real Smart City Please Stand Up? Intelligent, Progressive or Entrepreneurial?" *City* 12, no. 3 (2008): 303–320.

Holston, James. *The Modernist City: An Anthropological Critique of Brasilia.* Chicago: University of Chicago Press, 1989.

Honig, Bonnie. *Emergency Politics: Paradox, Law, Democracy.* Princeton, NJ: Princeton University Press, 2009.

Honig, Bonnie. "The Politics of Public Things: Neoliberalism and the Routine of Privatization." *No Foundations: An Interdisciplinary Journal of Law and Justice* 10 (2013): 59.

Hulchanski, David. "A Tale of Two Canadas: Homeowners Getting Richer, Renters Getting Poorer." *Centre for Urban and Community Studies Research Bulletin,* 2001. http://www.urbancentre.utoronto.ca/pdfs/researchbulletins/02.pdf.

Hulchanski, David. *The Three Cities within Toronto: Income Polarization among Toronto's Neighbourhoods, 1970–2005.* Toronto: Cities Centre, University of Toronto, 2010. http://neighbourhoodchange.ca/2011/05/12/research-paper-one/.

Hume, Christopher. "Urban Revival Balances Past and Present: Rejuvenation of Wychwood Barns Maintains Link to the Past While Successfully Creating Perfect Mix of Beauty and Utility." *Toronto Star,* November 20, 2008, p. A10.

Hunold, Christian, and Iris Marion Young. "Justice, Democracy, and Hazardous Siting." *Political Studies* 46, no. 1 (1998): 82–95.

Hunt, D. Bradford. *Blueprint for Disaster: The Unraveling of Chicago Public Housing.* Chicago: University of Chicago Press, 2009.

Ihlanfeldt, Keith R., and David L. Sjoquist. "The Spatial Mismatch Hypothesis: A Review of Recent Studies and Their Implications for Welfare Reform." *Housing Policy Debate* 9, no. 4 (1998): 849–892.

Ihlanfeldt, Keith R., and Madelyn V. Young. "The Spatial Distribution of Black Employment between the Central City and the Suburbs." *Economic Inquiry* 34, no. 4 (1996): 693–707.

Imbroscio, David. "American Cities and American Political Science: A Look at Thick Injustice." *Perspectives on Politics* 10, no. 3 (2012): 736–738.

Imbroscio, David. "From Redistribution to Ownership: Toward an Alternative Urban Policy for America's Cities." *Urban Affairs Review* 20, no. 10 (2013): 1–34.

Imbroscio, David. *Reconstructing City Politics: Alternative Economic Development and Urban Regimes.* London: Sage, 1997.

Imbroscio, David. *Urban America Reconsidered: Alternatives for Governance and Policy.* Ithaca, NY: Cornell University Press, 2011.

Ingram, James D. "The Politics of Claude Lefort's Political: Between Liberalism and Radical Democracy." *Thesis Eleven* 87, no. 1 (2006): 33–50.

Isaac, Jeffrey C. *Democracy in Dark Times.* Ithaca, NY: Cornell University Press, 1998.

Jacobs, Jane. *The Death and Life of Great American Cities.* Reissue ed. New York: Vintage, 1992.

James, Royson. "New Subway's Coming, but a Subdued Mood Is Here." *Toronto Star,* October 10, 2013.

Johnson, Lisa, and Tamara Baluja. "Transit Referendum: Voters Say No to New Metro Vancouver Tax, Transit Improvements." *CBC News,* July 2, 2015. http://www.cbc.ca/news/canada/british-columbia/transit-referendum-voters-say-no-to-new-metro-vancouver-tax-transit-improvements-1.3134857.

Jung, Courtney, and Evan Rosevear. "Economic and Social Rights across Time, Regions, and Legal Traditions: A Preliminary Analysis of the TIESR Dataset." SSRN Scholarly Paper. Rochester, NY: Social Science Research Network, March 4, 2013. http://papers.ssrn.com/abstract=2228399.

Juris, Jeffrey S. "Reflections on #Occupy Everywhere: Social Media, Public Space, and Emerging Logics of Aggregation." *American Ethnologist* 39, no. 2 (2012): 259–279.

Kain, John F. "Housing Segregation, Negro Employment, and Metropolitan Decentralization." *Quarterly Journal of Economics* 82, no. 2 (1968): 175–197.

Kant, Immanuel. *Kant: Political Writings.* Edited by H. S. Reiss. New York: Cambridge University Press, 1991.

Katzenstein, Peter J. *Small States in World Markets: Industrial Policy in Europe.* Ithaca, NY: Cornell University Press, 1985.

Kayden, Jerold S. *Privately Owned Public Space: The New York City Experience.* Toronto: Wiley, 2000.

Keene, Danya E., Mark B. Padilla, and Arline T. Geronimus. "Leaving Chicago for Iowa's 'Fields of Opportunity': Community Dispossession, Rootlessness, and the Quest for Somewhere to 'Be OK.'" *Human Organization* 69, no. 3 (2010): 275–284.

Keene, Derek. "Tall Buildings in Medieval London: Precipitation, Aspiration and Thrills." *London Journal* 33, no. 3 (2008): 201–215.

Kennedy, Geoff. *Diggers, Levellers, and Agrarian Capitalism: Radical Political Thought in 17th Century England.* Lanham, MD: Lexington Books, 2008.

King, Loren. "Democratic Hopes in the Polycentric City." *Journal of Politics* 66 (2004): 203–223.

Kingwell, Mark, and Patrick Turmel, *Rites of Way: The Politics and Poetics of Public Space.* Waterloo, ON: Wilfrid Laurier University Press, 2009.

Kipfer, Stefan, Parastou Saberi, and Thorben Wieditz. "Henri Lefebvre: Debates and Controversies." *Progress in Human Geography* 37, no. 1 (2013): 115–134.

Klein, Ezra. "Romney's Theory of the 'Taker Class,' and Why It Matters." *Washington Post*, September 17, 2012. http://www.washingtonpost.com/blogs/wonkblog/wp/2012/09/17/romneys-theory-of-the-taker-class-and-why-it-matters/.

Kohli, Atul. *Democracy and Discontent: India's Growing Crisis of Governability.* Cambridge: Cambridge University Press, 1990.

Kohn, Margaret. *Brave New Neighborhoods: The Privatization of Public Space.* London: Routledge, 2004.

Kohn, Margaret. "Civic Republicanism versus Social Struggle: A Gramscian Approach to Associationalism in Italy." *Political Power and Social Theory* 13 (1999): 201–238.

Kohn, Margaret. "Dreamworlds of Deindustrialization." *Theory & Event* 12, no. 4 (2009). https://muse.jhu.edu/article/368576/summary.

Kolers, Avery. *Land, Conflict, and Justice: A Political Theory of Territory.* Cambridge: Cambridge University Press, 2011.

Kuymulu, Mehmet Barış. "The Vortex of Rights: 'Right to the City' at a Crossroads." *International Journal of Urban and Regional Research* 37, no. 3 (2013): 923–940.

Laborde, Cécile, and John Maynor. *Republicanism and Political Theory.* Toronto: Wiley, 2009.

Laclau, Ernesto. *Emancipation(s).* London: Verso, 2007.

Laclau, Ernesto. *On Populist Reason.* London: Verso, 2007.

Lakoff, George. *Moral Politics: How Liberals and Conservatives Think.* Chicago: University of Chicago Press, 2002.

Landemore, Hélène. *Democratic Reason: Politics, Collective Intelligence, and the Rule of the Many.* Princeton, NJ: Princeton University Press, 2013.

LaVaque-Manty, Mika. *Arguments and Fists: Political Agency and Justification in Liberal Theory.* East Sussex, UK: Psychology Press, 2002.

Lees, Loretta. "Gentrification and Social Mixing: Towards an Inclusive Urban Renaissance?" *Urban Studies* 45, no. 12 (2008): 2449–2470.

Lefebvre, Henri. *Du contrat de citoyenneté.* Paris: Editions Syllepse, 2007.

Lefebvre, Henri. *Le manifeste différentialiste.* Paris: Gallimard, 1970.

Lefebvre, Henri. *The Urban Revolution.* Translated by Robert Bononno. Minneapolis: University of Minnesota Press, 2003.

Lefebvre, Henri. *Writings on Cities.* Edited by Eleonore Kofman and Elizabeth Lebas. Malden, MA: Blackwell, 1996.

Lefort, Claude. *Democracy and Political Theory.* Translated by David Macey. Cambridge: Polity Press, 1991.

Lefort, Claude. *The Political Forms of Modern Society: Bureaucracy, Democracy, Totalitarianism.* Edited by David Thompson. Cambridge, MA: MIT Press, 1986.

Leontidou, Lila. "Urban Social Movements in "Weak" Civil Societies: The Right to the City and Cosmopolitan Activism in Southern Europe." *Urban Studies* 47, no. 6 (2010): 1179–1203.

Ley, David. "Artists, Aestheticisation and the Field of Gentrification." *Urban Studies* 40, no. 2 (2003): 2527–2544.

Ley, David. *The New Middle Class and the Remaking of the Central City*. Oxford: Oxford University Press, 1996.

Lipsey, Richard G., and Kelvin Lancaster. "The General Theory of Second Best." *Review of Economic Studies* 24, no. 1 (1956): 11–32.

Locke, John. *Second Treatise of Government*. Edited by C. B. Macphereson. Indianapolis, IN: Hackett, 1980.

Locke, John. *Two Treatises of Government*. Edited by Peter Laslett. 3rd ed. New York: Cambridge University Press, 1988.

Logan, John R., and Harvey L. Molotch. *Urban Fortunes: The Political Economy of Place*. Berkeley: University of California Press, 2007.

Love, Nancy. "'You Are Standing on the Indian': The Settler Contract, Terra Nullis, and White Supremacy." Paper presented at the American Political Science Association meeting, Washington, DC, August 2014.

Low, Setha. *Behind the Gates: Life, Security, and the Pursuit of Happiness in Fortress America*. London: Routledge, 2004.

Machiavelli, Niccolo. *Selected Political Writings*. Translated by David Wooton. Indianapolis: Hackett, 1994.

Macpherson, C. B. *The Political Theory of Possessive Individualism: Hobbes to Locke*. Reprint ed. Edited by Frank Cunningham. Don Mills, ON: Oxford University Press, 2011.

Magnusson, Warren. *Politics of Urbanism: Seeing Like a City*. New York: Routledge, 2012.

Malleson, Tom. "Rawls, Property-Owning Democracy, and Democratic Socialism." *Journal of Social Philosophy* 45, no. 2 (2014): 228–251.

Malloy, Robin Paul, and Michael Diamond. *The Public Nature of Private Property*. Burlington, VT: Ashgate, 2011.

Mansbridge, Jane. "Using Power/Fighting Power." *Constellations* 1, no. 1 (1994): 53–73.

Marcuse, Peter. "From Critical Urban Theory to the Right to the City." *City* 13, no. 2–3 (2009): 185–197.

Marcuse, Peter, James Connolly, Johannes Novy, Ingrid Olivo, Cuz Potter, and Justin Steil. *Searching for the Just City: Debates in Urban Theory and Practice*. London: Routledge, 2009.

Markell, P. "The Rule of the People: Arendt, Archê, and Democracy." *American Political Science Review* 100, no. 1 (2006): 1–14.

Marshall, Thomas Humphrey. *Citizenship and Social Class*. London: Pluto Press, 1992.

Martens, Karel. "Basing Transport Planning on Principles of Social Justice." (2006). http://repository.ubn.ru.nl/handle/2066/45509.

Martens, Karel. "Justice in Transport as Justice in Accessibility: Applying Walzer's 'Spheres of Justice' to the Transport Sector." *Transportation* 39, no. 6 (2012): 1035–1053.

Martens, Karel. "Substance Precedes Methodology: On Cost-Benefit Analysis and Equity." *Transportation* 38, no. 6 (2011): 959–974.

Martens, Karel. *Transport Justice: Designing Fair Transportation Systems*. New York: Routledge, 2016.

Marx, Karl. *Capital:* vol. 1: *A Critique of Political Economy*. Reprint edition. London; New York: Penguin, 1992.

Mathur, Shishir. *Innovation in Public Transport Finance: Property Value Capture. Shishir Mathur*. Burlington, VT: Ashgate, 2014.

Mayer, Margit. "The 'Right to the City' in the Context of Shifting Mottos of Urban Social Movements." *City* 13, nos. 2–3 (2009): 362–374.

McBride, Keally D. *Collective Dreams: Political Imagination & Community*. Cambridge: Cambridge University Press, 2005.

McBride, Sarah. "Google Bus Blocked in San Francisco Gentrification Protest." *Reuters*, December 10, 2013. http://www.reuters.com/article/2013/12/10/us-google-protest-idUSBRE9B818J20131210.

McCann, Eugene J. "Inequality and Politics in the Creative City-Region: Questions of Livability and State Strategy." *International Journal of Urban and Regional Research* 31, no. 1 (2007): 188–196.

McCormick, John P. "Machiavelli against Republicanism." *Political Theory* 31, no. 5 (2003): 615–653.

McCormick, John P. *Machiavellian Democracy*. Cambridge: Cambridge University Press, 2011.

McGurty, Eileen Maura. "From NIMBY to Civil Rights: The Origins of the Environmental Justice Movement." *Environmental History* 2 (1997): 301–323.

McKenzie, Evan. *Beyond Privatopia: Rethinking Residential Private Government*. Washington, DC: Urban Institute Press, 2011.

McKenzie, Evan. *Privatopia: Homeowner Associations and the Rise of Residential Private Government*. New Haven, CT: Yale University Press, 1996.

Mendelsohn, Oliver. "The Supreme Court as the Most Trusted Public Institution in India." *South Asia: Journal of South Asian Studies* 23, supp. 1 (2000): 103–119.

Millar, Fergus. *The Crowd in Rome in the Late Republic*. Ann Arbor: University of Michigan Press, 2002.

Miller, David. *Principles of Social Justice*. Cambridge, MA: Harvard University Press, 1999.

Miller, David. "Territorial Rights: Concept and Justification." *Political Studies* 60, no. 2 (2012): 252–268.

Mills, C. W. "'Ideal Theory' as Ideology." *Hypatia* 20, no. 3 (2005): 165–183.

Mishra, Srijit. "Risks, Farmers' Suicides and Agrarian Crisis in India: Is There a Way Out?" *Indian Journal of Agricultural Economics* 63, no. 1 (2008): 38–54.

Mitchell, Don. *The Right to the City: Social Justice and the Fight for Public Space.* New York: Guilford Press, 2003.

Moore, Aaron A. "Trading Density for Benefits: Section 37 Agreements in Toronto." *IMFG Perspectives* 2 (2013): 1–7.

Moore, Margaret. *A Political Theory of Territory.* Oxford: Oxford University Press, 2015.

Moore, Margaret. "Which People and What Land? Territorial Right-Holders and Attachment to Territory." *International Theory* 6, no. 1 (2014): 121–140.

Morley-Fletcher, Edwin. "Vouchers and Personal Welfare Accounts." 9th B.I.E.N International Congress (2002).

Mouffe, Chantal. "Deliberative Democracy or Agonistic Pluralism?" *Social Research* 66, no. 3 (1999): 745–758.

Muecke, Stephen. *Ancient & Modern: Time, Culture and Indigenous Philosophy.* Kensington, NSW: UNSW Press, 2004.

Murdie, Robert, and Carlos Teixeira. "The Impact of Gentrification on Ethnic Neighbourhoods in Toronto: A Case Study of Little Portugal." *Urban Studies* 48, no. 1 (2011): 61–83.

Murphy, Liam, and Thomas Nagel. *The Myth of Ownership: Taxes and Justice.* Oxford: Oxford University Press, 2002.

Mutua, Makau W. "Savages, Victims, and Saviors: The Metaphor of Human Rights." *Harvard International Law Journal* 42, no. 1 (2001): 201–245.

Myers, Ella. *Worldly Ethics: Democratic Politics and Care for the World.* Durham, NC: Duke University Press, 2013.

Nozick, Robert. *Anarchy, State, and Utopia.* New York: Basic Books, 1974.

Oakley, Deirdre, and Keri Burchfield. "Out of the Projects, Still in the Hood: The Spatial Constraints on Public-Housing Residents' Relocation in Chicago." *Journal of Urban Affairs* 31, no. 5 (2009): 589–614.

O'Neill, Martin, and Thad Williamson, eds. *Property-Owning Democracy: Rawls and Beyond.* Malden, MA: Wiley-Blackwell, 2012.

Otsuka, Michael. *Libertarianism without Inequality.* Oxford: Oxford University Press, 2003.

Otsuka, Michael. "Self-Ownership and Equality: A Lockean Reconciliation." *Philosophy & Public Affairs* 27, no. 1 (1998): 65–92.

Page, Benjamin I., Larry M. Bartels, and Jason Seawright. "Democracy and the Policy Preferences of Wealthy Americans." *Perspectives on Politics* 11, no. 1 (2013): 51–73.

Paine, Thomas, and Nancy J. Altman. *Agrarian Justice: With a New Foreword, 'Social Security, Thomas Paine, and the Spirit of America.'* CreateSpace Independent Publishing Platform, 2015.

Parkinson, John. *Democracy and Public Space: The Physical Sites of Democratic Performance.* Oxford: Oxford University Press, 2012.

Pateman, Carole, and Charles Mills. *The Contract and Domination.* Cambridge: Polity Press, 2007.

Patil, Ashok Vikhe, K. V. Somasundaram, and R. C. Goyal. "Current Health Scenario in Rural India." *Australian Journal of Rural Health* 10, no. 2 (2002): 129–135.

Peck, Jamie. "Struggling with the Creative Class." *International Journal of Urban and Regional Research* 29, no. 4 (2005): 740–770.

Peñalver, Eduardo M., and Sonia Katyal. *Property Outlaws: How Squatters, Pirates, and Protesters Improve the Law of Ownership.* New Haven, CT: Yale University Press, 2010.

Pendall, Rolf. "Why Voucher and Certificate Users Live in Distressed Neighborhoods." *Housing Policy Debate* 11, no. 4 (2000): 881–910.

Pender, Kathleen. "$1 Million City: S.F. Median Home Price Hits 7 Figures for 1st Time." *SFGate,* July 17, 2014. http://www.sfgate.com/business/networth/arti cle/1-million-city-S-F-median-home-price-hits-7-5626591.php.

Permutt, Samuel D. "Manual Scavenging Problem: A Case for the Supreme Court of India." *Cardozo Journal of International and Comparative Law* 20 (2011): 277.

Pettit, Philip. *Republicanism: A Theory of Freedom and Government.* Oxford: Oxford University Press, 1999.

Pettit, Philip. *Just Freedom: A Moral Compass for a Complex World.* New York: Norton, 2014.

Piketty, Thomas. *Capital in the Twenty-First Century.* Cambridge, MA: Harvard University Press, 2014.

Pitkin, Hanna Fenichel. *The Concept of Representation.* Berkeley: University of California Press, 1967.

Piven, Frances Fox, and Richard Cloward. *Poor People's Movements: Why They Succeed, How They Fail.* New York: Vintage, 1978.

Pogge, Thomas W. *World Poverty and Human Rights.* 2nd ed. Cambridge: Polity Press, 2008.

Pontusson, Jonas. "Once Again a Model." In *What's Left of the Left.* Edited by James E. Cronin, George W. Ross, and James Shoch. Durham, NC: Duke University Press, 2011: 89–115.

Pucher, John. "Discrimination in Mass Transit." *Journal of the American Planning Association* 48, no. 3 (1982): 315–326.

Pucher, John. "Who Benefits from Transit Subsidies? Recent Evidence from Six Metropolitan Areas." *Transportation Research Part A*: 17, no. 1 (1983): 39–50.

Purcell, Mark. "Excavating Lefebvre: The Right to the City and Its Urban Politics of the Inhabitant." *GeoJournal* 58, no. 2–3 (2002): 99–108.

Purcell, Mark. "Possible Worlds: Henri Lefebvre and the Right to the City." *Journal of Urban Affairs* 36, no. 1 (2014): 141–154.

Purcell, Mark. *Recapturing Democracy: Neoliberalization and the Struggle for Alternative Urban Futures.* New York: Routledge, 2008.

Putnam, Robert D., Robert Leonardi, and Raffaella Y. Nanetti. *Making Democracy Work: Civic Traditions in Modern Italy.* Princeton, NJ: Princeton University Press, 1994.

Quint, Peter E. *Civil Disobedience and the German Courts.* New York: Routledge, 2008.

Radin, Margaret Jane. "Property and Personhood." *Stanford Law Review* 34 (1982): 957–1015.

Radin, Margaret Jane. *Reinterpreting Property.* Chicago: University of Chicago Press, 1993.

Rahman, M. "India's Slumdog Census Reveals Poor Conditions for One in Six Urban Dwellers." *Guardian,* March 22, 2013. http://www.theguardian.com/world/2013/mar/22/india-slumdog-census-poor-conditions.

Rajagopal, Balakrishnan. "Pro–Human Rights but Anti-Poor? A Critical Evaluation of the Indian Supreme Court from a Social Movement Perspective." *Human Rights Review* 8, no. 3 (2007): 157–186.

Rancière, Jacques. "Democracy, Republic, Representation." *Constellations* 13, no. 3 (2006): 297–307.

Rancière, Jacques. *Disagreement: Politics and Philosophy.* Minneapolis: University of Minnesota Press, 2004.

Rancière, Jacques. *The Philosopher and His Poor.* Translated by John Drury, Corinne Oster, and Andrew Parker. Durham, NC: Duke University Press, 2004.

Rawls, John. "The Justification of Civil Disobedience." *Collected Papers.* Cambridge, MA: Harvard University Press, 1999.

Rawls, John. *The Law of Peoples: With "The Idea of Public Reason Revisited."* 1st ed. Cambridge, MA: Harvard University Press, 2001.

Rawls, John. *A Theory of Justice.* Cambridge, MA: Harvard University Press, 2009.

Razsa, Maple, and Andrej Kurnik. "The Occupy Movement in Žižek's Hometown: Direct Democracy and a Politics of Becoming." *American Ethnologist* 39, no. 2 (2012): 238–258.

Right to the City Alliance. "We Call These Projects Home: Solving the Housing Crisis from the Ground Up." (2010). http://cdp.urbanjustice.org/sites/default/files/We_Call_These_Projects_Home_Summary.pdf.

Ripstein, Arthur. *Force and Freedom: Kant's Legal and Political Philosophy.* Cambridge, MA: Harvard University Press, 2009.

Roberts, Sam. "More Apartments Are Empty yet Rented or Owned, Census Finds." *New York Times,* July 6, 2011, sec. N.Y./Region.

Robichaud, David, and Patrick Turmel. *La juste part: Repenser les inégalités, la richesse et la fabrication des grille-pains.* Montreal: Atelier 10, 2012.

Robin, Corey. *The Reactionary Mind: Conservatism from Edmund Burke to Sarah Palin.* New York: Oxford University Press, 2011.

Robson, Garry, and Tim Butler. "Coming to Terms with London: Middle-Class Communities in a Global City." *Journal of Urban and Regional Research* 25, no. 1 (2001): 70–86.

Rosen, Gillad, and Eran Razin. "The Rise of Gated Communities in Israel: Reflections on Changing Urban Governance in a Neo-liberal Era." *Urban Studies* 46, no. 8 (2009): 1702–1722.

Rosenblum, Nancy L. *Membership and Morals: The Personal Uses of Pluralism in America*. Princeton, NJ: Princeton University Press, 1998.

Ross, Andrew. *The Celebration Chronicles: Life, Liberty, and the Pursuit of Property Value in Disney's New Town*. New York: Ballantine Books, 2011.

Rudolph, Lloyd I., and Suzanne Rudolph. *In Pursuit of Lakshmi: The Political Economy of the Indian State*. Chicago: University of Chicago Press, 1987.

Sack, Robert David. *Human Territoriality: Its Theory and History*. New York: Cambridge University Press, 1986.

Saffon, M. P., and N. Urbinati. "Procedural Democracy, the Bulwark of Equal Liberty." *Political Theory* 41, no. 3 (2013): 441–481. doi:10.1177/0090591713476872.

Salzano, Edoardo. "La città come bene comune: Costruire il futuro partendo dalla storia." *Historia Magistra* (2012). http://www.francoangeli.it/riviste/Scheda_rivista.aspx?IDArticolo=44992.

Sandel, Michael J. *What Money Can't Buy: The Moral Limits of Markets*. New York: Farrar, Straus and Giroux, 2013.

Scheuerman, William E. "Whistleblowing as Civil Disobedience: The Case of Edward Snowden." *Philosophy & Social Criticism* 40, no. 7 (2014): 609–628.

Schrader, Stuart, and David Wachsmuth. "Reflections on Occupy Wall Street, the State and Space." *City* 16, no. 2 (2012): 243–248.

Schuck, Peter H. "Judging Remedies: Judicial Approaches to Housing Segregation." *Harvard Civil Rights–Civil Liberties Law Review* 37, no. 2 (2002): 289–368.

Schwartz, Joseph M. *The Future of Democratic Equality: Rebuilding Social Solidarity in a Fragmented America*. London: Routledge, 2008.

Scott, Allen J. "Creative Cities: Conceptual Issues and Policy Questions." *Journal of Urban Affairs* 28, no. 1 (2006): 1–17.

Scott, Brittany. "Is Urban Policy Making Way for the Wealthy: How a Human Rights Approach Challenges the Purging of Poor Communities from US Cities." *Columbia Human Rights Law Review* 45 (2013): 863–895.

Sen, Amartya. "Equality of What?" In *Liberty, Equality, and Law: Selected Tanner Lectures on Moral Philosophy*. Edited by Sterling M. McMurrin. Cambridge: Cambridge University Press, 1987.

Sennett, Richard. *The Uses of Disorder: Personal Identity and City Life*. New York: Norton, 1992.

Shapiro, Michael J. "Street Politics." *Journal of Critical Globalisation Studies* 5 (2012): 127–128.

Siegel, Kevin D., and Matthew D. Visick. "Inclusionary Zoning for Affordable Housing under Attack" (2014). http://www.bwslaw.com/tasks/sites/bws law/assets/Image/Siegel%20Visick%20PLJ%20Article%20Summer%20 2014.pdf.

Skinner, Quentin. "The Republican Idea of Political Liberty." In *Machiavelli and Republicanism*. Edited by Gisela Bock, Quentin Skinner, and Maurizio Viroli. Cambridge: Cambridge University Press, 1990: 293–309.

Skinner, Quentin. *Visions of Politics*, vol. 2, *Renaissance Virtues*. Cambridge: Cambridge University Press, 2002.

Slater, Tom. "The Eviction of Critical Perspectives from Gentrification Research." *International Journal of Urban and Regional Research* 30, no. 4 (2006): 737–757.

Slater, Tom. "Municipally Managed Gentrification in South Parkdale, Toronto." *Canadian Geographer* 48, no. 3 (2004): 303–325.

Smith, Neil. *The New Urban Frontier: Gentrification and the Revanchist City*. London: Routledge, 1996.

Smith, William. "Civil Disobedience and the Public Sphere." *Journal of Political Philosophy* 19, no. 2 (2011): 145–166.

Smith, William. "Civil Disobedience and Social Power: Reflections on Habermas." *Contemporary Political Theory* 7, no. 1 (2008): 72–89.

Smithsimon, Gregory, and Sharon Zukin. "The City's Commons: Privatization vs. Human Rights." In *The Future of Human Rights in an Urban World*. Edited by Thijs van Lindert and Doutje Lettinga. Netherlands: Amnesty International (2014): 41–44.

Smolka, Martim O. *Implementing Value Capture in Latin America*. Cambridge, MA: Lincoln Institute of Land Policy, 2013.

Soja, Edward W. *Seeking Spatial Justice*. Minneapolis: University of Minnesota Press, 2010.

Solnit, Rebecca, and Susan Schwartzenberg. *Hollow City: The Siege of San Francisco and the Crisis of American Urbanism*. London: Verso, 2002.

Sorkin, Michael, ed. *Variations on a Theme Park: The New American City and the End of Public Space*. New York: Hill and Wang, 1992.

Spencer, Herbert. *Spencer: Political Writings*. Edited by John Offer. New York: Cambridge University Press, 1993.

Spivak, G. C. "Can the Subaltern Speak?" in *Marxism and the Interpretation of Culture*. Urbana: University of Illinois Press, 1988.

Stake, Jeffrey Evans. "The Uneasy Case for Adverse Possession." *Georgetown Law Journal* 89, no. 8 (2001): 2419–2474.

Stilz, Anna. "Nations, States, and Territory." *Ethics* 121, no. 3 (2011): 572–601.

Stilz, Anna. "Occupancy Rights and the Wrong of Removal." *Philosophy & Public Affairs* 41, no. 4 (2013): 324–356.

Stothard, Michael. "Corporation of London Draws Protesters' Ire." *Financial Times*, November 19, 2011, p. 2.

Swain, Ashok. *Struggle against the State: Social Network and Protest Mobilization in India*. Farnham, UK: Ashgate, 2013.

Tarrow, Sidney G. *Power in Movement: Social Movements and Contentious Politics*. 3rd ed. Cambridge: Cambridge University Press, 2011.

Taylor, Charles. "Modern Social Imaginaries." *Public Culture* 14, no. 1 (2002): 91–124.

Taylor, Charles. "What's Wrong with Negative Liberty?" In *The Idea of Liberty*. Edited by Alan Ryan. Oxford: Oxford University Press, 1979: 175–194.

Teichgraeber, Richard. "Hegel on Property and Poverty." *Journal of the History of Ideas* 38, no. 1 (1977): 47–64.

Tilly, Charles, and Sidney Tarrow. *Contentious Politics*. Boulder, CO: Paradigm, 2006.

Tocqueville, Alexis de. *Democracy in America and Two Essays on America*. Edited by Isaac Kramnick. Translated Gerald E. Bevan. London: Penguin, 2003.

Töngür, Ünal, and Adem Yavuz Elveren. "Deunionization and Pay Inequality in OECD Countries: A Panel Granger Causality Approach." *Economic Modelling* 38 (2014): 417–425.

Tuan, Yi-Fu. *Topophilia: A Study of Environmental Perception, Attitudes, and Values*. New York: Columbia University Press, 1974.

Tully, James. *A Discourse on Property: John Locke and His Adversaries*. Cambridge: Cambridge University Press, 1983.

Tully, James. "The Struggles of Indigenous Peoples for and of Freedom." In *Political Theory and the Rights of Indigenous Peoples*. Edited by Duncan Ivison and Paul Patton. Cambridge: Cambridge University Press, 2000: 36–59.

Vale, Lawrence J., and Erin Graves. "The Chicago Housing Authority's Plan for Transformation: What Does the Research Show So Far?" Cambridge, MA: Massachusetts Institute of Technology, Department of Urban Studies and Planning, 2010.

Van Parijs, Phillipe. "Basic Income: A Simple and Powerful Idea for the Twenty-First Century." *Politics & Society* 32, no. 1 (2004): 7–39.

Van Parijs, Phillipe. "Competing Justifications of Basic Income." In *Arguing for Basic Income: Ethical Foundations for a Radical Reform*. Edited by Philippe Van Parijs. London: Verso, 1992: 1–43.

Van Parijs, Phillipe. "The Second Marriage of Justice and Efficiency." *Journal of Social Policy* 19, no. 1 (1990): 1–25.

Van Parijs, Phillipe. "Why Surfers Should Be Fed: The Liberal Case for an Unconditional Basic Income." *Philosophy & Public Affairs* 20, no. 2 (1991): 101–131.

Van Trier, Walter. "Who Framed Social Dividend?" USBIG discussion paper no. 26 (March 2002).

Vatter, Miguel. "The Quarrel between Populism and Republicanism: Machiavelli and the Antinomies of Plebeian Politics." *Contemporary Political Theory* 11, no. 3 (2011): 242–263.

Verba, Sidney, and Norman H. Nie. *Participation in America: Political Democracy and Social Equality*. Chicago: University of Chicago Press, 1987.

Vigdor, Jacob, Douglas S. Massey, and Alice M. Rivlin. "Does Gentrification Harm the Poor?" *Brookings-Wharton Papers on Urban Affairs* (2002): 133–173.

Viroli, Maurizio, and Antony Shugaar. *Republicanism*. New York: Hill and Wang, 2001.

Volscho, Thomas W., and Nathan J. Kelly. "The Rise of the Super-rich: Power Resources, Taxes, Financial Markets, and the Dynamics of the Top 1 Percent, 1949 to 2008." *American Sociological Review* 77, no. 5 (2012): 679–699.

Wahi, Namita. "State, Private Property and the Supreme Court." *Frontline Magazine* 29, no. 19 (2012).

Wahi, Namita. "The Tension between Property Rights and Social and Economic Rights: A Case Study of India." In *Social and Economic Rights in Theory and Practice*. Edited by Helena Alviar et al. London: Routledge, 2014: 138–157.

Waldron, Jeremy. *God, Locke, and Equality: Christian Foundations in Locke's Political Thought*. New York: Cambridge University Press, 2002.

Waldron, Jeremy. "Homelessness and the Issue of Freedom." *UCLA Law Review* 39, no. 1 (1991): 295–324.

Waldron, Jeremy. "Two Worries about Mixing One's Labour." *Philosophical Quarterly* 33, no. 103 (1983): 37–44.

Walks, Alan, and Richard Maaranen. "Gentrification, Social Mix, and Social Polarization: Testing the Linkages in Large Canadian Cities." *Urban Geography*. 29, no. 4 (2008): 293–326.

Walzer, Michael. *Spheres of Justice: A Defense of Pluralism and Equality*. New York: Basic Books, 1984.

Warren, Mark E. "Citizen Participation and Democratic Deficits: Considerations from the Perspective of Democratic Theory." In *Activating the Citizen: Dilemmas of Participation in Europe and Canada*. Edited by Joan DeBardeleban and Jon Pammet. London: Palgrave Macmillan, 2009: 17–40.

Warren, Mark E. *Democracy and Association*. Princeton, NJ: Princeton University Press, 2000.

Weaver, Timothy. "Neoliberalism in the Trenches: Urban Policy and Politics in the United States and the United Kingdom." PhD dissertation, University of Pennsylvania, 2012.

Weintraub, Jeff, and Krishan Kumar. *Public and Private in Thought and Practice*. Chicago: University of Chicago Press, 1997.

Wenar, L. "What We Owe to Distant Others." *Politics, Philosophy & Economics* 2, no. 3 (2003): 283–304.

Wertheimer, Alan. *Coercion*. Princeton, NJ: Princeton University Press, 1990.

Western, Bruce, and Jake Rosenfeld. "Unions, Norms, and the Rise in U.S. Wage Inequality." *American Sociological Review* 76, no. 4 (2011): 513–537.

White, Stephen, and Evan Farr. "'No-Saying' in Habermas." *Political Theory* 40, no. 1 (2011): 32–57.

Wildt, Andreas. "Solidarität." *Historisches Worterbuch der Philosophie.* Band 9. Basel: Schwabe, 1995: 1004–1005.

Wilen, William P. "The Horner Model: Successfully Redeveloping Public Housing." *Northwestern Journal of Law & Social Policy* 1 (2006): 62–303.

Wiles, Ellen. "Aspirational Principles or Enforceable Rights: The Future for Socioeconomic Rights in National Law." *American University International Law Review* 22 (2006): 35–64.

Williams, Eric, and Colin A. Palmer. *Capitalism and Slavery.* Chapel Hill: University of North Carolina Press, 1994.

Williams, F. B. *The Law of City Planning and Zoning.* New York: Macmillan, 1922.

Williams, Patricia J. "Alchemical Notes: Reconstructing Ideals from Deconstructed Rights." *Harvard Civil Rights–Civil Liberties Law Review* 22 (1987): 401–434.

Williams, Robert A. *The American Indian in Western Legal Thought: The Discourses of Conquest.* Oxford: Oxford University Press, 1990.

Williamson, Thad. "Mobility and Its Opponents: Richmond, Virginia's Refusal to Embrace Mass Transit." Paper presented at the Urban Affairs Association meeting, April 2013.

Williamson, Thad, David Imbroscio, and Gar Alperovitz. *Making a Place for Community: Local Democracy in a Global Era.* New York: Routledge, 2003.

Winstanley, Gerrard. *"The True Levellers' Standard Advanced," "The Law of Freedom" and Other Writings.* Edited by Will Jonson. CreateSpace Independent Publishing Platform, 2014.

Wong, Aline Kan, and Stephen Hua Kuo Yeh, eds. *Housing a Nation: 25 Years of Public Housing in Singapore.* Singapore: Maruzen Asia, 1985.

Wong, Julia Carrie. "The Fight over San Francisco's Public Spaces." *New Yorker,* October 23, 2014. http://www.newyorker.com/tech/elements/dropbox-airbnb-fight-san-franciscos-public-spaces.

Wood, Allen W. "The Marxian Critique of Justice." *Philosophy & Public Affairs* 1, no. 3 (1972): 244–282.

Young, Iris Marion. "Residential Segregation and Differentiated Citizenship." *Citizenship Studies* 3, no. 2 (1999): 237–252.

Young, Iris Marion. *Responsibility for Justice.* Reprint. Oxford: Oxford University Press, 2013.

Young, Robert. "Egalitarianism and Personal Desert." *Ethics* 102 (1992): 319–341.

Ypi, Lea. *Global Justice and Avant-Garde Political Agency.* Oxford: Oxford University Press, 2012.

Zeveloff, Julie. "The 20 Most Expensive Housing Markets in America." *Business Insider,* November 12, 2014. http://www.businessinsider.com/most-expensive-housing-markets-2014-11?op=1.

Zick, Timothy. *Speech Out of Doors.* Cambridge: Cambridge University Press, 2008.

Zukin, Sharon. *Loft Living: Culture and Capital in Urban Change.* 25th anniversary ed. New Brunswick, NJ: Rutgers University Press, 2014.

INDEX

France
  republicanism in, 75–76
  right to mobility in, 132
  solidarism in, 14, 19, 195
Frank, Jason, 150
freedom, 77, 78, 100, 116, 118, 188
  equal, 123–24
  liberal theory of, 124
  private property and, 119
Freeman, Lance, 91
free markets, 93, 104
free public transit, 132
free speech, 116, 140, 223n19
French Revolution, 160
friendship, 171

GAHP. *See* Gautreaux Assisted- Housing
  Program
Gandhi, Sanjay, 50
gangs, criminal, 211n57
Garrett, Mark, 114
gated communities, 11
Gautreaux Assisted- Housing Program
  (GAHP), 79
general will, 228n43
gentrification, 9–10, 11, 63, 67, 73,
  86–89, 174
  city and, 93–94
  conclusion to, 111–12
  defined, 89–92
  democracy and, 102–6
  displacement and, 90–91
  homogeneity and, 106–11
  incomplete, 107
  libertarian approach to, 92–95
  luck egalitarianism and, 95–102
  place and, 102–6
  polarization and, 106–11
  public housing and, 92–93
  solidarism and, 100
  territoriality and, 102–6
geographic equity, 169
George, Henry, 204n8
German Hobbesianism, 10, 141
Germany, 151, 229n58
Gide, Charles, 19, 24–27, 30, 49, 87
Glass, Ruth, 89

global justice, 198
Goldberg, Lana, 147
Google shuttle buses, 113
Gotha Program, 86
governmentality, 187
grandfather clauses, 130
Groupe de Navarrenx, 191
Guesde, Jules, 190
Guilds, 180

Habermas, Juergen, 10, 141, 159,
  162–64, 166–67
Hackworth, Jason, 74, 90
Hague v. CIO, 140
Hardt, Michael, 195, 196
Harrington, James, 39
Harvey, David, 4, 11, 52, 194, 197
Hayek, Friedrich, 5, 92–95, 100, 101
Hayward, Clarissa, 121, 122, 213n24213 n 24
Hegel, Georg Wilhelm FriedrichI, 76–77,
  78, 84, 188
Henry Horner Annex, 82
Henry Horner Homes, 60, 63, 79–84
Henry Horner Mothers Guild, 79, 82–83
hetero-rights, 11, 178, 185, 188, 189, 191
heterotopia, 105–6, 178, 185, 188
hidden mechanisms, of redistribution, 194
Hirschman, A. O., 81
Hobbes, Thomas, 41, 54, 118, 140–42, 149, 151
Holmes, Oliver Wendell, 76
Holston, James, 47
homeless(ness), 3, 33, 42, 53, 56, 71, 74, 183,
  198, 215n60
"Homelessness and Freedom" (Waldron),
  77, 188
home-voters, 171–74, 200
homogeneity, 106–11
homogenization, 90, 91
Honig, Bonnie, 66
Hope VI, 9, 60, 64, 74
Horner Residents Committee, 83
housing, 8, 58. *See also* public housing
  bubble, in U.S., 4–5
  Cabrini-Green project, 9, 60,
  63–66, 73, 85
  de-commodifying, 101
  mixed-income, 64, 82